Katarzyna Stokłosa (Ed.)

Borders and Memories

Mittel- und Ostmitteleuropastudien

herausgegeben von

Gerhard Besier und Katarzyna Stokłosa
Sigmund-Neumann-Institut für Freiheits- und Demokratieforschung
(Technische Universität Dresden/University of Southern Denmark)

Band 13

LIT

Borders and Memories

Conflicts and Co-operation in European Border Regions

edited by

Katarzyna Stokłosa

LIT

Cover photo: Impression von einem französisch-schweizerischen Grenzübergang (Winter 2012). Photo: Katarzyna Stokłosa

This book is printed on acid-free paper.

Bibliographic information published by the Deutsche Nationalbibliothek
The Deutsche Nationalbibliothek lists this publication in the Deutsche Nationalbibliografie; detailed bibliographic data are available on the Internet at http://dnb.d-nb.de.

ISBN 978-3-643-91094-3 (pb)
ISBN 978-3-643-96094-8 (PDF)

A catalogue record for this book is available from the British Library.

Klosbachstr. 107
CH-8032 Zürich
Tel. +41 (0) 44-251 75 05
E-Mail: zuerich@lit-verlag.ch http://www.lit-verlag.ch
Distribution:
In the UK: Global Book Marketing, e-mail: mo@centralbooks.com
In North America: Independent Publishers Group, e-mail: orders@ipgbook.com
In Germany: LIT Verlag Fresnostr. 2, D-48159 Münster
Tel. +49 (0) 2 51-620 32 22, Fax +49 (0) 2 51-922 60 99, e-mail: vertrieb@lit-verlag.de
e-books are available at www.litwebshop.de

Contents

List of Figures

1 All Figures are privately owned (all date from 2016, except for figures 5.9 and 5.14 from 2009). Steffen Höhne thanks Marit Haferkamp and Kirsten Heyerhoff for making Fig. 5.15–5.18, Manfred Weinberg for making Fig. 5.19 and Sibylle Höhne for the others.

Joanna Frątczak-Müller and Anna Mielczarek-Żejmo

List of Abbreviations

ABS	Association for Borderland Studies
CBC	Cross-Border Cooperation
CBOS	Centrum Badania Opinii Społecznej (Public Opinion Research Center)
CEPA	Customized Educational Programs Abroad
DNR	Donétskaya Naródnaya Respúblika (Donetsk People's Republic)
EC	European Community
EGTC	European Grouping of Territorial Cooperation
ESNB	Euroregion Sprewa-Nysa-Bóbr (Spree-Neisse-Bober Euroregion)
ETC	European Territorial Cooperation
EU	European Union
FMP	Fundusz Małych Projektów (Small Projects Fund)
GDI	Gross Domestic Income
GfK	Growth from Knowledge
HDZ	Hrvatska Demokratska Zajednica (Croatian Democratic Union)
IEP	Institut d'Études Politiques (Institutes of Political Studies)
IS	Islamic State
JNA	Jugoslovenska Narodna Armija (Yugoslav People's Army)
MLG	Multilevel Governance
NGO	Non Governmental Organization
NKBG	North Karelia Border Guard
PiS	Prawo i Sprawiedliwość (Law and Justice)
ROC	Russian Orthodox Church

SNBE	Spree-Neisse-Bober Euroregion
SPF	Small Projects Fund
SPQR	Senatus Populusque Romanus (The Roman Senate and People)
SSR	Soviet Socialist Republic
SU	Soviet Union
TEIN	Transborder Euro-Institute Network
TIGR	Revolutionary Organization of the Julian March T.I.G.R. (Trst – Istra – Gorica – Reka)
Trst	Trieste
TsK	Tsentralnyj Komitet Vsesoyuznoj (Central Committee of the Communist Party)
UN	United Nations
US	United States
USA	United States of America
USSR	Union of Soviet Socialist Republics
VKP(b)	Vsesojuznaja Kommunističeskaja Partija (bol'ševikov) (All-Union Communist Party (Bolshevik))
WWI	World War I
WWII	World War II
YLE	Yleisradio Oy (General Radio/Broadcast)

Notes on Contributors

GERHARD BESIER is a historian (Ph. D.), theologian (DD and Habilitation) and psychologist (Diploma). In 2009, he received an honorary doctorate from the University of Lund, Sweden. He has held chairs in Contemporary (Church) History and European Studies at the Universities of Berlin, Heidelberg and Dresden, and is currently Director of the Sigmund Neumann Institute (Berlin, Dresden, Flensburg) and teaches at several universities in Europe and the USA. He has published widely on the themes of German-Polish antagonisms, transformation processes in Europe since 1945, European dictatorships, denominational controversies in Germany, Europe and the USA, and on stereotypes and prejudices. His latest books are (with Katarzyna Stokłosa), *Neighbourhood Perceptions of the Ukraine Crisis. From the Soviet Union into Eurasia?*, London and New York: Routledge 2017 and *How to deal with Refugees? Europe as a Continent of Dreams*, Zürich/Wien: LIT 2018.

JOANNA FRĄTCZAK-MÜLLER – is a lecturer at the Institute of Sociology at the University of Zielona Góra. Her main research interest is connected with functioning of public sphere, cross-border cooperation and the operation of social networks. She is an author and co-author of diagnoses regarding cross-border cooperation network, social policy and revitalization. She is involved in the programming process of regional and local development on the Polish-German border.

STEFFEN HÖHNE studied German language and literature, History and Political Science. 1987 to 1992 Assistant Professor in Düsseldorf, than in Prague at Charles University (1992–1996) and in Jena at Friedrich-Schiller University (1996–2000). Since fall 2000 Professor at the Institute for Musicology in Weimar-Jena, he teaches Cultural science and -management. Since 2013 he is Dean of faculty III. Board member of *Collegium Carolinum*, Munich and president of the *Johann Gottfried Herder Forschungsrat*; Editor in chief of *Brücken. Germanic Yearbook Czech Republic – Slovakia* and *Journal of Cultural Management: Arts, Economics, Policy.*

OLGA ILYUKHA is a researcher and a director (since 2015) of the Institute of Language, Literature and History (Karelian Research Center of the Russian Academy of Sciences). She studied the problems of the social history and culture of Karelia and Russian European North, history of education and school. She has published papers dealing with the issues of mutual perception of the nations separated by the border, and the border as an intercultural contact zone. Researcher stories primers.

DORTE JAGETIĆ ANDERSEN is Associate Professor at the University of Southern Denmark, Department of Political Science and affiliated with the Centre for Border Region Studies. She has a background in European Ethnology and European Continental Philosophy. Her main research interest is in identity-politics in border regions influenced by conflict, particularly in the context of the former Yugoslavia, and she is widely known in the field of border studies for her contributions to developing the concepts of the border multiple and Café Europa.

VOLODYMYR V. KRAVCHENKO is Professor at the Department of History and Classics, University of Alberta, Canada, where he teaches European, Russian, and Soviet history after transferring from Kharkiv in 2011. He is also founding Director of the Contemporary Ukraine Studies Program at the Canadian Institute of Ukrainian Studies. His research interests embraces Ukrainian and Russian imperial history, Ukrainian regional and border studies as well as intellectual history of Ukrainian studies and historiography. He is the author of about 170 publications.

JENNI MEROVUO is a researcher and a doctoral student at the Department of Geographical and Historical studies in the University of Eastern Finland (Joensuu). She has previously worked among collecting and organising the historical data on the Finnish Border Guard in North Karelia. In her Ph. D. project, Merovuo studies the state border and the borderland communities in the 18th-century context.

ANNA MIELCZAREK-ŻEJMO is an adjunct at the Institute of Sociology at the University of Zielona Góra in Poland. Her main research interest is social structure, cross-border cooperation and social cohesion particularly as a result of processes of social renewal (revitalization) of degraded areas. She conducts her scientific interests in practice in cooperation with local governments and non-governmental organizations operating on the Polish-German border.

KATARZYNA STOKŁOSA is Associate Professor in the Department of Political Science and Public Management, Centre for Border Region Studies, at the University of Southern Denmark. She finished her Ph. D. at the European University Viadrina in Frankfurt (Oder) and her habilitation thesis at the University of Potsdam. She has published various books and articles on European border regions in comparison and on European history. Her latest books are (with Gerhard Besier), *Neighbourhood Perceptions of the Ukraine Crisis. From the Soviet Union into Eurasia?*, London and New York: Routledge 2017 and *How to deal with Refugees? Europe as a Continent of Dreams*, Zürich/Wien: LIT 2018.

BIRTE WASSENBERG is Professor in Contemporary History at the Institute for Political Studies (IEP) of the University of Strasbourg and member of the Research Unit Dynamiques européennes (UMR). A former student of the College of Europe in Bruges, she holds a Jean Monnet Chair, is deputy director of the Franco-German Jean-Monnet Center of Excellence and is director of the Master in Border Studies, International Relations. From 1993 to 2006 she was responsible for cross-border cooperation at the *Région Alsace*.

CHLOE WELLS is a Ph. D. candidate in Human Geography at the University of Eastern Finland. Her Ph. D. research examines the transmission of the (post) memory of the 'lost' city of Viipuri, Finland (since World War II Vyborg, Russia) between groups in Finland, with a focus on youths' (post)memories of the city. Her forthcoming Ph. D. thesis monograph is provisionally titled 'Vyborg is ours': the memory and postmemory of a borderland city, and will be published by the University of Eastern Finland in 2019.

On Borders and Memories. Introduction

Katarzyna Stokłosa

Borders and border regions are shaped by many phenomena connected with both co-operation and conflict. The neighbourhood, cross-border contacts, illegal migration, border crossings, prejudices and stereotypes, border guards, and perceptions of borders are some of the key words that characterize the articles in this volume.

Until recently, scholars tended to differentiate between developments in Western and Northern European border regions, on the one hand, and Eastern, Central-Eastern and Southern-Eastern European border regions, on the other hand. While the former were viewed as being better developed and more active with regard to cross-border co-operation, the latter were characterized as being more problematic and still in the transformation process. This concept of differentiation has largely disappeared in response to recent challenges, in particular the refugee crisis. Nowadays, it is reasonable to say that almost all European border regions, as well as border regions outside Europe, are shaped by and come under the considerable influence of recent crises.[1]

The book deals with European border regions that have experienced numerous changes over the 20th century. Because of this changeable, frequently painful past, different human stories – mostly tragic or romanticized – individual and collective memories, mythologies with heroes, and divergent perceptions of history developed. Most authors in this volume deal with conflicts and co-operation that can either be remembered or forgotten. The interplay between regional, national and border discourses becomes very visible. Many authors ask questions about identity and memory, the borders in peoples' minds. Ethical and philosophical questions emerge about how, under which circumstances, why and by whom the borders were being applied in everyday life. For this reason, this volume relates to "Border and Memory Studies", concepts that have extended widely in the field of border studies research.[2]

Jenni Merovuo, historian, studies memories of the building of the border in Ilomantsi, located in North Karelia on the border with Russia. She analyses the social interaction between officials and civilians, as well as the structural changes

1 Cf. Katarzyna Stokłosa / Gerhard Besier (eds.) European Border Regions in Comparison: Overcoming Nationalistic Aspects or Re-Nationalization?, London-New York: Routledge 2014.

2 Cf. Angela Vaupel (ed.) Borders, Memory and Transculturality. An Annotated Bibliography on the European Discourse, Wien: LIT 2017.

following the 1917 establishment of the border and after its re-establishment in 1947. Merovuo uses interviews archived in the North Karelian Border Guard Heritage Collection to present the border guards' contribution to building the border region. She analyses relations between border guards and the locals. The Finnish Border Guard was established in 1919 to control movement across the Finnish-Russian border in the aftermath of Finland becoming independent in 1917 and the Civil War in 1918. After the re-establishment of the Finnish-Russian border in 1947, the border became more hermetical, as occurred in almost all Eastern and Central-Eastern European border regions. The majority of civilians accepted the concept of the closed and guarded border, as well as that of Russia being the "other" in their life. The issue of trust is very interesting in this context: Border guards started to help civilians in their every-day life in order to get to know them better and to win their trust. Consequently, the border guards represented not only the means of control for civilians, but also a means of help and, most importantly, the feeling of security. Merovuo emphasizes: "It was part of the professional border work to build a bond of trust between officials and civilians." (p. 12)

Chloe Wells, human geographer, combines ideas from Human Geography, Border Studies and Memory Studies in her work to examine collective memories and post-memories concerning the Finnish-Russian border region. She uses the example of the former Finnish city of Viipuri, which has been known as Vyborg, Russia, since World War II. Wells shows how the older generation of Finns from Vyborg tend to cultivate a certain mythology and nostalgia regarding the "lost Finnish city". Finnish media and social media discourses reinforce this picture of the "lost Vyborg". In contrast, the results of focus groups conducted by Wells indicate that Finnish youth appear to have only a very vague knowledge about the city's history and geographical location. However, in many cases, the Finnish youth also repeated clearly recognisable versions of the older generations' nostalgic images and memories of Finnish Vyborg and of discourses occurring in the Finnish media. Wells' contribution adds to our understanding of how and why certain groups remember border change and (lost) borderland cities, the nature of memories of place, and the emotions associated with these memories.

Olga Ilyukha, historian and anthropologist, also deals with the younger generation. She explores how the notion of the border was explained to children during the era of the Soviet Union. Soviet propaganda paid considerable attention to children in order to educate a new generation who would be part of the future communist system. Ilyukha shows how the border as a dividing line between "them" and "us" was an essential consolidating factor for the entire society in Soviet mythology, and for children in particular. The border had a function to protect citizens from danger, a foreign enemy that was often presented in the form of a metaphor, mostly a wolf. Children learnt about the borders of their homeland in almost all school subjects. They studied poems about border guards and learned grammar rules using texts about the border. In addition, in their leisure time, children were supposed to learn about the Soviet border when playing various border games. Based on children's drawings, children's modern perception of the state border is analysed.

Dorte Jagetić Andersen and Steffen Höhne deal with the topic of heritage in border regions.

Dorte Jagetić Andersen, ethnologist and philosopher, analyses the ways in which war heritage has solidified the national image of the Croatian town, Vukovar, located on the border with Serbia. Being turned into a national symbol has affected the townscape and its population, preventing as it is both the renewal of built structures and the overcoming of ethnic tension. In her analysis, the author focuses on the post-war initiatives aimed at developing new heritage infrastructures. After a brief introduction to Croatian nation-building after partition, Jagetić Andersen explores the concept of war heritage and its relationship to nation-building. Next, the author takes the reader on a tour of sites in Vukovar that have come to symbolize the memory of war. She explains how the Croatian presence in the Yugoslav conflict is being recast and how the war heritage is brought into play in the formation of spatial identity. The author also describes how collective memory is influencing the community. Vukovar's status in the national narrative highlights the ethnic divisions within the town; Serbs and Croats continue to live separately, which only emphasises how, "War narratives may attract tourists but they do nothing to overcome ethnic tensions." (p. 65)

Steffen Höhne, cultural scientist, analyses the cultural practices of memory of the Italian city Trieste (Trieste/Trst) and the Ukrainian city Chernivtsi (Černivci/Cernăuţi) in his article. Both of these cities are central, Habsburg-oriented cultural cities, relating back to their diverse multilingual literary development in the late 19th and 20th centuries. Höhne describes urban development and monuments in the cities, which, as a visual element and a historical-political medium, are an expression of publicly binding identity politics. Höhne concludes that urban monument policy obviously refers to the constitution of collectively binding spatial concepts and images, which are intended to have a group-stabilizing effect. As a supranational political entity, Trieste needed to be recoded nationally. While the concepts of Habsburg and Italianità are very visible, the Slovenian component appears to have been marginalised. Chernivtsi also wants to reach out to and engage in its multinational past.

Volodymyr Kravchenko, historian, deals with historical discourses in Ukraine and their function in the context of the Ukrainian-Russian conflict during and after the Euromaidan and the Russian annexation of the Crimea in 2014. After a brief description of Ukrainian-Russian relations following the dissolution of the Soviet Union, he analyses recent Ukrainian regionalism and its role in the symbolic reconfiguration of the Ukrainian-Russian borderland. Kravchenko highlights the fact that the desire to strengthen relations with the European Union is much stronger in Ukrainian society than the prioritisation of contacts with Russia. The gradual erosion of the Soviet space and the clash of Russian neo-imperialist policies with Ukrainian ethnic-cultural doctrines have contributed to the symbolic heterogenisation of the Ukrainian border territory and the emergence of regional discourses. These were used for political purposes during the Euromaidan Revolution of 2014, the Russian annexation of Crimea and the "hybrid war" in Donbass. These events were very important stimuli to both the Russian and the Ukrainian nation-building. With respect to the Ukrainian-Russian borderland, Kravchenko concludes that, it appears more consolidated on the

Russian side than it does on the Ukrainian side. He argues for the updating of the methodological arsenal of Ukrainian and Russian border and regional studies.

Gerhard Besier, historian and psychologist, explores the question, "Which factors trigger a feeling of togetherness and which ones cause feelings of separateness?" (p. 115) based on experiences from the Polish-Russian and Ukrainian-Russian border regions. This article aims to explain how emotional anthropological factors work to limit cross-border co-operation. Besier examines how people make use of old myths and archaic notions of an imagined "other one", concepts of a stranger who is different from "us". "The other" is mostly celebrated through stereotypes, prejudices and concepts of the enemy, a danger to "us". Moreover, people typically want to believe tales of conspiracy because they create a context of justification that is both emotionally believable and compatible with their expectations. Far too frequently, phenomena such as these asserting the need for mental separation are used to justify the existence of borders. Besier emphasises that it is very important that people identify how they need to change their own minds in order to overcome their prejudices against their neighbours and, consequently, to achieve successful cross-border co-operation.

Joanna Frątczak-Müller and **Anna Mielczarek-Żejmo**, sociologists, deal with the impact of the Euroregion Spree-Neisse-Bober on cross-border cooperation in the German-Polish border region as well as perceptions of the work of this Euroregion in the population.

The starting point for the development of neighbourhood relations in the German-Polish border region was not easy. The end of the Second World War, painful border changes and expulsions of the German population brought, above all, animosity and hindered good relations between Poland and Germany for many years. The German-Polish border was hermetically closed until 1991 (with a short opening period from 1972–1980). One of the consequences of cross-border co-operation after the opening of the border was the creation of Euroregions, which aim to strengthen co-operation. Research carried out by the authors in 2013–2014 indicates that most inhabitants of the region support activities of the Euroregion Spree-Neisse-Bober, which was created in 1993. Both Poles and Germans identify mutual contacts as significant. A very important effect of this support is the relatively high level of mutual trust demonstrated on both sides of the border. Nonetheless, respondents from the German side of the Euroregion declared more often that they have trust in their neighbours, when compared to inhabitants from the Polish side. German inhabitants stated more frequently that meetings with friends from a neighbouring country are very important. By contrast, Poles tend to perceive their neighbours as "others" and "strangers" more often than is the case for Germans.

To conclude the anthology, **Birte Wassenberg**, historian, presents the Jean Monnet project "Conflict and Cooperation in EU Border Regions (EU-Front)", which had the goal of exchanging experiences and debate on the role of the border in the process of European Integration. In addition, she describes diverse projects in European border regions that can be used as models and contribute to the process of European Integration. She also presents the development of border studies from the 1970s to the present day and highlights the variety of phenomena related to this topic. Wassenberg explains that "despite cooperation and reconciliation, conflict also remains a key characteristic in European border regions" and "many obstacles to cross-border cooperation still have to be overcome". (p. 142; 144)

Although the articles in this volume indicate that there has already been a great deal accomplished and written in the scholarly discipline of border and border region studies, it also becomes clear that much more research and further comparative studies are needed in order to understand and explain the border phenomenon fully.

I would like to thank all those who have contributed to the development of this anthology: Heather Rae for the translation and proofreading of numerous articles, Marie Jorun Breuer for the organisation of the notes, the preparation of the index of names and places and the list of abbreviations and Olaf Lange for the layout.

Sønderborg / Berlin, January 2019

Persistent operation

Memories of border work during transition periods

Jenni Merovuo

Introduction

My paper studies the official border work in the Eastern Finnish borderland in Ilomantsi municipality, focusing on the transition periods after the establishment of the Finnish Border Guard in 1919 and after re-establishment in 1947. I investigate the border work that Madeleine Reeves describes as the "business of making the territory integral". Reeves is talking about making the authoritarian boundaries stand out in a process that is messy and controversial. The borders are spatial but also temporal for they are under constant development.[1] My interest is especially focused on social interaction because I view it as essential to the border-building process.

Ilomantsi is located in North Karelia and borders Russia in the east. During the Second World War, as Finland ceded the southeast corner of the state to Russia, the borderline shifted southwards from Ilomantsi. The municipality became the easternmost part of Finland. In this paper, I focus on memories of the interaction. Although my focus is on the transition periods, I consider the border work perpetual. In my article, I argue that the border work was bidirectional. It was not always purpose-orientated, nor even conscious, but intertwined the professional and personal as well as state and local levels in an interesting manner.

The Finnish Border Guard was established in 1919, when responsibility for guarding the borderline was transferred from the Ministry of War to the Ministry of the Interior. Four districts were established on the eastern border: Salmi, Joensuu, Kainuu and Lapland. In 1922, the Karelian Isthmus was separated into a district of its own. The Joensuu border guard district included the borderline from Pielisjärvi (Lieksa from 1973 onwards) to Salmijärvi village in Suojärvi. During the Second World War, Finnish Border Guard personnel served under the defence forces, after which the institution was re-established. The North Karelia[2]

1 Madeleine Reeves, Border work. Spatial lives of the state in rural Central Asia, Cornell University Press, Ithaca-London 2014, 6–7.

2 The Joensuu Border Guard District was renamed upon re-establishment.

Border Guard District oversaw the stabilisation of the new borderline from Ilomantsi municipality southwards.

Methods and sources

In this chapter, I focus on two transition periods. The duration of the transition process cannot be precisely defined. However, post-war transition processes have been evaluated to last close to 20 years, as new practices replace the old ones. It is not a revolution but a slow, heterogeneous and sometimes selective process that may have little comprehensive significance at the state level.[3] The years following both the establishment of the Finnish Border Guard and the border change after the Second World War have features that are missing from the sources of the late 1960's and 1970's. The period after the Second World war was especially significant in the three southernmost Border Guard Districts since the border shifted westwards. The remains of the Karelian Isthmus and Salmi Districts were merged and became the Southeast Finland Border Guard District. The change affected the Joensuu Border Guard District significantly since the course of the borderline changed to the southwest from Virmajärvi in Ilomantsi municipality. Roughly half of the North Karelian borderline was re-established. In the reorganization, the Joensuu Border Guard District was renamed the North Karelia Border Guard, keeping its headquarters in Kontiolahti municipality.

As my main sources, I use the interviews archived in the North Karelian Border Guard Heritage Collection. By analysing interviews collected by the North Karelian Border Guard, I present the border guards' contribution to building the border region. I understand the region as historical and constantly becoming in interaction. This building process that forges the state boundary occasionally provokes conflict. I concentrate on the transitional periods of the 20th century – Finland's independence from Russia and the Second World War. I will investigate the structural changes in society that strained relations between border guards and locals, but also border guarding as a profession.

I have analysed altogether 26 audio recordings that include interviews of 34 people. Four of the informants are civilians and 12 of the 30 officials talk specifically about the Ilomantsi border area. Ilomantsi municipality is in the middle of the North Karelia Border Guard district. The northern borderline follows a centuries-old conception of the boundary. The southern part was redefined in the 1940's. The border zone was sparsely populated throughout the research period.

All the interviews are conducted by retired border guards. The first audios were recorded in 1961 and 1983 on a multitrack recorder and have since been digitised. Other interviews happened in 2008 and 2009 as the border guard guilds organised the profession's heritage gathering. Former colleagues conducted tens of interviews in North Karelia. A few civilians were also interviewed. The interviews meander around various topics. The significance the interviews have for a

---

3 Antti Räihä, Jatkuvuus ja muutoksen hallinta. Hamina ja Lappeenranta Ruotsin ja Venäjän alaisuudessa 1720–1760-luvuilla, in: Jyväskylä studies in humanities 183 (2012), 20–22.

researcher may not have been apparent when the recordings were made since the aim was to preserve what is considered the border guards' heritage.[4]

The interviews were conducted among the border guards that maintain contact with the guilds. Some of the informants have since passed away. The heritage interviews were collected during a "calm" period in the border's existence. This has allowed the former border guards to distance themselves from the years during which the border was considered threatened. Interviews conducted later[5] may highlight different aspects. A memory always embodies the present moment.

The familiarity of the interviewer may have spurred the conversation. The arrangement whereby former border guards interview each other poses an atmosphere of collectiveness. The interviews followed a common structure, with much variety in detail. Professional issues regarded as self-evident, however, were occasionally neglected. Also, knowingly avoiding a subject occurred. In some interviews, the interviewer manipulated discussion of contested experiences. Group pressure is reflected in the outcome. Presumably, the informants were initially chosen due to their potentially "right" attitude and ability to provide good stories that are well known in the profession. On the other hand, where there are common perspectives, it might have been easier to talk to a former colleague. The arrangement has potentially encouraged or prevented remembering.

Oral history brings certain conditions to the analysis. The interviews do not particularly focus on the topic. I study the memories of the relationship between the border guards and the civilians. How did the border guards experience their position? On one hand, the border guards represented the state. On the other hand, they populated the fringes of the state and experienced the same struggles as the rest of the inhabitants. How did controversy manifest itself between the civilians and the border guards during the transition periods? Jukka Partanen mentions the tensions in the history of the North Karelia Border Guard District. Disputes were not as numerous, however, as in the more densely populated southeastern borderland.[6]

In analysing oral history, it is the researcher's task to sense the stories beyond the words, stories that are to be found in meaningful gaps or tones of voice. In written, the nuances manifest in a different form, if at all. From the interviews, I seek the significance given to the interaction in memories. Conflict or co-operation is remembered or forgotten depending on the meaning given to it. Informants should not be expected to tell their story in an unbiased way. Taking sides

---

4 Patricia Leavy, Oral history, New York 2011, 7–9.

5 In 2017, traffic across the border decreased while the number of the asylum seekers increased. The previous year, only three people sought asylum at the North Karelian border. In the spring of 2017, the number of asylum seekers peaked when a total of eight people sought asylum in North Karelia between April and July. 33 people attempting to cross the border were turned back. These few uneasy episodes in the border district that has been calm for decades alerted the Border Guard to reallocate resources to the "green border" where relations with the borderland civilians provide an additional advantage. North Karelian Border Guard overview 4.5.2017, 5.6.2017, 5.7.2017, 3.8.2017, http://www.raja.fi/tietoa/tiedotteet?466_year=2017. [Accessed: 20.07.2018].

6 Jukka Partanen, Turvana rajalla. Pohjois-Karjalan rajavartiosto 1947–2017, Saarijärvi 2017, 46–48.

is a pre-condition of the interview situation. In this sense, remembering *right* is secondary, if we think of the past as socially constructed. Memories develop.[7]

Identifying collective memory and self-identifying memory as the two intertwining aspects of remembering will foreground the likely patterns of forgetting. Professional secrecy stands for retirement of the border guard and may have affected communication. The setting in which the interviews took place may have discouraged personal reminiscences. The interviews were collected for the institution, organised by the border guard guilds and covered the professional lives of the officials.[8]

Establishing the modern Finnish national border

Eiki Berg has described the Russian-Estonian border of the early 20th century as a space for communication, building and controlling neighbourliness, and protecting territory. In other words, building the borders of newly seceded nations consisted of selective social acts.[9] Before Finland became independent in 1917, the eastern boundary was a customs border. After Finland seceded from Russia, army troops were stationed on the border. In the disorderly state of affairs caused by the First World War and the Russian revolution, the main motivation was to control the flow of travellers and ideas. The internal tension was an overriding concern, yet an attack from Russia was also considered possible. The civil war erupted at the beginning of 1918. In March 1919, the Council of State established the Finnish Border Guard, which took over guarding the border under the Ministry of the Interior, releasing the army from border-guarding duties. The head of the Border Guard District steered the operational activity under the county governor during the initial years. Hence, so-called paramilitary order was established from the start.[10]

The Finnish Border Guard began with organising shelter and equipment. Little was provided beforehand as the whole institution was based on precarious periodical funding. Erikki Raappana was selected as the new commanding colonel in 1921. He described the first years as a time of stabilising the operating base without the certainty of continuity[11]. The ideological ambition of the newly established institution was to build a dividing line between the nations of Finland and Russia. From the headquarters' viewpoint, the national borders were to be considered sacred and untouchable. However, the idea was foreign to the borderland's inhabitants to whom the national boundary was an abstraction that happened to cross

7 Paul Thompson, Believe it or not: Rethinking the Historical Interpretation, in: Jaclyn Jeffrey & Glenace Edwall (Eds.) Memory and history. Essays on Recalling and Interpreting Experience, Maryland 1994, 1–16; here: 8; Aleassandro Portelli, What makes oral history different? in: Robert Perks & Alistair Thomson (Eds.) The Oral History Reader, New York 1998, 63–74; here: 65–73.

8 See Thompson, Believe it, Loc. Cit. (Note 7), 5–7; Markus Heiskanen, Rajakeisarin uudet (v)aatteet. Käsiteanalyysi rajaturvallisuudesta. Acta Electronica Lapponiensis 124 (2013), 647.

9 Eiki Berg, Deconstructing border practices in the Estonian-Russian borderland, in: Geopolitics 5 3 (2000), 78–98; here: 82.

10 See Heiskanen, Rajakeisarin uudet, Loc. Cit. (Note 8), 642; See Partanen, Turvana rajalla, Loc. Cit. (Note 6), 11–12.

11 Interview 1, 8.4.1961, North Karelia Border Guard (NKBG).

the living space to which they were accustomed. The ideologies of the centre and the periphery dissented.[12]

> "... it was hard work and a fight for the Border Guard for the first years, not so much with border guarding as you know it now, but with constructing the attitude of the state authorities. [The] scope of action among the people [was] very small, effectively non-existing. [...] So, border guarding was all about stabilizing. To build a comprehension that we are one. It was more than enough of a task."[13]

Raappana looked back on the early years of the Border Guard as poorly focused. He served as commanding colonel of the Joensuu Border Guard District from 1921 until the Second World War erupted. In an interview recorded in 1961 – a year before his passing – Raappana recollected that it was well into the 1920's before any institutionalized form of border control or consistent procedure was established. The border work was inconsistent as there was no coherent ideological basis. Per Raappana, the governmental authorities did not have a proper perspective on the special characteristics of Finland's eastern border.[14] Thus, there was call for an ideology in addition to equipment and funding.

The commanding colonel had assumed the border to be settled via diplomacy and a political ruling. Per his statement, much was left to the border guards to define. Establishing the border at grassroot level happened via interaction. Raappana believed a lack of knowledge about local conditions prevented the centralized political steering of border work. He tackled the problem unprompted. In the interview, Raappana mentions that the parliament had a vision of a very porous borderline, much like the token boundary Finland had with Sweden following River Tornio.[15] For many, this was inadequate.

The memory of not being fully endorsed by the Government arose from the confused situation the commanding colonel was thrown into during his first year in office. In 1922, the so-called East Karelian Uprising in Russia was supported by Finnish volunteers. The uprising aspired Russian Karelia independence from the Soviet Union, but failed miserably. The retreating troops, with Soviet soldiers at their heels, sought asylum from the Finnish Karelia side. Concerned about the consequences, Raappana was granted permission to close the border. However, the Border Guard District lacked the manpower to keep a solid guard. The funding was at an all-time low in 1922, as the Government debated on the necessity of the institution.[16] Raappana felt unsupported by the state. The Border Guard's persistent mission to 'sacralise' the border was overlooked. The psychological dividing line, though, would symbolise national independence and increase national safety.

---

12 See Partanen, Turvana rajalla, Loc. Cit. (Note 6), 12–18.

13 Interview 1, 8.4.1961 Joensuu, commander colonel 1921–1939, NKBG. "... kyllä Rajavartiolaitos ensimmäiset vuodet sai taistella ja tehdä työtä, ei niinkään paljon rajavartioinnin kanssa ja rajavartiopalveluksessa, siis nykyisessä mielessä, kun piti luoda Suomen valtiovallan käsitykset. Toimintamahdollisuudet kansan keskuuteen oli olemattomat, niitä ei ollut olemassakaan. [...] Siis koko tämä rajavartiostotoiminta oli pelkästään vakiinnuttaa. Saada kansa siihen käsitykseen, että me olemme yhtä. Siinä olikin hommaa enemmän kuin tarpeeksi."

14 See Interview 1, 8.4.1961, Loc. Cit. (Note 13) NKBG.

15 See Interview 1, 8.4.1961, Loc. Cit. (Note 13) NKBG.

16 Jukka Partanen & Juha Pohjonen, Rajakomendanttina, in: Jukka Partanen & Juha Pohjonen, E. I. Raappana: Rajan ja sodan kenraali, Keuruu 2007, 59–137; here: 63–68.

Forging the dividing line

Before Finland gained independence, the cross-border interaction was lively. The post-revolution incoherence, Russian concern about the German invasion through Finland, the Finnish Civil War and the Karelian Uprising all strained the relations between Russia and its newly seceded former grand duchy.[17] Throughout the 1920's and 1930's the position of the Border Guard as a defence organisation was on the table. Military control seemed unnecessarily provocative to some. On the other hand, the former Jaegers[18] holding office within the Border Guard were enthusiastic to ideologically differentiate the Finnish borderland from Russia. The Border Guard management portrayed spying, smuggling and military threat as the greatest dangers to the state boundary and the borderland. Before the Second World War erupted, the chief of the Border Guard, Wiljo Tuompo, highlighted the soldierly duties of the organization.[19] Interest in guarding the state border was not economic but ideological and defensive.

According to Raappana, the locals did not regard crossing the border a significant act or a statement but a part of their everyday life. Nor did they fear the beyond. The cross-border region and its occupants were part of their regional habitat. Many had relatives or friends living across the border, which had not previously prevented communication. The officers, however, saw crossing the border as a security risk. The major general, Tuompo, saw the sanctity of the border as embodied in the national sovereignty and therefore crossing the border was to be subjected under strict official control. Both, Tuompo and Raappana, underlined the Finnish identity as opposing the Russian.[20] To secure the border, the community had to become stronger, an "us" in opposition to "them" – the Russians. In Joensuu Border Guard District, the challenge was the peripheral borderland population.

The locals needed to be persistently persuaded and convinced to support the institution's mission by practical means of persuasion. The poor of the borderland, in particular, were interpreted to be in need of national cultivation of culture. Due to a severe food shortage in the early years the poor were prepared to follow anyone who could bring food, as Raappana recalled. In the 1920's, an institutional-

17 Marja Simola, Sotilaskotityötä rajoillamme. Rajasotilaskotiyhdistys viisikymmentä vuotta, Joensuu 1996, 11; Maunu Häyrynen, The Adjustable periphery: Borderlands in the Finnish National Landscape Imagery, in: Lars-Folke Landgren and Maunu Häyrynen (Eds.), Dividing Line. Borders and National Peripheries, Renvall Institute Publications 9, Helsinki 1997, 103–112; here: 108; Matti Kosonen, I–IV, in: Matti Kosonen & Juha Pohjonen, Isänmaan portinvartijat. Suomen rajojen vartiointi 1918–1994, Keuruu 1994, 11–240; here: 61.

18 Jaegers were a group of Finnish separatists who trained and served in the German Army 1914–1918. After the Finnish Civil War in 1918, they became national heroes and an essential group in building the Finnish National Army. Anders Ahlbäck, Sotasankaruus miehuuden esikuvana, in: Ulla-Maija Peltonen & Ilona Kemppainen (Eds.), Kirjoituksia sankaruudesta, Suomen Kirjallisuuden Seuran toimituksia 1283, Helsinki 2010, 47–88; here 52–63.

19 See Interview 1, 8.4.1961, Loc. Cit. (Note 13) NKBG; Wiljo Tuompo, Rajavartiostojen tehtävät ja niiden suoritus, in: Itärajan vartijat. Piirteitä rajavartiostojen 20-vuotistaipaleelta, Joensuu 1939, 9–20; here: 9–12.

20 See Tuompo, Rajavartiostojen tehtävät, Loc. Cit. (Note 19), 9–12; See Interview 1, 8.4.1961, Loc. Cit. (Note 13) NKBG.

ized effort was made to educate the borderland inhabitants on national ideal. The borderland work undertaken together by the Finnish Border Guard, the Soldiers' Home Association and the Civil Guard aimed at building Finnish patriotism. However, the myth of "us" – the Finns as keepers of the last outpost of the West – seemed foreign to the people. Civilians daily concerns revolved around their immediate surroundings, not the national ideology. Little did they fear Russia, but many were suspicious of the Civil Guard with the Civil War having just come to a devastating end.[21] The common ideology would not find its way into people's thinking by merely informative means. Thus, the borderland work continued to be persistently incorporated into the border guarding duties.

Raappana began consciously improving relations between the inhabitants and the border guards. The goal was to build trust to encourage the public to report information to the border guards about smugglers, defectors, and any suspicious activity near the border. In *Guidelines and Orders for the Stations*, Raappana defined the guidelines for communicating with the public. The border guards were to behave calmly and politely to feed positive attitudes. Every border guard represented the institution and must therefore serve all Finns. Specific neutralism was to be used with those sympathetic to the "Reds"[22] who had lost the Civil War and those proclaiming themselves unbiased. One was required to refrain from having an opinion one way or another. Civilians were to be kept out of the Border Guard premises, but the guards were to approach the civilians in their own habitat to establish rapport while also performing risk analysis.[23] These instructions foregrounded the internal border work.

The border work as ordering and bordering is a multifaceted process happening simultaneously at several levels of society. Everyday activities, brief encounters, concepts, definitions and narratives all construct the border.[24] North Karelian borderland civilians remembered with gratitude the favours the border guards did for them. In an interview recorded in 2008, one informant, still a child in the 1930's, tells how the border guards acknowledged the civilians by bringing them their post and calling on them socially, gradually building efficiency and trust. The civilians benefitted from the presence of officials and the border guards received information in return. Also, the borderland households produced foodstuffs for the border guards in exchange for money, special goods and assistance. The guards volunteered for farm work and assisted with tasks while on patrol.[25] The border guarding was rather place-specific and independent in the 1920's and 1930's. The challenges posed by the poor infrastructure put the same strain on the border guards and the civilians, and highlighted their personal relationships.

---

21 See Interview 1, 8.4.1961, Loc. Cit. (Note 13) NKBG; See Simola, Sotilaskotityötä, Loc. Cit. (Note 17), 11; See Häyrynen, The Adjustable periphery, Loc. Cit. (Note 17), 108; See Kosonen, I–IV, Loc. Cit. (Note 17), 61; Kimmo Katajala, Finland – the Last Outpost of Western Civilization, in: Kirchliche Zeitgeschichte 27 (2014), 299–309; here: 301–303.

22 By the "Reds" I am referring to the working-class based party of the Civil War defeated by the "Whites".

23 Guidelines and Orders for the guards in the field 21.12.1925, North Karelia Border Guard District, Joensuu (NKBG).

24 See Reeves, Border Work, Loc. Cit. (Note 1), 5–6, 241–242.

25 Interview 2, 29.12.1982, NKBG; Interview 6 7.2.2008 Lieksa, two civilians 1930–, NKBG.

To build a chain of trust between the borderland civilians and the headquarters of the Border Guard District, the border guards in the field needed to be trustworthy. To strengthen the institutional profile, locals were rarely employed as border guards because of their potential contradictory affiliations with the civilians. They might sympathize with the suspicious behaviour of their friends and relatives, or create unwanted controversy via their personal relationships. Nevertheless, some managed to pursue a career in their own region. A North Karelian, hired as a border guard in 1929, confirmed in an interview conducted in 1982 that headquarters was suspicious of locals in service. He did not remember having any objectivity issues but tells a story of another local border guard who concealed his relatives' dealings across the border. The outcome convinced him that the mistrust was justified, he remembered. Therefore, he accepted the attitude.[26] Headquarters' suspicion in relation to all border guards manifested itself in personal life restrictions, such as permitting marriage only by courtesy of the commanding colonel.[27] A neutral and diligent border official winning the trust of both headquarters and the locals was an ideal. The guards were living in the borderland, not as locals but as state officials, which put them in a somewhat precarious position.

Most border guards came to North Karelia from Ostrobothnia or Southern Finland. For many, border guarding was merely temporary employment. In the 1920's, contracts were short, and troublemakers were let go easily. Usually the border guards served for a maximum of a few years and returned home. Turnover was high and the motivation often low. The out-of-towners faced the challenge of building trust among the locals. The Ostrobothnians fitted the headquarters' profile but were not welcomed with neutrality among the civilians. Ironically, many locals treated them as outsiders – the "other" – with no understanding of local conditions.[28] The borders of identification followed no administrational, political or physical boundary. In fact, Raappana defined people as Russians based on their faith and social contacts. When in need, he said in the interview, they would turn to the East for support. Piia Einonen points out that Finnishness as opposed to other nationalities, was not common in Eastern Finland at the beginning of the 20th century. In addition to heavy emigration, there was immigration as well.[29]

The border guards remember intermittent controversial encounters with the locals. Civilians, especially in Ilomantsi municipality, where the border ribboned through the wilderness, were not used to the constant presence of the officials. Now the border guards intruded on their habitat to control the borderland civilians. Per the border guard orders, encroaching on another official's remit was for-

26 Guidelines and Orders for the guards in the field 21.12.1925, NKBG; Interview 2, 29.12.1982, NKBG.

27 See Partanen, Turvana rajalla, Loc. Cit. (Note 6), 45–46.

28 Samuel Juutinen, Rajavartiokoulu Lieksassa, in: Asko Saarelainen (Ed), Hukan hännän mitalla: Rajaseudun historiaa Lieksasta, Jyväskylä (2004), 378–399; here: 381–382; Marja Walling, Pitkä partio: Rajavartijan taival havumetsistä Schengenin ulkorajoille. Rajavartioliitto 50 vuotta (1954–2004), Kajaani (2006), 18–20, 137.

29 See Interview 1, 8.4.1961, Loc. Cit. (Note 13) NKBG; Interview 2, 29.12.1982 Ilomantsi, border guard 1929–1939, NKBG; Piia Einonen, Vyborg's Two Faces: Drawing National, Religious, and Spatial Boundaries in the First Half of the 19th Century, in: Kimmo Katajala (Ed), Meanings of an Urban Space: understanding the historical layers of Vybor, Mittel- und Ostmitteleuropastudien 12, Wien 2016, 153–157.

bidden but acting when necessary essential. Poaching and illegal distillation were contradictory issues. Border guard Otto Moilanen wrote a reminiscence in the local newspaper in 1953 about confronting a game-bird-poaching civilian with an illegal trap in the 1920's. As an official, Moilanen felt obligated to discipline him although he was aware of the food shortages. The man admitted knowingly breaking the law but educated Moilanen on the hunger the people were suffering from. The informant from 1982 mentioned similar situation, this time involving illegal distilling. Far from the trade centres, the people made moonshine; the border guards empathised since it was unreasonable to expect people to travel to the commercial centres. Alcohol was in demand at the periphery for medicinal purpose, the informants emphasised.[30] In these cases, the challenge of striking a balance between the professional and personal becomes evident. Favourable decisions were presented as good policy, although they were not in accordance with orders.

Border zone – Back to square one?

State borders are more than mere lines on a map. Forging in multiple complex processes, the territoriality of the state, argues Reeves, often contrasts with local interests. Not only the physical act of creating a border, but the mental and conceptual aspects of the border work ground the spatiality of a nation state. Everyday conflicts and cooperation between the officials and the civilians of the borderland should be investigated as an essential expression of the border work.[31] Between the state and the civilians, the border guards upheld the space for control, bargaining and reciprocity.

Minor restrictions for movement near the border already stood in the 1920's, but there was no systematic enforcement of the border zone. But, as an outcome of the Second World War, Finland established a new borderline and a restricted border zone to control the eastern boundary. Since 1939, before Finland waged war with Russia, movement within the borderland became firmly limited. Approaching the borderline was restricted. Visitors needed permits for travel near the border. During the war, the border guards were assigned under military order. The peace treaty of Moscow in 1940 reshaped the south-eastern boundary of Finland as she ceded part of Karelia to Russia. In 1947, the year the Finnish Border Guard was re-established, Finland established border zone legislation delimiting the surroundings of the immediate border. The border zone was defined as projecting up to the state border maximum of three kilometres. Any visits to the zone required a border zone permit. The inhabitants needed a valid permit and were expected to adhere to the special behavioural code, for example refraining from pointing light directly towards the border.[32]

---

30 Guidelines and Orders for the guards in the field 21.12.1925, NKBG; Interview 1, 8.4.1961, NKBG; See Interview 2, 29.12.1982, Loc. Cit. (Note 29) NKBG.

31 See Reeves, Border work, Loc. Cit. (Note 1), 241–242.

32 See Pohjonen, Isänmaan portinvartijat, Loc. Cit. (Note 17), 264, 356–359; Ville Thomsson, Elämää rajavyöhykkeellä: erityismääräyksien vaikutus rajaseudulla asuneiden elämään vuosina

The people whose everyday lives were not significantly affected by the border change adapted more easily to the new situation. The border zone as such was not an attraction except to the occasional adventurer. However, in cases where the new restrictions affected returning to everyday life after the war, subjecting to the regulations presented a challenge. During the Second World War, Finland evacuated a great number of people from ceded Karelia. The evacuees were relocated within the state borders after the war. Thus, social networks shifted along with the border, producing a different situation than in the 1910's. The cross-border contacts did not pose the same challenge as during the first transition period, but the loss of home, land and fishing grounds was difficult on many. A company commander, and later commanding colonel, of the reorganised, re-established and renamed Karelia Border Guard highlighted the situation after the war. There was increasing bitterness among the borderland people about lost possessions and the rationing of goods.[33] Resources were remote and there was no clear outlook with regards to the future.

The civilians accepted the idea of the closed and guarded boundary between states but, for some, the restricted border zone was unreasonable. Although the restrictions were in place for years before the border zone legislation, the discontent lived on. To establish the border after the war required determination from the officials to steer behaviour in accordance with the new law.[34] In a documentary by The Finnish broadcasting company YLE, disputes over the usufruct of the border zone was described as a war. When asked if they had problems with the border guard officials, an inhabitant answered:

> "Why, yes, I did, back then, when the war ended, we always clashed over fishing. We fished on the border zone and supposedly it was forbidden. […] Well, now [1973] that war has ended once and for all, I can fish there as long as I apply for the [border zone] permit."[35]

The locals felt entitled to the usufruct of the border zone on the grounds of tradition. From the state's viewpoint, the zone was established to reassert the linear state border. The controlled zone was hardly a novelty in border security, yet for the locals seeking to normalise their lives after the war, it was sometimes construed as further oppression. Others mistook the zonal boundary as a Russian stipulation and were less eager to protest. The idea of Russia as the "other" had gained wider acceptance now. As much as for securing against external threats, the boundary was about controlling the interior. In the beginning, the boundary markers and injunctions needed to be accompanied by diligent surveillance to fully establish the

---

1944–1954, unpublished master's thesis, UEF 2010, 34; See Kosonen, I-IV, Loc. Cit. (Note 17), 95–99, 147; See Partanen, Turvana rajalla, Loc. Cit. (Note 6), 37, 43.

33 Interview 4 21.1.2008 Kontiolahti, commander colonnel etc. 1947–1968, NKBG; Interview 5 21.10.2008 Kontiolahti, commander colonnel etc. 21.10.2008, NKBG; Interview 18, 27.3.2008 Lieksa, border guard 1968–1995, NKBG.

34 See Pohjonen, Isänmaan portinvartijat, Loc. Cit. (Note 17), 360.

35 "No, oli aikoinaan, silloin sota kun loppui, niin silloin oli kahnauksia aina tuossa kalastuksessa. Kun kalastettiin rajavyöhykkeellä ja siellä ei kuulemma oikeastaan olisi ollut lupa kalastaa. […] No, nyt on rauhoittunut se sota pois kokonaan, että nyt saadaan kalastaa siellä, kun saadaan vaan [rajavyöhyke]luvat." Arvi Auvinen/ Yleisradio 25.4.1973, http://yle.fi/elavaarkisto/artikkelit/myo_oomme_kun_luonnonlapset_risukossa_11262.html#media=11265, [Accessed: 20.07.2018].

new borderline. In memories, most of the border zone complications were caused by animals, fishermen, hunters and simple-minded people who did not understand the restrictions of the border zone. The troublemakers were a minority.[36]

The narrowing down of the border zone began in the 1960's. The stabilised practices along with the calm international border and developing international politics enabled this improvement. The Border Guard aimed to exclude most civilian dwellings from the restricted zone, thus lightening the bureaucracy by further isolating the area. The work became more risk-oriented as movement at the border slowed down. The border zone was narrowed down significantly between the 1960's and the 2000's.[37]

Reciprocity and reciprocal mistrust

A station benefitted the borderland community in many ways. Help and access to a phone are mentioned frequently in the interviews as increasing a sense of security. From the 1960's onwards, televisions brought villagers to the stations. Though the instructions were not to encourage the public to make themselves too comfortable at the stations, in everyday life relations became rather unreserved. However, the benefits did not come gratuitously. The Border Guard insisted on setting up watch towers and phone lines on civilian property, for example. Also, the inhabitants of the border zone needed permits for any guests. Windows facing east were to be covered.[38] On one hand, the surveillance provoked a sense of security, but it restricted privacy.

To get to know the locals, the border guards applied the old practice of helping the civilians.[39] In Ilomantsi, the border guards also rented accommodation in civilians' houses before the funding for the new stations was organised. Once again, the locals made an income from providing food supplies and the border guards volunteered for hay-making and harvesting, although they could not help everyone, which created jealousy.[40] The interdependence was inevitably built on efficiency, yet social differences existed in the periphery as well. Contact seemed to be focused on people with favourable attitudes and reasonable living stand-

36 Interview 15 17.6.2008 Ilomantsi, seven border guards 1950–2000, NKBG; See Interview 18 27.3.2008, Loc. Cit. (Note 33) NKBG; Interview 19 28.3.2008 Lieksa, border guard 1969–1996, NKBG; Interview 22 2009, Tohmajärvi, civilian 1930–, NKBG; Interview 25 13.8.2009 Ilomantsi, five border guards 1960–2000, NKBG.

37 Interview 7 7.2.2008 Lieksa, two civilians, NKBG; Interview 12 11.3.2008 Ilomantsi, border guard 1974–1999, NKBG; See Interview 25 13.8.2009, Loc. Cit. (Note 36) NKBG; Interview 26 28.10.2009 Tohmajärvi, civilian 1955–, NKBG; Map: Narrowing down of the border zone, 2013, NKBG.

38 Interview 9 3.3.2008 Ilomantsi, border guard 1957–1978, NKBG; Interview 10 2008, Lieksa, Four border guards 1960–1999, NKBG; See Interview 12 11.3.2008, Loc. Cit. (Note 37) NKBG; Interview 16 25.3.2008 Lieksa, border guard 1958–1983, NKBG; Interview 21 2009, Tohmajärvi, civilian 1930–, NKBG.

39 See Partanen, Turvana rajalla, Loc. Cit. (Note 6), 46–47.

40 Interview 13 11.3.2008 Ilomantsi, border guard 1974–1999, NKBG; Interview 14 17.3.2008 Ilomantsi, border guard 1966–1990, NKBG; See Interview 10 2008, Loc. Cit. (Note 38) NKBG; Interview 23 22.10.2008 Ilomantsi, border guard 1960s–1980s, NKBG.

ards. The marginalised poor, such as the man in the documentary film mentioned above, were not discussed very much in the interviews. The closest bonds seemed to have been built with the landowners and the families, since social and practical interests brought people together.

According to Jukka Partanen, significant violations took place in more densely populated areas. In Ilomantsi, he argues, there were few problems because the population close to the immediate border was scarce. However, the interviews suggest that the border guards did indeed face reluctance to submit to the new border regulations. In general, the public was frustrated with the disciplining officials after the war was over. To the evacuees, the injunction on visiting their homes on the Soviet Russian side, or even walking along the border to look across, seemed unjust. Furthermore, the out-of-towners as border guards put an additional strain on relations. The practice of hiring guards from Ostrobothnia was adopted on the same grounds as before the war. Headquarters was suspicious of locals due to their personal entanglements in relation to border crossings and border zone violations.[41] Locals felt these strangers had a poor understanding of the region its people.[42] The commanding colonel ordered the border guards to resort to kindness with the civilians. "The best asset in gaining the trust of the borderland inhabitants lies in [doing] favours out of love and kindness."[43]

In the interviews with the Ilomantsi border guards, the universal suppression of negative collective memories is present, nonetheless. "Not the slightest problem,"[44] reacted some, yet the statement is accompanied by long pauses and heavy sighs indicating hesitation. Surely many border guards had good relationships with the civilians. It was part of the professional border work to build a bond of trust between officials and civilians. The civilians enjoyed the company of the officials, recalled one guard[45]. No major fights or quarrels arose. It may be that the lack of open conflict invalidated the memories of minor friction, which might have been hard to recognise retrospectively. The question regarding problems is passed over quickly. Some hint of discontent still lives on in the memories. For example, the border guards recall being considered feeble. The high turnover suggested that the quality of the men was not satisfactory. In the eyes of some civilians, sitting on guard duty or skiing along the border zone seemed the kind of lazing around that anyone was capable of.[46] This was experienced as unjust, as well as embarrassing, within the profession.

41 See Interview 4 21.10.2008, Loc. Cit. (Note 33) NKBG; Ilmari Kirjavainen, Sotavuodet ja sotien välinen aika, in: Uuno Peltoniemi & Kai Säteri & Ilmari Kirjavainen (Eds), Rajavartiolaitos 1919–1969, Mikkeli 1969, 217–454; here: 357; See Pohjonen, Isänmaan portinvartijat, Loc. Cit. (Note 17), 264, 348, 356–359, 509; See Thomsson, Elämää rajavyöhykkeellä, Loc. Cit. (Note 32), 34; See Partanen, Turvana rajalla, Loc. Cit. (Note 6), 85–86, 107; See Walling, Pitkä partio, Loc. Cit. (Note 28), 138.

42 See Interview 10 2008, Loc. Cit. (Note 38) NKBG; See Interview 4 21.10.2008, Loc. Cit. (Note 33) NKBG; See Partanen, Turvana rajalla, Loc. Cit. (Note 6), 100–108.

43 Order of the day 1./R3, 12.12.1944, NKBG, "Parahin keino rajaseudun asukkaiden luottamuksen saavuttamiseksi on rakkaudenpalveluksen ja avuliaisuuden osoittaminen."

44 See Interview 14, 17.3.2008, Loc. Cit. (Note 40) NKBG.

45 See Interview 13 11.3.2008, Loc. Cit. (Note 40) NKBG.

46 See Interview 10 2008, Loc. Cit. (Note 38) NKBG; See Interview 4 21.10.2008, Loc. Cit. (Note 33) NKBG; See Partanen, Turvana rajalla, Loc. Cit. (Note 6), 100–108.

The arrangement whereby former border guards interviewed each other seems to have encouraged foregrounding some issues, and overriding others. When the mind is set on a certain task, memories adapt to the situation. A recalled memory moulds into the setting it is brought back to instead of reappearing immutable every time. Therefore, the memory and the concept of the past develop. The present is always connected to the recollection. Collectively upheld conceptions therefore affect the way we tend to remember the past.[47] One of the retired border guards carried out six of the interviews I used. I paid especial attention to him as he joined the primary informant in reminiscing about the past.

In the first two interviews of the six, the informant cannot remember any problems with the civilians, and neither can the interviewer. The third informant defined trust as following the rules and cannot remember a case of a civilian defying them. In the fourth interview, the interviewer admits that surely there were some people who were not happy with him. In the next interview, the informant speaks of *"a few Red men who did not like border guards"*. In another, an informant mentions that the educated respected the profession, but problems occurred with the working class. Also, the young were remembered as having adapted the easiest in relation to control. In the sixth talk, the interviewer opens discussion on the topic by spontaneously stating that he did not personally remember any problems and even that girls were imposed on him. Several out-of-towners settled in Ilomantsi and married into the community but conflicts still occurred between men of approximately same age.[48] The jealousy over women seems to have been an issue between the border guards and the male civilians, highlighting the former's position as dwellers yet not locals, and foregrounding the mutual spatial and social territory-marking.

The entrenched border

In practice, the border guards were on duty round the clock until the law on working hours was amended to their advantage. Until 1972, the staff in stations had no fixed working hours and they wore uniforms whenever they appeared in public. Work was a significant part of a border guard's public persona. The State's presence in the borderland was embodied by them. Work and leisure time became more clearly differentiated, as the guards now had regular free time. After the legislation on working hours became applicable to border guards in the field, they could apply for accommodation. The close connections between the border guards and civilians began to break up but the same relationships were strengthened in the civilian context. The law on working hours allowed the officials to accept additional and less formal roles in the community. As owning a car became more

47 Marigold Linton, Phoenix and Chimera: The Changing Faces of Memory, in: Jaclyn Jeffrey & Glenace Edwall (Eds.) Memory and history. Essays on Recalling and Interpreting Experience, Maryland 1994, 69–88; here: 70–73; See Thompson, Believe it, Loc. Cit. (Note 7), 3–7.

48 See Interview 9 3.3.2008 Loc. Cit. (Note 38); See NKBG Interview 10 2008, Loc. Cit. (Note 38) NKBG; Interview 11 6.3.2008 Ilomantsi, border guard 1967–1995, NKBG; See Interview 12 11.3.2008 Loc. Cit. (Note 37) NKBG; See Interview 13 11.3.2008, Loc. Cit. (Note 40) NKBG; See Interview 14 17.3.2008, Loc. Cit. (Note 40) NKBG.

common, guards could move closer to the population centres. The guards made commitments to the local community as private people through sports clubs and local politics, for instance. Parallel development of infrastructure and technology, accompanied by the narrowing down of the border zone, altered the work significantly. Also, border guarding gradually became a potential career for locals as headquarters relaxed its attitude.[49] The profession no longer overrode the personal but signalled trustworthiness and determination.

The rural exodus hit the peripheral borderland hard from the 1960's. Due to authoritative cooperation and intensification on the border areas, the border guards soon appeared to be the last remaining authorities. The uniform and proximity of the station invoked a sense of security. Guarding the border gradually turned into cooperative borderland security, altering the authoritative duties of the borderland officials. Decreasing resources and growing expenses forced the Border Guard to rationalise activities. The Border Guard had established its place on the borderland and provided service, work and a sense of security in the periphery. General official assignments had brought them among the people.[50]

Conclusions

During the transition periods, the border work aimed to establish a stable and controlled border area. To succeed, the officials controlled the activity and participated in educating the inhabitants on the ideological grounds, simultaneously justifying their own position. The intermediary role between the State and the local community posed a challenge for the border guards since they represented the 'internal other'. For civilians, the border guard uniform represented control but also, in time, help and security. The border work was not a unidirectional development but reshaped continuously, depending on the current circumstances.

The most efficient relationship developed around neighbourhood and utility. During these two periods, the newly established border regulations clashed with everyday life. The civilians did not submit to rules without resistance. The issue was not the linear boundary but the state's interference with the regional networks, usufruct and ownership, income and ownership. Though instructions highlighted neutrality and kindness, relations were more control-based with the poor and ideological adversaries than with the cooperative group.

Educating the borderland inhabitants about the sanctity of the border was a mission the border guards participated in actively. In the interviews, the memories of the conflicts occurred within Finland's borders. The state border was not something definitive, but its significance had to be justified and regulated by communication and sanctions. Though the conversations about relations with the ci-

49 Interview 24 10.3.2009 Tohmajärvi, border guard 1965–1990, NKBG; See Kirjavainen, Sotavuodet ja, Loc. Cit. (Note 41), 357; See Pohjonen, Isänmaan portinvartijat, Loc. Cit. (Note 17), 348, 509; See Walling, Pitkä partio, Loc. Cit. (Note 28), 138–144, 150–151, 283–288.

50 Interview 17 27.3.2008 Lieksa, border guard 1972–1999, NKBG; See Pohjonen, Isänmaan portinvartijat, Loc. Cit. (Note 17), 485–487, 492–493; See Walling, Pitkä partio, Loc. Cit. (Note 28), 177; Jenni Merovuo, Turvaksi kaikissa oloissa. Rajavartiosto Ilomantsissa, in: Lähde: historiatieteellinen aikakauskirja 10 (2013), 114–134; here: 129–130.

vilians were short and elusive, they reveal the challenges and the utility of the border work. The people living in the border zone or nearby were few and in general relations were friendly or at least polite, partially out of necessity. Civilians protested when regulations were considered unreasonable. Testing the rules was an attempt to regain the lost milieu or to mark spatial and social territory. The out-of-towner border guards were considered suspicious. On the other hand, endorsing the border guards and reporting one's sightings presented a way to actively enhance one's own sense of security.

During the transition periods, conflicts were an inevitable part of the border work. As practices stabilised, the conflicts became fewer and more personal in nature. In North Karelia, the border remained rather calm after the Second World War. The precautions and measures against severe violations were essential in memories about controlling the green border, yet the greatest threat was never actualised. Problems of a private nature, such as jealousy, were not considered essential in the interview agenda and, thus, not widely discussed, though the guards were on duty round the clock and the personal and professional inevitably intertwined.

In the interviews, the 'civilians' involved a highly colourful group socially, territorially and in terms of age range. The border guards formed a more unified group. All were adult males and most were out-of-towners. Within the Border Guard institution, though, people were of different personality and professional position. The ideology of the headquarters was not always reflected in the operative work in the periphery. Personal relations not considered as part of the border guarding affected the social dynamics, nevertheless. The border work executed during the transition periods has greatly affected the experience of eternal and unchangeable boundaries, but has nonetheless proven that the borders are subject to a process of perpetual adjustment.

Abstract

The article studies the border work in the Eastern Finnish borderland during two transition periods of the first half of the 20th century. Border work is understood as a controversial social process of strengthening official national borders. First, after Finland became independent in 1917, and second, after the border shift of 1940 (reasserted in 1944), the border work aimed to establish new borders and to inhibit border crossings. The main source material consists of the interviews with the former border guards and the borderland civilians. To establish strong borders, the border guards educated, helped, controlled and disciplined the borderland community. The most successful cooperation between the border guards and the civilians built around neighborhood and utility. However, conflicts were inevitable as the local community resisted submitting to the new order. Though the trouble was reluctantly discussed in the interviews, the border work is remembered to have caused controversy of personal and professional nature. In the local community, the border guards were considered as the 'internal other' but in time they became trusted members of the community whose presence increased the sense of security. Thus, the dividing national borders did not fall into place naturally, but they have formed gradually in a complex and continuous social process.

The 'lost city' of Vyborg and the construction of remembered borders between Finland and Russia

Chloe Wells

Introduction

The most recent re-drawings of the Finnish-Russian border, which took place during World War Two (WWII), entailed large scale forced population movement with around 407,000 people or almost 11 % of Finland's total population moving from territories ceded by Finland into the Finnish interior and being re-settled there.[1] This happened twice: once in 1940 and again in 1944. The ceded territories were retaken and held by Finnish forces between 1941 and 1944. The loss of Finnish territory and the forced evacuation and resettlement of the Finnish population can be understood as a traumatic event, both for the individuals involved and for the imagined community of Finland, one which still resonates over 70 years later. This article explores Finnish discourses which represent these events as an historical injustice.

The nation-state feels loss of territory as a 'territorial phantom pain,' as a missing limb.[2] Loss of nation-state territory is also traumatic for groups and individuals, and may be regarded by them as an injustice, if they have been spatially socialized into an understanding of 'their' national state territory which includes the ceded territories as a 'natural' part of that state.[3] Spatial socialization describes the processes through which people "become members of territorial entities and internalize narratives and memories related to collective identities and shared traditions."[4] In this case how 'Finns' come to feel part of 'Finland' via the adoption of narratives and memories of Finland's history.

---

1 This number is from Ulla Savolainen, The Return: Intertextuality of the Reminiscing of Karelian Evacuees in Finland, in: Journal of American Folklore 130 516 (2017), 166–192; here: 170.

2 Franck Billé, Territorial phantom pains (and other cartographic anxieties), in: Environment and Planning D: Society and Space 31 (2014), 163–178; here: 163.

3 For more on the theory of spatial socialisation see Anssi Paasi, Bounded spaces in a 'borderless world': Border studies, power and the anatomy of territory, in: Journal of Power 2 2(2009), 213–34. And Anssi Paasi, Dancing on the graves: Independence, hot/banal nationalism and the mobilization of memory, in: Political Geography 54 (2016), 21–31.

4 See Paasi, Dancing, Loc. Cit. (Note 3), 24

The loss of Vyborg,[5] which was Finland's second city, the capital of the trans-border Karelia region and 'the Karelians' city', is emblematic of the feelings of injustice and traumatic loss which surround the ceded Finnish territories as a whole. As Farrar has pointed out: "the loss of a city is a devastating national crisis… When we lose places, we *grieve* them, individually and collectively."[6] This article examines how Vyborg is collectively remembered in Finland within the context of this loss.

Vyborg is located on the Gulf of Finland around 130 km northwest of St. Petersburg and around 40 km from the Finnish-Russian border. The 700 year old borderland settlement is located geographically on the Karelian Isthmus[7] and administratively the town is part of the Leningrad Oblast. Vyborg has 'changed sides' or 'direction' several times during its long history. The borderline on the Karelian Isthmus which nowadays divides the territories of the nation-states of Finland and Russia has been fixed by seven different peace treaties since 1323 and been decided between 5 different territorial-political powers.[8] These border changes all affected the castle and settlement of Vyborg and its inhabitants.[9]

Vyborg was the eastern outpost of the Russian Grand Duchy of Finland from 1812–1917 and then of the Republic of Finland from 1917 until WWII. During the inter war years Finnish Vyborg grew exponentially, increasing its area and more than doubling its population, and became a centre of culture and trade.[10] This brief period of Vyborg's history, barely 20 years, determines the image of Vyborg within the post war tradition of memorizing the 'lost city' in Finland. It is remembered within a context of nostalgic longing for a 'better place in a better time.' Vyborg was ceded to the Soviet Union in 1940, reoccupied by the Finns in 1941, taken by the Red Army in 1944 and again officially ceded to the Soviet Union as per the Paris Peace Treaty of 1947. Vyborg is frozen in collective memory as

5 Originally Viborg, the town is normally called Vyborg in English language texts. In Finnish it is called *Viipuri*. Vyborg is the standard transliteration to Latin characters of the Cyrillic *Выборг*, the Russian name of the town. I use the name Vyborg here without ideological or political agenda or implication. Cf Kimmo Katajala / Jussi Semi, Introduction in: Kimmo Katajala (ed.), Meanings of an Urban Space: Understanding the historical layers of Vyborg, Zurich 2016, 11–20; here:18).

6 Margaret E. Farrar, Home/Sick: Memory, Place, and Loss in New Orleans, in: Theory & Event 12 4 (2009), np. Emphasis in original.

7 The strip of land between the Gulf of Finland and Lake Ladoga. Since after WWII the Isthmus has been within the territories of the Leningrad Oblast, and the Republic of Karelia, Russia.

8 The Swedish Empire, the Novgorod Republic, The Russian Empire or Tsardom, Independent Finland, The Soviet Union.

9 Marika Tandefelt, Vyborg: Free trade in Four Languages, in: Kurt Braun-Müller / Gisella Ferraresi (eds.), Aspects of multilingualism in European Language History, Amsterdam 2003, 85–105; here: 85.

10 Yrjö Kaukiainen, Viipurin suomalaistuminen in: Pentti Paavolainen / Sanna Supponen (eds.), Monikulttuurisuuden aika Viipurissa, Viipurin Suomalaisen Kirjallisuusseuran toimitteita 17 Helsinki, 2013, 74–88, especially: 76–77. For population growth statistics see Suomen Tilastot, Suomen tilastollinen vuosikirja 1925, http://www.doria.fi/handle/10024/69243 [Accessed: 13.08.2018]. And Suomen Tilastot, Suomen tilastollinen vuosikirja 1940, http://www.doria.fi/handle/10024/69230 [Accessed: 13.08.2018]. Population statistics for Vyborg 1815–2010 in tabular and graph form available at: https://fi.wikipedia.org/wiki/Viipuri#V.C3.A4est.C3.B6 [Accessed: 13.08.2018].

a golden, prospering, 1930s city. This article seeks to look beneath this mythologising and nostalgia at the idea of the loss of Vyborg as historical injustice.

The 'holy' border and the Karelian question

The "politico-ideological border with Russia has been at the core of the narration of [Finnish] national identity since 1917 and even earlier."[11] The Finnish state "as a national 'We' has typically been constructed in exclusive terms in relation to Russia/ the Soviet Union ('The Other')."[12] This othering was done via highlighting of the perceived "differences between the Finnish and Russian nations, between the 'Civilised West' (Finland, 'us') and the 'Barbarian East' (Russia, 'them', the Other)."[13] An exert from a 1931 Finnish poem sums up this viewpoint and Finland's positioning as an 'outpost of the West against the East':

> "Like a chasm runs the border:
> In front, Asia, the East;
> In back, Europe, the West:
> like a sentry, I stand guard."[14]

During WWII othering of Russia intensified: Finnish news media appealed to the "cultural difference of the Finns and the Russians and the Russians' difference from the western people" and portrayed the Soviet Union as "the archenemy [...] 'that old tormentor' which throughout history had attacked Finland and forced every generation to defend the country."[15]

The physical border between Finland and Russia was and is important in this mental bordering. Of Finland's different borderlines, the 1812 border between the Russian Grand Duchy of Finland, Sweden and the Russian Empire, which was replicated in the 1920 border between the independent Republic of Finland and the Soviet Union, is seen (by some) as 'natural' or correct. There is an idea in Finland of the 'holy border.' This idea refers to the border between Finland and Soviet Union in the 1920s and 1930s. Vyborg is seen by some as 'naturally' being a part of Finland as it was on the Finnish side of both the 1812 and 1920 borderlines. The later, post-WWII, border redrawing is still seen by some as an unjust or 'bad' border dividing from Finland a town and territory which it sees as rightfully its own. This perception of Vyborg is strictly unofficial. There is no official or government standpoint in Finland to the effect that Vyborg and the other ceded areas 'rightly' belong within Finland's borders. But one can certainly find this view

---

11 See Paasi, Dancing, Loc. Cit. (Note 3), 25.

12 Ibid.

13 Katariina Kosonen, Making maps and mental images: Finnish press cartography in nation-building 1899–1942, in: National Identities 10 1 (2008), 21–47; here: 28.

14 Uuno Kailas, 1931, Rajalla (On the Border) translated to English and quoted in Sinikka Wunsch, Image Research and the Enemy Image: The Soviet Union in Finnish Newspapers during the Winter War (November 30, 1939 – March 13, 1940), in: Kari Alenius / Olavi K. Fält / Seija Jalagin (eds.), Looking at the Other – Historical Study of Images in Theory and Practice, Oulu 2002, 73–88; here: 78

15 See Wunsch, Image Research, Loc. Cit. (Note 14), 77–78.

unofficially circulating amongst some sections of the Finnish population and in societal discourses.[16]

The question of "whether Russia should reassign the territories in Karelia to Finland," the so called Karelian Question, is "not a neutral or purely historical one."[17] The Finnish *ProKarelia* association, founded in 1999, "aims at returning the Finnish [territories] [...]back to the context of Finland and the EU."[18] They plan to achieve the return of the "stolen territory"[19] "peacefully and by negotiations"[20] beginning with Finland raising the question of the ceded territories with Russia – something which has never officially happened. The association uses the idea of injustice in its argumentation; *ProKarelia* stated via its spokesman in 2003 that: "it is unjust that Estonia, Latvia, and Lithuania, which were also affected by the Molotov-Ribbentrop Pact, are now independent states, while Karelia remains part of Russia."[21] However, despite *ProKarelia*'s assertion that "the return is possible"[22] "return of the ceded areas [...] has not been regarded as realistic or feasible" by the majority in Finland.[23] Thus Vyborg remains a town firmly situated within the Russian Federation.

"Like watching a thief driving your car"[24]: Finnish media portrayals of Vyborg and online reactions to these

An image can be understood as a "mixture of memories, hopes, myths, love and hate."[25] Analyzing popular media representations gives us an insight into how the place image of Vyborg is created, maintained and circulated within Finland. Finn-

---

16 Cf. Savolainen, The Return, Loc. Cit. (Note 1), 4. And Karen Armstrong, Remembering Karelia: a family's story of displacement during and after the Finnish wars. Oxford 2004; here: 2.

17 See Savolainen, The Return, Loc. Cit. (Note 1), 4.

18 ProKarelia ry, Pro Karelia Mission, nd a, http://prokarelia.net/en/?x=prokarelia [Accessed: 13.08.2018].

19 Veikko Saksi, KARELIA – STOLEN TERRITORY, ProKarelia ry 19th March 2013, http://prokarelia.net/en/?x=artikkeli&article_id=2070&author=61 [Accessed: 13.08.2018]. NB I have quoted from the association's English languages web publications here. In Finnish they have published as recently as 04.06.2018 on the topic of the return of Karelia. Their website features hundreds of Finnish language articles tagged as being about this topic. Cf ProKarelia ry, Kategoria [02]: Karjalan palautus, nd b, http://prokarelia.net/fi/?x=kategoria&knum=2&article_id=2218&author=61 [Accessed: 13.08.2018].

20 Veikko Saksi, CURRENT INTERPRETATIONS OF THE AGGRESSION OF THE SU AGAINST FINLAND, ProKarelia ry 2nd November 2012, http://prokarelia.net/en/?x=artikkeli&article_id=2066&author=61 [Accessed: 13.08.2018].

21 Charles Carlson, Finland: Soviet Annexation Of Karelia Still A Taboo Subject, in: Radio Free Europe Radio Liberty 1st July 2003, https://www.rferl.org/a/1103688.html [Accessed: 13.08.2018].

22 See Saksi, Current, Loc. Cit. (Note 20), np.

23 Jukka Oksa, Six Images of Karelia, 2003, http://www.lammasoja.net/joksa/6images/ [Accessed: 13.08.2018].

24 Comment, Suomi 24 online discussion forum. Available at: http://keskustelu.suomi24.fi/t/14664246/epaisanmaallinen-yle--piruilee-kansalle Author's translation from the Finnish.

25 Peterson, 1960, VII referenced in Olavi K. Fält, Introduction in: Kari Alenius / Olavi K. Fält / Seija Jalagin (eds.), Looking at the Other – Historical Study of Images in Theory and Practice, Oulu 2002, 7–11; here: 9.

ish tabloid magazines about Vyborg, for example, are a type of *lieux de memoire*[26] made up of "images and texts [...] pictures and postcards"[27] which represent Finnish Vyborg. These ‹icons› will all have an impact on how the place is remembered.[28] The photos in the magazines are projected onto, conceptualised and contextualised in different ways using collective memory and postmemory. Postmemories are "belated or inherited" memories which take the form of stories and images 'remembered' and told by the "generation after."[29] Postmemory is "not actually mediated by recall but by imaginative investment, projection, and creation."[30] Without these stories and their interpretations "there are no ghosts and no sense of place."[31] Postmemories of Vyborg, "particular pieces of the past", often stories and images sourced from evacuees from the Finnish city, are "resurrected and presented in a particular order and context"[32] within Finnish tabloid media.[33]

Use of certain photographs of Finnish-era Vyborg in the tabloid magazines creates a simplified picture of life at that time and in that place. This "stereotyping freezes differences and makes possible conflicts and disputes invisible."[34] Ownership of urban space, who is permitted to be visible in the cityscape, is always contested but any conflicts over space in Finnish-era Vyborg are masked by photos of a prosperous, successful city and its inhabitants. Streetscape photographs from Vyborg's interwar Finnish era (1920s, 1930s) featured in two tabloid magazines demonstrate this.[35] In these 70 photographs there are no visible signs of poverty, violence, vandalism or other negative but natural features of urban life.[36]

---

26 Cf. Pierre Nora, Between Memory and History: Les Lieux de Mémoire, in: Representation 26 (1989), 7–24.

27 Börries Kuzmany, Brody always on my mind: the mental mapping of a Jewish city, in: East European Jewish Affairs 43 2 (2013), 162–189; here:162.

28 Ibid.

29 Marianne Hirsch, The Generation of Postmemory, in: Poetics Today 29 1 (2008), 103–128; here: 106–107.

30 Ibid.

31 Petri Raivo, In this very place: war memorials and landscapes as an experienced heritage, Thingmount working paper series on the philosophy of conservation, University of Lancaster, Department of Philosophy, 1999; here: 4.

32 Carolyn Kitch, Anniversary journalism: Collective memory and the cultural authority to tell the story of the American past, in: Journal of Popular Culture 36 1 (2002), 44–67; here: 50–51.

33 An example would be the Finnish tabloid magazine *Viipuri – Muistot (Vyborg – Memories)* which features '100 touching stories' from evacuees and their descendants.

34 Jussi Semi, Representing the places of Vyborg: town space as lieux de mémoire. Paper presented at the European Association of Urban History Conference, Helsinki, 24–27 August 2016, https://www.researchgate.net/publication/307475724_Representing_the_places_of_Vyborg_town_space_as_lieux_de_memoire [Accessed: 13.08.2018]; here: 11.

35 For reasons of space analysis is limited here to the Finnish tabloid magazines *Viipuri (Vyborg)* published 03.05.2012 and *Viipuri – Muistot (Vyborg – Memories)* Published 14.02.2013. These magazines are both representative and important sources. I use these magazines in my focus groups (see below). For another analysis of photos of pre-WWII Vyborg see Semi, Representing, Loc. Cit. (Note 34).

36 I counted 33 streetscapes from prewar Finnish Vyborg in the magazine *Vyborg* and 37 in *Vyborg – Memories* I have excluded photos from WWII era Vyborg as these, naturally *do* feature damage and destruction. The point here is how prewar Finnish Vyborg is presented today via the the use of certain photographs. One finds the same or very similar photos in each of the magazines.

Viewed together back to back and side by side in the magazines the photographs present the city as impossibly ‹perfect›, a representation both validating and being validated by personal stories of ex Finnish Vyborgians who declare "Vyborg was the best city in the world."[37] Nostalgic, idealized representations of Vyborg may seem innocent but "from a sense of things having once been better […] come harder emotions such as anger and loss"[38] which may lead to feelings of injustice and a desire for retribution. Nostalgia is not always an innocent emotion; the term was originally coined to denote a mental illness.[39] Vyborg's imperfect present reality cannot compete with the idealised image of Finnish Vyborg.

National and communal collective historical memory of a perceived historical injustice can do harm leading to the persistence and renewal of "rancour and resentment […] and the determination to exact revenge for injuries both real and imagined."[40] Obsessively recalling a past wrong can do "an injustice to the present."[41] Remembrance "may be the ally of justice, but it is no reliable friend to peace, whereas forgetting can be."[42] It is then of concern what is remembered about Vyborg and what emotions are stirred by these collective postmemories. Shikalov has stated that "Finns [still feel] very bitter about losing Vyborg […] Vyborg is still seen as an 'old Finnish town' or a lost treasure."[43] Böök has argued that feelings of "bitterness, anger and nostalgia" associated with the ceded Finnish territories persist[44] and one can easily imagine these being channeled into a sense of injustice.

Repeated popular representations of pre-WWII Finnish Vyborg in the Finnish media have allowed the city to "inscribe itself […] successfully"[45] in Finnish memory. It is not primarily Vyborg, the living town of today, which is inscribed but second hand, past representations of Vyborg 'as it once was'. Although these representations are fairly pervasive they are not picked up by all sections of society (see below). These representations of pre-war Finnish Vyborg must be in place before the modern-day town can be meaningful within Finnish memory. This is exemplified in the Finnish documentary *Viipuri 360* (2017) which, although focusing on the modern day town, begins with a reminder of Vyborg's Finnish past by

37 Eeva Nikkilä-Kiipula, Veljekset Abi ja Tevi Kagan ovat kokeneet Viipurin kauneuden ja sodan kauheuden, Helsingin juutalaisen seurakunnan Hakehila-lehti 5 2002 2 5763 (2002), http://www.jcviipuri.org/#!epilogi/b9jbi [Accessed: 13.08.2018].

38 Ian Jack, A generation hooked on nostalgia is trying to return Britain to the past, in: The Guardian 1st April 2017, https://www.theguardian.com/commentisfree/2017/apr/01/generation-nostalgia-britain-past-brexit-immigration [Accessed: 13.08.2018].

39 Susan J. Matt, You Can't go Home Again: Homesickness and Nostalgia in US History, in: The Journal of American History 94 2 (2007), 470–497; here: 470

40 David Rieff, The cult of memory: when history does more harm than good, in: The Guardian, 2nd March 2016, https://www.theguardian.com/education/2016/mar/02/cult-of-memory-when-history-does-more-harm-than-good [Accessed: 13.08.2018].

41 Ibid.

42 Ibid.

43 Yuri Shikalov, Russian, Lost, Fairy-tale: Images of Vyborg from the 1940s to the 2010s, in: Kimmo Katajala (ed.) Meanings of an Urban Space: Understanding the historical layers of Vyborg, Zurich 2016, 223–249; here: 238.

44 Netta Böök, Border Karelia through rose-coloured glasses? Gazes upon a ceded territory, in: Fennia 182 1 (2004), 33-45; here: 41.

45 See Kuzmany, Brody, Loc. Cit. (Note 27), 162.

including footage from the 1940 Finnish short film *Vanha Wiipurimme (Our Old Vyborg)*.[46] The opening seconds of *Viipuri 360* are a close up of the Russian flag flying from Vyborg castle tower. The castle tower, coupled with the *Finnish* flag flying, is an enduring symbol of Finnish Vyborg.[47] This opening image may therefore be jarring for those who still in some sense believe Vyborg should be part of Finland. The voiceover also states a few minutes later (after showing the footage from *Vanha Wiipurimme*) that "Memories are remembered, but Vyborg is no longer ours and never will be" a harsh 'wake up call.' The title, *360*, implies a complete view but the documentary is mostly positive. As in Finnish representations of pre-WWII Vyborg, in today's Vyborg it is always summer and the residents are proud of their home town and Vyborgian identity. Vyborg is a good place to be.

The Finnish online reaction to this documentary brought to the surface the idea of injustice surrounding Vyborg. One commenter on the busy online discussion forum *Suomi 24*, Finland's largest online community,[48] reacted to *Viipuri 360* as follows: "Russian Vyborg? Give the finger to these unpatriotic people. In Finland there are thousands of people who will always feel what was once Finland's second largest city will never become Russian."[49] It is interesting the commenter feels they share an opinion with thousands of others. Another commented: "Russkie ruined Vyborg [...] who wants to watch [this]. It's like watching a thief driving your car"[50] expressing a sense of injustice that Vyborg is not part of Finland.

There were varied reactions to *Viipuri 360* on the Facebook group *Puskaradio Viipuri (The Vyborg Grapevine)* an active and growing Finnish language group with over 3,200 members.[51] The group is a re-creation in the virtual realm of a Finnish community centred on Vyborg. It is notable that members of the group often have parents or grandparents from Vyborg and also enjoy visiting the town and sharing photos of Vyborg as it is today. Such online 'places' become spontaneous dynamic virtual archives (though rather chaotic ones sometimes lacking any kind of search or cataloguing functions), virtual memorials and places of memory, even imagined communities.[52] Within these groups one can see communal history-making as it happens. These histories are personalised with national events and past places linked to family histories and stories. One posted story will likely generate more similar tales.

---

46 *Viipuri 360* can be viewed at: http://areena.yle.fi/1-3457603 [Accessed: 13.08.2018]. *Vanha Wiipurimme* is available at: https://youtu.be/frculJMx5fQ [Accessed: 13.08.2018].

47 Cf. Jani Karhu / Chloe Wells, Vyborg Castle as a Symbol of Power Institutions: Imagined and remembered borders between generations in Finland, in: The Journal of Power Institutions in Post-Soviet Societies, 18 (2017), np; here: paragraphs 11; 12; 19; 20; 23; 26; 34; 36. And Jani Karhu / Ludmila Ryabova, Meanings of the Urban Space of Vyborg, in: Kimmo Katajala (ed.), Meanings of an Urban Space: Understanding the historical layers of Vyborg, Zurich 2016, 263–299; here: 281, 293; 294.

48 https://www.suomi24.fi/ [Accessed: 13.08.2018].

49 Available at: http://keskustelu.suomi24.fi/t/14664246/epaisanmaallinen-yle--piruilee-kansalle [Accessed: 13.08.2018]. Author's translation from the Finnish.

50 Ibid.

51 https://www.facebook.com/groups/puskaradio.viipuri/ [Accessed: 13.08.2018]. Membership as at 13.08.2018.

52 Cf. Anne Heimo / Kirsi Hänninen, Participatory, community and spontaneous archives and digitally born cultural heritage, in: Folklore Fellows Network 47 (2015), 4–11.

One member of *Puskaradio Viipuri* group posted: "Yesterday I watched […] *Viipuri 360*. Have you watched it and what kind of thoughts did it awaken? From my perspective something like this […] Present day Vyborgians approach us as neutral neighbours. I hope for the same from Finns." The first reply reacted strongly against this viewpoint, echoing the *Suomi 24* commender above:

> "My grandparents have been living in the Vyborg region for hundreds of years [sic] and I was born there, that is, in Finnish Vyborg. Finland fought two wars to secure our survival, albeit with heavy losses. Over 90,000 fallen and we lost 12% of national territory, 450,000 residents torn after hundreds of years from the areas where they lived. This was a serious tragedy […] After all this I can never take a neutral view of Vyborg. In my mind it is always Finnish."

The original poster replied: "I feel present day Vyborg is my home area, even if it's behind the border […] even if I was born long after the war. I don't blame anything or anyone but I don't know who you could be bitter towards about this now. I don't believe it's worth it, even if the correct target could be found." These comments represent the different ways of remembering Finnish Vyborg: 'neutrally' as the original poster hopes for or negatively based on the remembered trauma of the events of WWII. These ways of remembering influence the meanings given to the present-day town ("in my mind it is always Finnish").

On another thread in the Facebook group about *Viipuri 360*, a promotional video for the documentary which starts with the slogan "Vyborg is Russian,"[53] comments included the idea that: "Finns were driven away from" Vyborg, that Vyborg "should be Finland's own" and the comment "I'm not interested in Russian Vyborg, only lost Vyborg." There was also a discussion which focused on the guilt and innocence of today's Russian Vyborgians and moved on to issues of war crimes and occupied territories. This shows that the idea of injustice connected to Vyborg can evolve from thinking about its loss, mention of which was prompted by presentation of the idea that "Vyborg is Russian." One poster simply commented "Return Vyborg!" However it is worth remarking that this comment received no attention from members of the group.

Groups such as *Puskaradio Viipuri* where members post images of Vyborg's Finnish past may be dubbed spontaneous archives[54] where one can witness history-making and telling, and collective memory formation 'as it happens.' Online communities represent a new expression of collective memory and a continued yearning for Finnish Vyborg expressed through these attempts to create it anew in the virtual realm. The online realm needs to be acknowledged in any research into collective ideas, images and memories as "the web has become a searchable and crunchable database for questions of any kind, a living cultural memory whose implications are complex and wide reaching."[55]

In the online realm a sense of injustice associated with Vyborg is sometimes strongly expressed but also countered. The internet can be a forum for airing extremist viewpoints and it is worth noting that in a recent survey of Finns with

---

53 Available at: https://www.facebook.com/ylelappeenranta/videos/1817127715173971/ [Accessed: 13.08.2018].

54 See Heimo / Hänninen, Participatory, Loc. Cit. (Note 52).

55 Meg Leta Jones, Ctrl + Z. The Right to be Forgotten, New York 2016; here: 55.

some connection to Vyborg "there were only a few [respondents] who mentioned the 'wrong ownership' as a negative thing."[56] The respondents' main concern was instead the current poor condition of Vyborg's infrastructure and buildings.[57] This fits with popular media portrayals which compare a perfect Finnish before with a 'ruined' Russian after.[58] This comparison is not neutral but laden with meaning: most Finnish discourse about Vyborg "is based on memories and imaginaries going back to the town's 'golden age', its last Finnish years [...] and bitter feelings of loss."[59] This is the basis for these comparisons of then and now which can also be seen as comparisons of 'us' with 'them': today's Vyborg must compete with the image of a perfect lost place.

Finnish youth and Vyborg

My research aims to discover the knowledge, ideas and postmemories of Finnish Vyborg expressed by Finnish youth who are in High School education: have they inherited the above discussed discourses or do they have different ideas? I have worked with high schoolers from 11 different geographic milieus around Finland: the eastern borderlands (the cities of Joensuu, Lappeenranta, and Imatra), central Finland (Jyväskylä), western Finland (Vaasa) northern Finland (Oulu, Rovaniemi), southern Finland (Lahti, Turku) and the Helsinki capital region (Helsinki and Vantaa).

Preliminary analysis of the focus group data indicates that Finnish youth commonly express only a vague knowledge of Vyborg's history and location. Initial results show that the focus group participants demonstrated some confusion over where Vyborg was or is in terms of both geographical and geopolitical location. This may be a result of the mixed message that Vyborg is Russian but also, somehow, Finnish. Overall it seems that Vyborg does not matter or resonate for Finnish High School students the way it does for some cohorts of older Finns for whom Vyborg is "a site of memory connected to a short period of time, and [...] a symbol of collective trauma."[60] We need to ask why. Is it that they are still too young to consider adopting the postmemories of Finnish Vyborg swirling in Finnish discourse as their own, uninterested at this stage of their lives in stories of personal and national loss and trauma? Or is it that they are they too far removed from the events of WWII? Will they tell the Finnish history of Vyborg differently than older generations, will Vyborg have a different meaning and significance for them?

In the focus groups the participants looked through the tabloid magazines *Vyborg – Memories* and *Vyborg* (see above) and there was some evidence that, by the end of the focus groups some participants were beginning to identify with the

56 See Karhu / Ryabova, Meanings, Loc. Cit. (Note 47), 278

57 Ibid.

58 See Böök, Border Karelia, Loc. Cit. (Note 44), 42. And a recent example of this Outi Salovaara, Kuvia Viipurista: Suomi rakensi, Venäjä jätti remontoimatta – Moni asuu asuinkelvottomassa talossa, in: Suomen Kuvalehti 28th December 2016, https://suomenkuvalehti.fi/jutut/ulkomaat/eurooppa/__trashed-11/?shared=949988-15ed1594-50%200 [Accessed: 13.08.2018].

59 See Karhu / Ryabova, Meanings Loc. Cit. (Note 47), 276.

60 See Karhu / Ryabova, Meanings Loc. Cit. (Note 47), 263.

common story about Vyborg as told in the magazines. One female participant in Oulu commented that "The city looked so beautiful [in the magazine pictures]" and that Vyborg seemed "a place so beautiful that I feel so sad that we lost it back then." A typical response when participants were asked at the end of the focus group discussion to briefly describe Vyborg ran along the lines of: "Viipuri (*sic*) was an important place which Finnish army tried to keep but failed. And Viipuri is still an important place to a lot of people, Finnish people."[61]

A female participant in a different group in Oulu summed up Vyborg's 20th century history in a way that matches popular Finnish views by saying: "I think before the wars it was rich and beautiful city but when it was part of the Soviet Union the city became kind of poor and dirty and broken."[62] A Joensuu participant summed up what their group had discussed and again reflected circulating Finnish discourse by writing: "Vyborg would have been different if it would have stayed in Finland. An important town for Finland. The forced evacuation of Karelia need not have happened." This expresses a sense of injustice, that things 'could have been different'.

At the start of each group the participants individually wrote down anything they associated with the word 'Vyborg.' I have gone through these lists to see if they express any sense of injustice regarding Vyborg's 'ownership.' Most references to this issue were quite subtle: comments such as Vyborg is "nowadays part of Russia"[63] or "right now it belongs to Russia"[64] showing that the city's 'changing sides' over 70 years ago is somehow still 'fresh' or perhaps still (wistfully or not) seen as temporary. There were 33 comments (14 % of total comments) which expressed some idea of injustice by using words like "lost." Two lists stated that Vyborg is "Finnish."[65] One Turku participant wrote that they associated Vyborg with "anger and bitterness" showing these emotions are sometimes passed on. The strongest expression of injustice was: "The Russians took it from Finland."[66] There were no comments in the lists that Finland 'should get Vyborg back.' However when I asked the groups towards the end of our time together "Should Vyborg be a part of Finland?" there were some strongly expressed opinions that it should and / or this has been the stated majority opinion.[67] In contrast some other participants felt that Vyborg "is a part of [our] history" but "in the end it doesn't matter who owns [it]."[68] Participants also sometimes felt separate from older generations of Finns and the emotions some of them express: "I think our generation doesn't even care anymore about Viipuri. It's, like, the older people that are still bitter."[69] Overall the focus groups have revealed a variety of viewpoints and levels

61 Female participant, Oulu, focus group data.
62 See above and Böök, Border Karelia, Loc. Cit. (Note 44) for a discussion of the media views.
63 Participant, Jyväskylä, focus group data.
64 Participant, Turku, focus group data.
65 Participant, Lappeenranta, and participant, Jyväskylä, focus group data. This may have been an error of geography rather than a political statement. Other participants (in Oulu, Turku and Jyväskylä) also got Vyborg's geopolitical location wrong.
66 Participant, Imatra, focus group data.
67 For example in a group in Turku where we voted on the issue 10 vs. 2 thought Vyborg should be part of Finland
68 Participant, Joensuu, focus group data.
69 Female participant, Lahti, focus group data.

of knowledge showing that the transmission of the collective memory of Vyborg and feelings association with it has not (yet) succeeded in all cases.

Conclusion

This article has demonstrated that, in the Finnish case, injustice in borderland situations emerges through cultural bordering processes: The loss of Vyborg, still regarded in some ways and by some sections of Finnish society as an injustice, is conceptualised via processes of mental bordering whereby the Finnish city is preserved in collective memory as a lost place and as a perfect place. This collective memory is transmitted via all kinds of media such as tabloid magazines and online discussions and attempts to challenge the collective image, for example the documentary *Viipuri 360*, can be met with hostility. Research with Finnish youth shows a repetition of the established image, memory and (to a lesser extent) emotions associated with Vyborg down the generations but also some new conceptions of Vyborg emerging which may point to it in future losing some of its aura of nostalgic longing.

Abstract

This article examines collective ideas, memories and postmemories, and socio-spatial frameworks concerning the Finnish-Russian border. The article focuses on the formerly Finnish borderland city of Viipuri (today Vyborg, Russia). Before World War Two (WWII) Vyborg was Finland's second city and the capital of Finnish Karelia. Its loss to the Soviet Union at the conclusion of the Fenno-Soviet Winter War in March 1940 and again (after a brief re-occupation by Finnish forces) in June 1944 is often represented in Finnish discourses as an historical injustice. This idea of injustice is framed by conceptions of a 'holy' Finnish Eastern border and maintained by processes of spatial socialisation, especially the representations of Vyborg and the events of WWII in Finnish popular media. Successive Finnish governments have never officially raised the question of 'getting Vyborg back.' Vyborg being returned is not now thought by the majority to be realistic or feasible but the idea that things 'should have been different' lingers. Vyborg's Finnish era is conceptualised in terms of nostalgic longing. An idealised, mythic, 'golden Finnish Vyborg' is presented in stark contrast to its sudden, traumatic loss and its current Russian identity. Memories of Vyborg in Finland are informed and shaped by the 'loss' of the city and by an understanding of Vyborg as, historically, a Swedish / Finnish place, an 'outpost of the West against the East.' Alongside an analysis of Finnish media portrayals of Vyborg this article presents the preliminary results of new research with Finnish youth, airing their neglected opinions and thoughts on these issues. This article examines whether today's Finnish youth have adopted the idea circulating in Finnish popular and familial discourses that Vyborg, Russian now for over 70 years and only part of the independent state of Finland for around 20 years, 'should' be part of Finland, and that the loss of Vyborg was an historical injustice.

References

Karen Armstrong, Remembering Karelia: a family's story of displacement during and after the Finnish wars, Oxford 2004.

Franck Billé, Territorial phantom pains (and other cartographic anxieties), in: Environment and Planning D: Society and Space 31 (2014), 163–178.

Netta Böök, Border Karelia through rose-coloured glasses? Gazes upon a ceded territory, in: Fennia 182 1 (2004), 33–45.
Charles Carlson, Finland: Soviet Annexation Of Karelia Still A Taboo Subject, in: Radio Free Europe Radio Liberty 1st July 2003, https://www.rferl.org/a/1103688.html [Accessed: 13.08.2018].
Margaret E. Farrar, Home/Sick: Memory, Place, and Loss in New Orleans, in: Theory & Event 12 4 (2009), np.
Olavi K. Fält, Introduction, in: Kari Alenius / Olavi K. Fält / Seija Jalagin (eds.), Looking at the Other – Historical Study of Images in Theory and Practice, Oulu 2002, 7–11.
Anne Heimo / Kirsi Hänninen, Participatory, community and spontaneous archives and digitally born cultural heritage, in: Folklore Fellows Network 47 (2015), 4–11.
Marianne Hirsch, The Generation of Postmemory, in: Poetics Today 29 1 (2008), 103–128.
Ian Jack, A generation hooked on nostalgia is trying to return Britain to the past, in: The Guardian 1st April 2017, https://www.theguardian.com/commentisfree/2017/apr/01/generation-nostalgia-britain-past-brexit-immigration [Accessed: 13.08.2018].
Meg Leta Jones, Ctrl + Z. The Right to be Forgotten, New York 2016.
Jani Karhu / Ludmila Ryabova, Meanings of the Urban Space of Vyborg, in: Kimmo Katajala (ed.), Meanings of an Urban Space: Understanding the historical layers of Vyborg, Zurich 2016, 263–299.
Jani Karhu / Chloe Wells, Vyborg Castle as a Symbol of Power Institutions: Imagined and remembered borders between generations in Finland, in: The Journal of Power Institutions in Post-Soviet Societies, 18 (2017), np.
Kimmo Katajala / Jussi Semi, Introduction in: Kimmo Katajala (ed.), Meanings of an Urban Space: Understanding the historical layers of Vyborg, Zurich 2016, 11–20.
Yrjö Kaukiainen, Viipurin suomalaistuminen, in: Pentti Paavolainen / Sanna Supponen (eds.) Monikulttuurisuuden aika Viipurissa, Viipurin Suomalaisen Kirjallisuusseuran toimitteita 17 Helsinki, 2013, 74–88.
Gene Keyes, Stalin's Finland Fiasco: Nonviolent Defense Clues from the Winter War, 2007, http://www.genekeyes.com/Stalin%27s_Finland-Frames.html [Accessed: 13.08.2018].
Carolyn Kitch, Anniversary journalism: Collective memory and the cultural authority to tell the story of the American past, in: Journal of Popular Culture 36 1 (2002), 44–67.
Katariina Kosonen, Making maps and mental images: Finnish press cartography in nation-building 1899–1942, in: National Identities 10 1 (2008), 21–47.
Börries Kuzmany, Brody always on my mind: the mental mapping of a Jewish city, in: East European Jewish Affairs 43 2 (2013), 162–189.
Susan J. Matt, You Can't go Home Again: Homesickness and Nostalgia in US History, in: The Journal of American History 94 2 (2007), 470–497.
Eeva Nikkilä-Kiipula, Veljekset Abi ja Tevi Kagan ovat kokeneet Viipurin kauneuden ja sodan kauheuden, in: Helsingin juutalaisen seurakunnan Hakehila-lehti 5 2002 2 5763 (2002), http://www.jcviipuri.org/#!epilogi/b9jbi [Accessed: 13.08.2018].
Pierre Nora, Between Memory and History: Les Lieux de Mémoire, in: Representation 26 (1989), 7–24.
Jukka Oksa, Six Images of Karelia, 2003, http://www.lammasoja.net/joksa/6images/ [Accessed: 13.08.2018].
Anssi Paasi, Bounded spaces in a 'borderless world': Border studies, power and the anatomy of territory, in: Journal of Power 2 2 (2009), 213–234.
Anssi Paasi, Dancing on the graves: Independence, hot/banal nationalism and the mobilization of memory, in: Political Geography 54 (2016), 21–31.
ProKarelia ry, Pro Karelia Mission, nd a, http://prokarelia.net/en/?x=prokarelia [Accessed: 13.08.2018].

ProKarelia ry, Kategoria [02]: Karjalan palautus, nd b, http://prokarelia.net/fi/?x=kategoria&knum=2&article_id=2218&author=61 [Accessed: 13.08.2018].

Petri Raivo, In this very place: war memorials and landscapes as an experienced heritage. Thingmount working paper series on the philosophy of conservation, University of Lancaster, Department of Philosophy, 1999.

David Rieff, The cult of memory: when history does more harm than good, in: The Guardian, 2nd March 2016, https://www.theguardian.com/education/2016/mar/02/cult-of-memory-when-history-does-more-harm-than-good [Accessed: 13.08.2018].

Outi Salovaara, Kuvia Viipurista: Suomi rakensi, Venäjä jätti remontoimatta – Moni asuu asuinkelvottomassa talossa, in: Suomen Kuvalehti 28th December 2016, https://suomenkuvalehti.fi/jutut/ulkomaat/eurooppa/__trashed-11/?shared=949988-15ed1594-50%200 [Accessed: 13.08.2018].

Veikko Saksi, CURRENT INTERPRETATIONS OF THE AGGRESSION OF THE SU AGAINST FINLAND, ProKarelia ry 2nd November 2012, http://prokarelia.net/en/?x=artikkeli&article_id=2066&author=61 [Accessed: 13.08.2018].

Veikko Saksi, KARELIA – STOLEN TERRITORY, ProKarelia ry 19th March 2013, http://prokarelia.net/en/?x=artikkeli&article_id=2070&author=61 [Accessed: 13.08.2018].

Ulla Savolainen, The Return: Intertextuality of the Reminiscing of Karelian Evacuees in Finland, in: Journal of American Folklore 130 516 (2017), 166–192.

Jussi Semi, Representing the places of Vyborg: town space as lieux de mémoire. Paper presented at the European Association of Urban History Conference, Helsinki, 24–27 August 2016, https://www.researchgate.net/publication/307475724_Representing_the_places_of_Vyborg_town_space_as_lieux_de_memoire [Accessed: 13.08.2018].

Yuri Shikalov, Russian, Lost, Fairy-tale: Images of Vyborg from the 1940s to the 2010s, in: Kimmo Katajala (ed.), Meanings of an Urban Space: Understanding the historical layers of Vyborg, Zurich 2016, 223–249.

Suomen Tilastot, Suomen tilastollinen vuosikirja 1925, http://www.doria.fi/handle/10024/69243 [Accessed: 13.08.2018].

Suomen Tilastot, Suomen tilastollinen vuosikirja 1940, http://www.doria.fi/handle/10024/69230 [Accessed: 13.08.2018].

Marika Tandefelt, Vyborg: Free trade in Four Languages, in: Kurt Braun-Müller / Gisella Ferraresi (eds.), Aspects of multilingualism in European Language History, Amsterdam 2003, 85–105.

Sinikka Wunsch, Image Research and the Enemy Image: The Soviet Union in Finnish Newspapers during the Winter War (November 30, 1939 – March 13, 1940), in: Kari Alenius / Olavi K. Fält / Seija Jalagin (eds.), Looking at the Other – Historical Study of Images in Theory and Practice, Oulu 2002, 73–88.

Soviet and post-Soviet borders in texts for children and as perceived by children

Symbolic figures, images, meanings[1]

Olga Ilyukha

The image of the national border has been one of the basic component parts of the worldview of Soviet people. Citizens' ideas about the borders of the country were of major concern for propaganda and the educational system, which were closely interrelated. The Soviet power, like many other 'new regimes', paid much attention to children. Raising children in the spirit of the communist ideology was a central task for school education, and literature was also engaged to this end.[2] Soviet literature, including opinion journalism, pedagogy and the entire educational system were gradually and consistently shaping the myth of the Soviet border, and modifying it to suit the changing political situation. In post-Soviet time, the border stopped being a 'painful topic' for the information space of propaganda and education, but Soviet-time stereotypes and clichés in the representation of the homeland frontiers were retained in the ideological polyphony.

This paper considers the characteristics of texts about the border written for children, exposes the lingo and implications of the governmental and pedagogical discourses on the subject, and the techniques of impressing it upon children. How were complex concepts of political-ideological nature explained to children? How were 'adult' topics adapted to the mindsets of younger generations? How were the ideological formulae accentuated when addressed to children? An attempt is made, relying on texts published both in editions for children and in those meant for school teachers, youth organization leaders, day-care teachers, to identify the basic constituents of the Soviet canon for representing the border and its later adjustments.

Valuable sources for this paper are the results of research on the ideological component in the literature for children and in the Soviet educational system, as

1 The study was carried out under state order (project № AAAA-A18-118030190093-9).

2 Evgueny Dobrenko claimed that in the Soviet time the family lost its former reader-shaping role, ceding it to school. Furthermore, in what concerned upbringing, the lines followed by the school and the literature not just intersected but, in fact, merged together. Cf Evgueny Dobrenko, Formovka sovetskogo chitatelya: sotsialnye i esteticheskie predposylsi retseptsii sovetskoi literatury, St. Petersburg: Akademicheskiy proekt, 1997, 136–148.

well as recent (two years) developments on the anthropology of the Soviet childhood and school.[3] Exceptionally important are also the conclusions made by researchers of Soviet subjectivity: actively writing himself into the Soviet order and mastering a new language of power became crucial in order for the individual to integrate into the Soviet system.[4] Naturally, children are no exception in this sense. On the other hand, it is obvious that the language of power was constructed not only by means of traditional cultural elites (namely writers and journalists), but also through involvement of 'the community', for instance 'ordinary' school teachers, educators, education methods specialists.

The border as a part of the myth of the Soviet Homeland

Soviet myth-making, a socio-political rather than an artistic process, relying on the mythological nature of mass consciousness, was especially intense in the 1930s, which was a time of ardent construction of the Soviet identity, as the Stalin's government strove to establish the basis for uniting the Soviet society. Soviet mythology was born through complex interactions of propaganda and the target audience, which reflected each other and lived in a world of interwoven and interpenetrating rationality and the 'collective unconscious'. Authorities involved specialists in literature, art, education and so forth to shape new ideals into myths. Old myths were re-created in a new social 'coat' on the basis of archaic models from olden times and through manipulations with cultural symbols.[5]

This kind of creativity resulted in a sophisticated combination of spontaneous 'grassroots' mythology, with all the inherent complexes of national self-sentiment (exceptionality/discrimination), and 'artificial' mythology, designed for ideological and political purposes by intellectuals and representatives of power groups.[6]

In Soviet mythology, the border – a dividing line between 'them' and 'us', was meant to be an essential consolidating factor for the entire society, including children. The frontier was a topic around which an ideological construct was built – a particular myth, which was integrated seamlessly into the Soviet sphere of concepts, the grandiose mythologized image of the 'new' Russia, but with distinctive features and traits of its own.

The relative openness of the USSR in the 1920s, stemming from the idea of the global revolution, brought about the motto "Communism shall eliminate

3 First of all studies by Evgueny Dobrenko, Catriona Kelly, Lisa Kirschenbaum, Maria Litovskaya, Svetlana Maslinskaya (Leont'eva), Alla Sal'nikova.

4 This has been demonstrated by Jochen Hellbeck and Igal Halfin, who 'read the Soviet experience as textuality' using diaries and autobiographies: See Jochen Hellbeck, Working, Struggling, Becoming: Stalin-Era Autobiographical Texts, in: Language and Revolution: Making Modern Political Identities, ed. Igal Halfin, London 2002, 135–159; Igal Halfin, "Intimacy in an Ideological Key: The Communist Case of the 1920s and 1930s", ibid., 185–213.

5 Roland Barthes in the 1950s wrote convincingly about modern 'universal' mythologization (Roland Barthes, Mifologii, Moscow, 1996 – translation from English "Mythologies"). See also: Eleazar Meletinskii, Mif i dvadtsatyi vek, in: Izbrannye statji. Vospominaniya, Moscow, 1998; Sergey Neklyudov, Struktura i funktsiya mifa, in: Mify i Mifologiya v sovremennoi Rossii, eds. Karl Eimermacher, Falk Bomsdorf, Gennadii Bordyugov, Moscow: AIRO-XX, 2000, 7–38.

6 See Sergey Neklyudov, Struktura i funktsiya mifa, ibid., 17–38.

borders". Propaganda and the educational system encouraged cooperation with "proletarians of the world" in both children and adults. Early in the 1930s, internationalism as part of the ideology addressed to children was questioned.[7] The metaphor of the Soviet country as a besieged fortress was gradually imprinted by various mass media, the background being escalation of patriotic moods and growing suspiciousness towards foreigners.

Ideas about the border were a part of the mythological, tripartite model of perceiving the space of the country: centre – the rest of the territory – foreign land. The sacrality of the centre rose from the fact that Moscow was the capital of the world's only socialist state, and that Stalin, the farther and the cherished leader of "all times and nations", was there.

Spatial marking out also followed the folklore scheme: the USSR stood for light and progress, the rest of the world was darkness. This other, dark world, which began beyond the border post, was the enemy abode. The enemies born by the other, dark space of foreign land were often described as zoomorphic creatures – wolves, hyenas, dogs, rats, foxes, sea serpents, octopuses, vultures, snakes, etc. Soviet border guards were metaphorized as vigilant sentries, likened to bylina hero Ilya of Murom. They safeguarded the 'piece' of the Homeland – a fortress surrounded by enemies, severing the stings of serpent-like foes with their swords.

The most popular metaphor for the external enemy in texts for children from the 1920s-1930s was the wolf. It was meant to denote a clever and cruel adversary, always ready to maul its prey, and blended smoothly into the information space of the childhood, as there were linkages to many national children-oriented folklore and literary traditions. This metaphor was, among other authors, used by Leib Kvitko and Sergey Prokofiev, each in their respective genres. In Kvitko's poem "Lullaby" (1937), a boy lost in the woods was saved from angry wolves by Stalin, who sent a tank to rescue. In Prokofiev's fairytale symphony "Peter and the Wolf", pioneer Peter lived with his caring grandfather behind a tall fence sheltering them from the perils of the outer world inhabited by the wolf. The script of this musical masterpiece by Prokofiev contains the ideologeme "pioneers aren't afraid of wolves", dispelling any doubts that this composition might be unrelated to ideology.[8] One of the fundamental principles of socio-psychological engineering applied to young citizens was: scare while entertaining, and suggest the solution. From very early age Soviet children were raised to feel the danger coming from across the border, and to believe they were protected by their "native state".

A finely fitting back-up for the mythical image of the Soviet country was the metaphor "border under lock", which became very common after being used in 1934 by the Commander of the Special Far Eastern Army V. K. Blücher.[9] The Soviet country was pictured as an island of happy childhood in the midst of a hostile world. The happy Soviet childhood project, which took shape in the 1930s,

7 Catriona Kelly, Malenkie grazhdane bolshoi strany: internatsionalism, deti i sovetskaya propaganda (authorized translation from English by Ya. Tokareva), in: Novoe literaturnoe obozrenie, 60 2 (2003), 218–251. http://magazines.russ.ru/nlo/2003/60/katrion.html. [Accessed: January 2015].

8 Liliya Safiullina, Utopicheskii i antiutopicheskii diskursy v animatsionnykh versiyakh simfonicheskoj skazki "Petya i volk" S. Prokofieva, in: PHILOLOGY AND CULTURE 3 29 (2012), 188.

9 Konstantin Dushenko, Russkie politicheskie tsitaty ot Lenina do Yeltsina. Chto, kem i kogda bylo *skazano*, Moscow: Jurist, 1996, 124.

came along with a new social contract: in this symbolic exchange between power and children the price for 'unclouded childhood' was self-sacrificing love for the leader and the homeland, readiness for a heroic feat in anticipation of a war. The ideological paradigm of a happy Soviet childhood was getting crystallized alongside the 'manufacturing' of child heroes.[10]

A key emotional-psychological technique suggested to be used when moulding a Soviet child into a 'new man' was heroic figures: "Heroism always attracts. Children are especially fond of heroes, keen on them, seeking to copy them. Our school should utilize the images and feats of the heroes of the Soviet country to raise courage, bravery, commitment to our proletarian ideals, and the feeling of implacable hatred towards the class enemy in children."[11]

In times of piece, the frontier and the railway were the special loci where one had a chance to commit a heroic feat, which children so dreamt of.[12] Mass media stressed that "the frontier remains the fighting line also in peacetime, the fighting line with all its hardships, its hazards". They also broadcasted F. Dzerzhinsky's idea about cooperation between border troops and border zone locals to secure the frontier 'imperviousness': "Together with border guards, the frontiers of our homeland are protected by collective farmers, Komsomol members, pioneers living in the border zone – most devoted patriots of the Soviet country, faithfully fulfilling their duty to the home country. Our frontier is under secure lock!"[13] The romantic and heroic gloss of life at a frontier post, as well as the hazard emanating from across the border were the psychological foundation for building up the interest of young USSR citizens in this subject. It fit seamlessly in the general context of school militarization. The frontier issue was set firmly in the system of patriotic upbringing of children and youth.

How the Soviet canon of representing the border was formed: educational and didactic texts and practices

At the service of politically charged upbringing of schoolchildren were not only extracurricular activities, but also school subjects and, naturally, school books.[14]

10 A trial balloon was the creation of the ideological myth about Pavlik Morozov. See Yuri Druzhnikov, Donoschik 001, ili Voznesenie Pavlika Morozova, Moscow: Moskovskii Rabochii, 1995; Catriona Kelly, Comrade Pavlik: The Rise and Fall of a Soviet Boy Hero, London: Granta Books 2005.

11 Rol' obshchestvovedeniya v kommunisticheskom vospitanii uchashchikhsya. Metodicheskoe pis'mo prepodavatelyam obshchestvovedeniya nachalnoy i nepolnoy sredney shkoly, Moscow: Uchpedgiz, 1935, 7.

12 As Sergei Shvedov observed, there were two loci in Stalin-time primer and reading books, where there was 'real life': alongside the national border it was the railway. See S. Shvedov, Uroki bukvarya, in: Znanie-sila 11 (1991), 41–47.

13 Nashsa respublika – pogranichnaya, Krasnaya Karelia, August 1st, 1937, 3.

14 Impregnation of school books, including primers and abecedaries, with politics is not an exclusively Soviet phenomenon. See Franz Pöggeler, Politik im Schulbuch, Bonn: Bundeszentrale für politische Bildung, 1985; Franz Pöggeler, Politische Inhalte in Fibeln und Lesebühern des "Dritten Reiches, in: Joachim S. Hohmann (Hg). Erster Weltkrieg und Nationalsozialistische "Bewegung" im deutschen Lesebuch 1933–1945, Frankfurt am Main u. a.: Lang, 1988, 75–104.

Children learned about the borders of the Homeland not only in humanities classes: this topic was addressed in a variety of school disciplines. Thus, information about the length of the national border was included in both mathematics problem books and geography textbooks.[15] The teacher was supposed to deliver any information about borders proceeding from the premise of the country's hostile neighbourhood: "Capitalists hate the country of Soviets, they are preparing for war. Working people in our country are preparing for defense. The gates of our homeland are safely locked". In a manual for teachers of social studies published in Moscow in 1935, the elementary school course syllabus was preceded by the warning that "remembering of the enemy is a primary task for every school employee."[16]

Primers and reading books published in Petrozavodsk in the 1930s – first half of the 1950s and meant for schools of Karelia (a region at the border) offered a wider coverage of the border theme than the unified textbooks coming from publishers based in the capital. Of special interest are Russian language textbooks for non-Russian children and the corresponding teacher's manuals, which provided explanations for the 'simple' concepts that needed not be explained to native Russian speakers. One may say that the ideological capacity of a primer is limited. Yet, the authors of the Russian language primer for Karelian schools, which covered only 400 lexemes, managed to 'squeeze' the topic of the border in.[17] Italicized phrases "The soldier shall not let the enemy approach the border", "Our defense is robust and reliable", and so forth were to be recited or written down repetitively. Such muted, inconspicuous practices of subjectivization, of implanting ideological clichés into the subconscious are known to be very productive, and assimilation of the suggested templates is a huge resource for influencing individuals.

There is a common plot in the stories "An episode at the border", "Druzhok", "A story told by a border guard", as well as in numerous poems on the same topic. It is explicated through an incident at the border, a situation involving seizure of a spy. Given the 'didactic' significance of the topic, the Ministry of Education of Karelia instructed teachers to explain the meaning of the notions "footprints at the frontier", "hands up", "spy" to children, emphasizing that only enemies can trespass the border.

The topic of protecting Soviet borders was addressed regularly. Children in classes learnt poems about border guards, recited them in chorus, studied grammar rules using texts about the border. One such exercise was to expand the following simple sentences: "Evening is coming. Border guard is listening. Rustle is heard. A man is slinking. The border guard waits. A shot sounds. The man falls. The enemy is captured."[18]

---

15 See, e.g., Geografiya SSSR. Uchebnye Materialy. Sed'moy Klass, Moscow: Izdatel'stvo Narkomprosa RSFSR, 1950, 7–8.

16 Rol' obshchestvovedeniya v kommunisticheskom vospitanii uchashchikhsya. Metodicheskoe pis'mo prepodavatelyam obshchestvovedeniya nachalnoy i nepolnoy sredney shkoly, Moscow: Uchpedgiz, 1935, 4.

17 Ivan Belyaev / Alexandra Bonch-Osmolovskaya, Osnovy metodiki obucheniya russkomu yazyku v nachal'nykh nerusskikh shkolakh Karelo-Finskoy SSR. Posobie dlya uchiteley, Petrozavodsk: Gosudarstvennoe izdatel'stvo Karelo-Finskoy SSR, 1946, 8; 102; 123; 186; 244.

18 Nikolai Anisimov, Grammatika karel'skogo yazyka. Chast' I. Uchebnik dlya nepolnoy sredney i sredney shkoly, Petrozavodsk: Karel'skoe gosudarstvennoe izdatel'stvo, 1939, 10.

A creative exercise of writing an essay also had to follow a ready-made scheme: learners were given keywords or plan strictly leading the situation in the same direction. An interesting variant of that was the task to make up a story using core words: "Border guards, frontier post, border, spy, pioneers, dog, Moscow."[19] The final word was meant not just to highlight the territorial unity of remote borders and the country's central city, but also to convince children, as the teacher asked them a series of suggestive questions, that a heroic feat committed at the border would surely become known to those 'within the Kremlin walls'.

In literature for children and even in opinion journalism, the outcome of the incidents was usually optimistic. Moscow sent over honours, and if the heroic border guard was wounded, there came medical help. In his poem "Border guard" (1938), Samuil Marshak depicted, in his specific formulaic manner, a classic ending of an incident at the border:

«Бандиту конец. Пограничнику слава.
Героя с почетом встречала застава.
Теперь его лечат в Москве доктора…
Такая была у мальчишек игра».[20]

("The outlaw is done with. The border guard is praised.
The post crew salutes the hero.
Doctors in Moscow shall treat him now…
This was a game boys used to play")

A well-known educationist and teaching methods specialist from Karelia Alexandra Bonch-Osmolovskaya "summarized the experience" of teachers of the republic to provide recommendations on studying the topic of the border in elementary school. Authenticated by the Ministry of Education of the Karelian-Finnish SSR, an instruction was published on the 'proper way' to read the story "Druzhok" in class. Let us look at the concepts and images used to first introduce the topic of the border to 7–8-year-old children, and at the associations used to anchor these concepts.

"… A picture entitled 'The border' is put up. Pupils read the title… Then the teacher points out the following in the picture: this is our land; this is foreign land; this is the border: where our land ends and foreign land begins. – Who is this? – This is a border guard. – What does he do? – He protects the border. – Protects, i. e. doesn't let strangers in, safeguards. You safeguard, protect your home, your kitchen garden in autumn, when vegetables are ripening. The poster 'Border guard protecting the border' is put up … Against whom does the border guard protect the border? – Against enemies, spies. – Who do we call a spy? – Someone who crosses someone else's border, spies out important secrets and returns to where they came from. – The poster 'Spy' is put up. Pupils read the title. The teacher says: 'A spy crosses the border; the border guard's dog heard the enemy coming. The border guard hides away to watch, and then the dog attacks the enemy' … The story 'Druzhok' is supplied with the following picture: forest, man lying on the ground, dog on the man,

19 Anna Galaktionova / Aleksandra Volkova, Sbornik uprazhnenii po karel'skomu yazyku. Chast' I. Fonetika i morfologiya. Dlya nepolnykh srednikh i srednikh shkol, Petrozavodsk: Kargosizdat, 1939, 13.

20 Samuil Marshak, My voennye, Moscow-Leningrad: Detizdat, 1938.

another man aiming a gun at the dog, and the border guard, in turn, aiming at that other man …"[21]

The above fragment of the methods guidelines shows convincingly that the defense reflex and vigilance were cultivated not only by the most traditional methods of dividing the social reality into 'us' and 'them', but also by exploiting the deep-seated ownership spirit. In the seemingly queer example where the national border is likened to a kitchen garden the reference is to household rather than collective property. To get the message through to the pupils the teacher had to diverge from another ideological task of raising a collectivist, who would work not 'for the sake of profit', so a spy was compared to a thief, an 'internal enemy'.

The geographic attribution of the border in educational texts for children was usually fuzzy: at western frontiers, at southern frontiers, in eastern borderlands, at the Nth frontier post. A frequent tool for geographic referencing in outright propagandistic journalistic texts was historical-cultural markers, often having negative connotations: borderline clashes with samurai, szlachta, lahtari. These texts are surrounded by a halo of state secret to justify their geographic vagueness.

Children were supposed to learn about the country's borders not only in class but also during leisure time. A variety of fun educational means were used to this end. For instance, tabletop game "A Tour of the USSR Borders" for junior schoolchildren was published in 1937 as a supplement to the "Murzilka" magazine, which was delivered to all schools in the country. The scope of generalization of the map on the game board was at its extreme: geographic units of the USSR were situated inside a circle, and the country's borders were evenly rounded up. The bright yellow circle against a grayish blue background symbolized a sunlit, happy country. On the other hand, it can be interpreted also as a symbol of a dream come true, a marvel island surrounded by a hostile ocean. The image was intensified by the semantics of visual graphics: the colour of the entire 'foreign land' was of a cold hue.[22]

The educational function of the game was limited to learning geographical names within the USSR as the players moved round the yellow disk. The players were advised to look for matches for places around and inside the circle on the USSR map. This procedure equated the sunny circle and the map of the homeland, made them appear equivalent to each other.

This journey was sanctified by the name of Lenin: the starting point was the border city of Leningrad. Having traveled in a circle around the sacral centre – the capital of the country, which is denoted in the map by a star, the players enclosed the Homeland in a symbolic loop of borders. They returned to the western, most dangerous borders having gained experience from the journey, after the challenge of meeting infiltrators at the Chinese border. The journey included small side trips deeper into the country, towards interesting (the stylistic choice in the source was

21 Alexandra Bonch-Osmolovskaya, Ob'yasnitel'noe chtenie v nerusskoy shkole, in: Metodicheskii byulleten' Ministerstva prosveshcheniya i Instituta usovershenstvovaniya uchiteley Karelo-Finskoy SSR 3 (1946), 31; 34.

22 The authors took into account the colour perception psychology. It was considered methodologically appropriate to use warm hues to render positive phenomena and cold hues for negative ones.

"remarkable") objects. At western borders, where the probability of encountering a spy was much higher, the players did stop over once, to visit the village of Mikhailovskoe (the game was issued on Pushkin's anniversary). This was however just a curious detail. In this game, like in many similar ones, in addition to gaining scientific knowledge about borders, schoolchildren were supposed to assimilate 'proper' political-ideological reference points. The mission was to build a certain world model, shape an individual's mind map.

A fun learning element in the study of the basics of geography in elementary school was to follow the physical map while reading the textbook, and image oneself on a plane.[23] Map-centered fantasies and games, habituating oneself to the imaginary Homeland were at the core of projects for building "living mock-ups" of the USSR. Such mock-ups depicted a dream country, and thus excited both teachers and children. In the summer of 1940, e. g., specialists in methods of pioneer activities disseminated experience from the play park in Sovetskiy district of Moscow, where 800 sq. m were allocated for creating a map on the ground. The Caspian Sea there was the size of a desktop, and the Gulf of Finland was suited for launching ship models. A highlighted object was the "Karelian-Finnish SSR, reunited with the family of socialist union republics" and its border.[24]

A common motif in the general propagandist discourse on westward expansion of the USSR was restoration of historical justice, "liberation of consanguine Ukrainians and Byelorussians from *panstvo* oppression", and a technique tailored specifically to children's audience was to integrate child characters in such texts. A good illustration of how much the literature for children was affected by the political mainstream is the history of revisions made to a story by future 4-time Stalin's prize winner Nikolai Virta. The story "Inostranka" (*Foreigner*) was first published in 1937. The main character, little Asya, unintentionally crossed the brook running along the borderline. Soviet border guards temporarily took her to a kindergarten. She liked it there so much that she was unwilling to go back to Poland, where poverty and hunger awaited her, especially because "she spoke the same language as all those children, with only a brook dividing them."[25] In its original version, the story ended with Asya's compelled return home. In the kindergarten the girl was given a bath, dressed in a new frock, presented with toys. As Asya was walking away, she "kept turning around, her shoulders were shuddering: she was sobbing."[26] After Soviet western borders had been expanded in 1939 to comprise new territories, N. Virta updated the plot by adding an optimistic ending. Asya's dream came true as people with red stars on service caps arrived from across the border and converted the rich neighbour's home into a kindergarten just as good as the one across the brook. "And so Asya was no longer a foreigner."[27] Helping miserable children, rescuing them from the tyranny of 'the bourgeois' was the key to 'comprehensibly' reasoning the shift of borders in texts addressed to little

---

23 Svetlana Samolyota, in: Lidiya Terekhova, Vladimir Erdeli, Geografiya. Uchebnik dlya 4 klassa nachal'noy shkoly, Moscow: Uchpedgiz, 1938, 54–55.

24 Ivan Rozanov, Karta na zemle, in: Vozhatyi 12 (1940), 13.

25 Nikolai Virta, Inostranka, Moscow-Leningrad: Detizdat, 1938, 11.

26 Virta, Inostranka, Loc. Cit. (Note 25), 15.

27 Nikolai Virta, Inostranka, in: Vozhatyi 13 (1939), 30.

citizens of the USSR. The archetype of a suffering child was widely employed by Soviet propaganda in general as a highly effective one.

Game practices were another way to explain the reasons for expanding Soviet borders to younger children. For instance, a recommendation to all educators in the country from "Igrushka" magazine was to use know-how from the Moscow City Pioneer Centre, where children supervised by instructor worked out a game plot "Red Army meets children of Western Byelorussia and Western Ukraine". The routine was described in detail:

> "A table was brought outside, surrounded by trees. Let's pretend it's a landowner's home. Where are then the landowners? Girls brought their dolls:
> – Please have perseverance: today you'll act as noble pany.
> One doll was dressed in a top hat and a cape collar. It was to portray a fat landowner. Another doll wore a bonnet – it was a peasant-offending evil landlord wife.
> – Just you wait! We shall defeat you! Our Red Army is strong!
> A mock-up church was built next to the house. Dolls were seated at the windows. Polish officers, two cannons were added.
> A bridge was built on the road to the manor house. Raya was unanimously chosen to be the commander. Children took shotguns, grenades (made of pieces of construction materials).
> – Units, fall in! – commanded Raya. – Comrade soldiers! We're going to liberate our brotherly Byelorussians and Ukrainians, those who live in Poland. Gentry and landowners made them toil, taking everything produced to themselves and not giving anything to the workers. They starved, they didn't have collective farms, not even their own schools. Come on, soldiers, for the Homeland, for Stalin! …"[28]

Children's feelings were sacrificed to ideological causes: children had to betray their dear dolls, which were transformed following the will of 'pedagogues' into diabolized landowner, bourgeois, spy characters.

Border guard, spy, child: images of the Soviet border and their transformations

Border guard and spy,[29] embodiments of good and evil, were the main symbolic figures in representations of Soviet borderlands. Collisions at the border in texts for children usually had in their centre a child, who made a strictly predetermined choice.

In the pantheon of Soviet heroes and the listing of professions with a halo of heroism, which were occasionally updated over the 70 years of Soviet history, the border guard was a resident, and the legendary Karatsupa was its personification.[30] Late in the 1930s, the border guard figure became one of the favorites among Soviet children. It fit better than other heroic images in the logic of the pioneer movement, which adopted a lot from the scout movement (scout = pathfinder, stalker), but was

28 Natalia Panova, Voennye igry oktyabryat, in: Igrushka 11–12 (1939), 20
29 Interestingly, other designations of trespassers (defector, infiltrator, outlaw etc.) typical of the Soviet propaganda discourse were hardly ever used in publications for children.
30 Nikita Karatsupa (1910–1994), Hero of the Soviet Union. Famed for border raids with well trained dogs.

modified to suit Soviet realities, cleared of the moral/ethical rules and the Christian spirit of Scouting. The protagonist of the border guard was the chekist. Both 'safeguard the country's tranquility', the 'peaceful sleep' of children. In the gallery of Soviet heroes, the border guard was the most watchful and the most alert, i. e. having a special skill of spotting the enemy. The logic suggested to the teacher was the following: "Why can't enemies infiltrate into the Soviet Union? – Because border guards *closely watch* the border and *see everything* going on there..."[31] A border guard "cannot be fooled or deceived". Watchful, alert, vigilant are the key words in texts about border guards. These exceptional qualities were backed up technically – vigilance was enhanced by binoculars, and a well-trained friend, the dog, helped stay alert. Children dreamed of having these two attributes of a contemporary *bogatyr* border guard. Self-made paper or wooden binoculars and a mongrel living in the yard were the easy-to-get substitutes, which let boys 'try on' the 'real' border guard image.

In texts for children, a border guard without a loyal service dog is unthinkable. It is the dog, which is described as an ingenuous creature with a "living soul", that makes the image of a border guard so attractive to junior children. No wonder writer Raisa Torban in her novelette "Yeti" (1938) kept calling the border guard "the master of the dog's soul".[32] The dog was made a full-fledged, and sometimes even the main character of various texts about the border, like for example in the film "Julbars" (Mezhrabpomfilm, 1935, script by Gabriel El-Registan). The guard dog there came to help on the most critical moments, when the situation appeared to be a deadlock. To prove that Julbars had conquered the hearts of the young audience, the dog's name became popular for decades, and was given to a variety of pets – from shepherd dogs to mongrels.

In the border-related frame of reference the hero border guard is opposed by antihero spy, whose ideological role is to provide evidence for the unparalleled qualities of the border guard. This opposition is vividly depicted in a story by Yuri Guerman. He described the border guard as an all-good character "...a tall, strong, handsome and very brave man. And very smart, too. Nobody could outsmart him, not a single enemy managed to cross the border – it was impossible to deceive comrade Avdeev." The spy had totally different looks: "...huge, angry look on fear-paled face, eyes gleaming like a wolf's, as if he's about to growl."[33]

A spy was subhuman, if at all human. Thus, Zhen'ka in a popular Soviet film "Timur and his Squad" (Soyuzdetfilm, 1940, script by Arkady Gaidar) said to the dog attacking her: "You go catch bandits or spies and I... am human". In the folklore tradition, the spy/enemy was labeled as 'foul', 'putrid' (fiend), with religious connotations to pagans, non-Christians. In children's literature, these characteristics may be attached to a spy in a literal sense, through their appearance. In the novelette by Ruvim Fraerman "The spy"[34] (1937), for instance, a Japanese infil-

31 V pomoshch shkole, in: Metodicheskii byulleten' Ministerstva prosveshcheniya i Instituta usovershenstvovaniya uchiteley Karelo-Finskoy SSR 3 (1946), 37.

32 The novelette was published as a book by Detizdat publishers in 1938 and appeared in the same year in "Pionerskaya pravda" newspaper. Hereinafter cited after Raisa Torban, Snezhnyi chelovek, in: Raisa Torban, Povesti dlya detey, Lipetsk: Infol, 2002, 21; 92.

33 Yuri Guerman, Rasskaz pogranichnika, in: Kniga dlya chteniya vo vtorom klasse karelo-finskoy shkoly, Ivan Belyaev, Petrozavodsk: Gosizdat Karelo-Finskoy SSR, 1952, 116; 119.

34 Ruvim Fraerman, Shpion, Moscow-Leningrad: Detizdat, 1937.

trator organized subversive operations from a Far East leprosarium, and looked leprose himself.

The protagonist of the spy was the bourgeois (thin, in a top hat and with a monocle – personifying evil, or fat – personifying an insatiable exploiter and thief). A spy was usually supplied with physical traits that make them stand out: lame, round-shouldered, with red beard, stout or lanky, shorty, etc. In drawings and photographs a spy would be either in caricature style or prostrate. Women spies were rarely found in these texts: they were usually disguised as pilgrims or nuns, dressed in old clothes, limped, leaned on a walking stick.

A foreign enemy was often described as a thief, a predator encroaching on the country's wealth. This is what they had in common with an internal enemy-thief. As sacral meanings were attached to the notion of 'the border', the focus of interest of an external enemy shifted towards the 'secret of the great country'. It is not often that the content of this secret would be explained in texts. The literature taught children to keep the Great Secret no matter what it takes, to pick up secret messages and packages. The sign of 'secrecy' was stated very definitely: "If they hide it, it's surely important."[35]

A spy in fiction and opinion journalism was marked out by turnskin symbolism. Placing a turnskin into a borderscape is in line with the mythological tradition, where the junction between worlds (appropriated/unappropriated, own/strange), the border between them is the most frequent locus for reincarnations, transformations, turning skin.[36] In Russian folk tales, borderlands were also positioned at the interface of two worlds – life and death – and were inhabited by 'evil creatures'. In texts directed at children, spies often appeared as beastlike humans, such as Kondiy the forester in Torban's novelette "Yeti": "Short, stout, hairy-faced, he moved around the house in a light-footed animal manner in his soft, skin-soled sharp-toed boots. To make the likeness to a beast even greater, there were the black spots of little spiteful eyes and a short neck. The split lip exposed a row of healthy yellowish teeth."[37] The night and crossroads were the typical time and place for meeting a spy, adding intensity to the reincarnation motif.

The resolution of the January 1938 TsK VKP(b) plenum demanded that one must "know enemy from friend and friend from enemy" and be able to "unmask a well-disguised enemy."[38] Children were 'assisted' in this tough challenge by the literature, which provided recipes for discerning enemy, even if clad in Red Army uniform.

A stranger could be given away by:
- "viper look"[39]; eyes gleaming "like a wolf's;"[40]

35 See Torban, Povesti, Loc. Cit. (Note 32), 130.

36 Neonila Krinichnaya, Russkaya narodnaya mifologicheskaya proza: Istoki i polisemantizm obrazov. 2, (Petrozavodsk, 2000), 350–351.

37 See Torban, Povesti, Loc. Cit. (Note 32), 40.

38 Umet' razlichat' vraga ot druga, Komsomolets Karelii, January 28, 1938, 1.

39 The hero of R. Fraerman's novelette "The spy", Korean pioneer Ti Soo-yevi, who lived in the Soviet Primorye region, felt suspicious about the looks of a Chinese boy "looking around like a little viper".

40 See Guerman, Rasskaz, Loc. Cit. (Note 33), 119.

– unauthentic, 'too correct', learned speech, cushioned voice,[41] or deliberately 'vernacular' retention of unstressed 'o';[42]
– forced laughter: a spy would roar with laughter to resemble a Soviet citizen, as they've heard "people have a joyful life in the Soviet land";[43]
– smile: forced, 'rigid', 'wry';[44]
– dress: deliberately shabby or irrelevant (elegant overcoat or hat, which look out of place in the countryside or woods); colour and details (strangely tailored hat or service cap), an eye-catching sign of a 'stranger' is a striped or checkered suit (or its elements). Striped clothes signaled danger, and stripes retained the traditional 'diabolical' connotations.[45]

On the other hand, the capacity to metamorphose, the cryptic 'second nature' of a spy figure added volume to it and thus made it more interesting and attractive for a young reader.

Firing squad for an enemy trespasser as a solution was a usual formula suggested in texts for children. Pre-school children were also deemed 'prepared' to understand such a behavioural model. In 1938 Igrushka magazine published, with a G. Hitrova, teacher from a kindergarten in Moscow, as the contributor, a script of a puppet performance allegedly made up by children. The characters in this play for a makeshift puppet theater were a border guard, a dog, a spy and "the chief". The formulae of the 'children's dialogue' echoed the ideological clichés adapted for young citizens, and the related didactic assumptions:

> "... – Oh, what a dangerous spy that is! He must be executed by shooting. – A border guard leads the spy away.
> – Forgive me, I'll never do it again, – begs the spy.
> – No, we shall not forgive you, – answers the chief, – it's too late now! And you, comrade border guard, will be awarded for protecting the borders well."[46]

In texts of various genres, children living near the border were ascribed all the qualities of vigilant Soviet citizens, always ready to lend a helping hand to border guards. They are good at smelling, spotting or tracking down a stranger by a cracking twig, footprints on sand, a whispering talk. Sweet treats used by the enemy to tempt children would only signal danger but could be accepted.[47]

In texts about border incidents children could only be present as border guard helpers. They acted as signalers or as messengers reporting an enemy emergence to the border post, or occasionally as lurers. The latter role consisted in luring a stranger to the border post or setting them on a wrong track to then inform

41 See Torban, Povesti, Loc. Cit. (Note 32), 129.
42 Nikilai Yakovlev, "Medvezhiy kogot'. Rasskaz", Komsomolets Karelii, April 16, 1938, 4.
43 Arkady Gaidar, "Marusya", (1939–1941), in Arkady Gaidar, *Sochineniya*, Vol. II (Moscow-Leningrad: Detgiz, 1949), 335.
44 See Torban, Povesti, Loc. Cit. (Note 32), 109; 158.
45 See Michel Pastoureau, *D'yavolskaya materiya. Istoriya polosok i polosatykh tkaney* (Moscow: Novoe literaturnoe obozrenie, 2008) – Russian translation from French: Michel Pastoureau, *L'étoffe du diable: une histoire des rayures et des tissus rayés* (Seuil, 1991)
46 Galina Hitrova, "Igra v teatr", *Igrushka*, 12 (1938), 15.
47 See Galaktionova / Volkova, Sbornik, Loc. Cit. (Note 19), 5; See Torban, Povesti, Loc. Cit. (Note 32), 40; 128.

border guards of where the enemy was heading. In these roles children not just appeared as 'mini adults', but excelled them in astuteness, reactions, wit.

Participation in capturing of a spy denoted a successful ritual of initiation evidenced by a portrait in a newspaper or a watch presented by the chief of the border post, or other symbolic gestures by men in power, including handshake (border guard "shook hands with the children, like they were grown-ups"[48]). Toddy Rohkimainen, a boy who came to northern Karelia from Canada (Raisa Torban's "Yeti"), also passed an initiation rite. He differed from Soviet peers in many things carried over from his native land: checkered trousers, thick-soled boots, foreign fashion cap, as well as an unfamiliar toy – handcuffs for "a game of gangsters", and even his dream of becoming a millionaire. After the trial of living at the border, he concluded, quite cynically, that "becoming rich is of no use in this country, while being a hero does make sense: earns you honors and rewards", especially given that "the government in the Soviet country often awarded cars to heroes."[49] In a while, he acquired a new dream, shared with Soviet children – to catch a spy. For Toddy, it was also a way into the dream country that the Soviet Union was turning into, as the boy was getting more familiar with it. The boy imagined he'd "capture that Kondiy and take the man, rifle aimed at him, to the village. And all lumberjacks would say: "What a hero he is, this boy from Canada! We should ask him to stay here in the Union for good."[50] Toddy realized that the only way for him to get recognized as 'one of us' in his new homeland was to give the enemy, the spy he had conspired with for money, in to the investigator. This would signify maturity, both socially and age-wise. No wonder the youngest character of the same novelette, even if afraid of spies, secretly dreamed of meeting one and thus getting a chance to "become a grown-up": "What if one such spy wanders in here! – said Juriki fearfully, yet secretly hopefully ..."[51] Like millions of his peers, he was eager to commit a heroic feat to gain recognition among adults.

At the same time, both propagandist literature and life realities *de facto* encouraged, although not so outspokenly, suspiciousness and whistle-blowing, artifice and shift. A textbook, an extra reading book, a game would engineer models for the behaviour of an ideal Soviet child in specific situations. Such an engineered child, a little Octobrist, a pioneer, would set a suspicious stranger on a wrong track, eavesdrop on adults (spies might be found even in the nearest surroundings), distract people to check the contents of their bag, demonstrate incredible ingenuity in fighting the enemy. Children throughout the country learned about Valya Vitushko, who "played dead, and sank her teeth into a spy's leg."[52]

This topic, first introduced through serious genres, has been gradually reconsidered, but remained attractive. In post-war years, publications appeared where the images were not so clichéd as before, irony and humour in relation to this subject became possible. The moves in this direction were very cautious and gradual. The tendency could spread out fully only after Stalin's death. In 1957, a book

48 See Torban, Povesti, Loc. Cit. (Note 32), 149.
49 See Torban, Povesti, Loc. Cit. (Note 32), 113; 114.
50 See Torban, Povesti, Loc. Cit. (Note 32), 139.
51 See Torban, Povesti, Loc. Cit. (Note 32), 80.
52 Elizar Smirnov, Prionery-geroi, in: Vozhatyi, 10 (1938), 49–50.

of verses "Seryozha catches a spy" by Ada Blank was published, where the subject is rendered ambiguous by moving the plot to the domain of the hero's night dreams.[53] In our days, the poem will be perceived as a pastiche of the "topicality" of the time, if not a mockery. With the action set in a dream, one gets a feeling of an unclear genre and conventionality of the action.

New dimensions of the border topic conceptualization through art appeared during the Thaw period, which revitalized internationalism in Soviet culture. Even journalistic representations of the border became more diverse. A soft-key version appeared in newspaper story "Hurricane" by A. Gordov (1958). Agitation at the border post was caused by a moose calf, whose mother had been killed by a bear. The "detainee" was not just given shelter, but even "put on rations", as evidenced by an accompanying photograph of a military cook feeding the calf, whom the border guards nicknamed Hurricane (Uragan).[54]

The harmfulness of spy mania and its paranoid nature were demonstrated in Raisa Torban's novelette "The enchanted ward" (Zakoldovannaya palata) (1962). Children staying in a sanatorium have taken to spy games. This interest was kept up by an elderly housemistress, who kept telling 'spy stories' to the little patients. Eventually, children themselves turned into spy mania critics as they chalked up a caricature of the housemistress "with a huge Nagant revolver stealing after an unknown spy all across the blackboard…"[55] To put an end to the unhealthy hobby, the Chief Physician of the sanatorium urged the woman to overcome the "Earth's gravity", "head for space", since "a new era has begun in the history of the humankind."[56]

Another method for a 'liberal' interpretation of the border theme is to put the central collision on stage, as has been done by a classic Soviet children's writer Viktor Dragunsky in his story "The death of spy Gadyukin,"[57] included in the "Denis's stories" series written by the author in the late 1950s – early 1960s. His sense of humour and writer's mastery enabled Dragunsky to expose the burlesque nature of Soviet spy fiction characters, everybody was sick and tired of. In a narrative by an eight-year-old Denis Korablyov, the author described a school play "A dog's death for a dog", with the title coming from a fixed phrase widely used by the 1930s–1940s Soviet propaganda to express satisfaction with ignoble death of a despised person.[58]

Both the 'positive' and the 'negative' characters of the espionage plot taken by Dragunsky up to the school stage appeared very comic in Denis Korablyov's description:

> "There stood a boy from fourth grade, wearing a black suit, with chalk on hair, as if he was silver-haired; he was holding a gun, and another boy, also from fourth

53 Ada Blank, Seryozha lovit shpiona, Simferopol: Krymizdat, 1957.

54 Aleksandr Gordov, Uragan, Yunye lenintsy, September 24, 1958, 4.

55 See Torban, Povesti, Loc. Cit. (Note 32), 209–210.

56 Ibid., 209.

57 This surname is derived from the colloquial word 'gad' = 'reptile'. Semantically, there is a hint at the chthonic nature of a spy, as a visitor from "the other" world. The figurative meaning of the word is 'a mean, disgusting person'.

58 In 1937 this fixed phrase turned into an ideologeme, which was used to cover up for the lawlessness in the country, for mass repressions of innocent people. It was included both in party leaders' speeches and resolutions of workers' meetings.

> grade, stood next to him. That other boy was glued to a beard, with blue eyeglasses sitting on his nose, and he was wrapped in an oilcloth coat with the collar up."

The 'dramatic composition' of the play was also entirely of a parody genre:

> "And there was a desk on the stage, and the black-suit boy sitting at it, and I knew he had a gun in his pocket. The boy with a beard was strolling opposite that boy. First he told he'd spent much time abroad, and now he came back again, and then he started bothering the black-suit boy begging him in a boring voice to show the airfield plan.
>
> But the other one said:
>
> – You shall not get this from me, mister Gadyukin!"[59]

The play had blunders and gaffes which back in the 1930s could have cost a life to both teachers and children's parents. Yet, this story reflected a different era, both politically and didactically.

Habitual clichés from Soviet and foreign spy fiction were obviously parodied in the cartoon "Passions of spies" (Soyuzmultfilm, 1967. Script by Lazar Lagin), where even the formerly untouchable Julbars did not avoid irony: it is safely disguised here in kitten 'costume'.

In post-Soviet times, even straightforward patriotic texts about the border had their storyline modified and cast away whatever was considered 'false romanticization'. Writings for teenagers from the 1970s–1980s were supplied with a character of a border guard lacking the zeal for service when conscripted but acquiring the 'taste' for service owing to the border/frontier post environment.[60] In the volume of stories "Zaslon" (Shield) by Nikolai Makhnev, border guard conscripts are not all courageous, there is space for doubt, for weakness.

The school canon of representing border images was also getting revised, although with a time lag. For instance, local study textbooks for schools of Karelia published in 1967 and 1970 still contained stories about the "perilous border", about children helping to arrest spies (the "dangerous country" was not however named).[61] These texts, which used to form a kind of a 'mind map' of Karelia, vanished from the 1978 edition: contacts with the neighbour country were developing, thousands of Finns were at that time building the town of Kostomuksha in Karelia.[62] The Soviet society in general was however still governed by the psychological laws of a 'besieged fortress'.

In the 1990s–2000s, the border was reconsidered to be perceived as a contact zone, the interface of different cultures. The post-Soviet period associated with the emergence of new political realities, apprehension of the national borders di-

---

59 Cited after Viktor Dragunsky, Smert' shpiona Gadyukina, http://deti-online.com/skazki/rasskazy-dragunskogo/smert-shpiona-gadyukina.

60 See e. g.: Nikolai Makhnev, "Vtoroe dykhanie", in: Nikolai Makhnev, Zaslon, Petrozavodsk: Karelia, 1985, 17–28.

61 Aune Blyudnik / Raisa Kotova / Gali Ogienko, Mladshim shkol'nikam o Karelii: kniga dlya chteniya, Petrozavodsk: Karel'skoe knizhnoe izdatel'stvo, 1967; Aune Blyudnik /Raisa Kotova / Gali Ogienko, Mladshim shkol'nikam o Karelii: kniga dlya chteniya. 2nd expanded edition, Petrozavodsk: Karelia, 1970.

62 Aune Blyudnik / Raisa Kotova / Gali Ogienko, Mladshim shkol'nikam o Karelii: kniga dlya chteniya. 3rd expanded edition, Petrozavodsk: Karel'skoe knizhnoe izdatel'stvo, 1978.

viding the former Soviet Union, the new united Europe with its transparent borders – these and other large-scope processes brought to life new images and symbols. A trend that showed up was to get rid of Soviet stereotypes, to parody them. There appeared numerous jokes about the border, something not to be heard in the USSR.[63] Yet, old clichés persisted, surfacing occasionally and covertly, which proved the images were deep-rooted and essentially archetypical.[64] Primers from the 1990s reproduced illustrations showing border guards protecting the country's frontiers, reflecting the opposition and intertwining of the Soviet and post-Soviet discourses in the life of the society.[65] The range of readings for children generally retained pieces of Soviet literature with ideologemes characteristic of their respective times.[66]

Russian educational policies of the 1990s – early 2000s, which followed the pan-European mainstream, numerous international programmes in the sphere of school education, development of international tourism, etc. altered the general perception of the border, turning it into a bridge to the neighbouring world for many children. Yet, recent political realities have been modifying children's worldview in general and their perception of the border in particular. We have a chance to analyze these changes relying on drawings by schoolchildren from Karelia.

The small data pool available now is made up of two collections of drawings by children aged 7 to 17.[67] The first one was assembled in 2010 and comprises 110 drawings; the second one, which is being assembled in the current year 2015, is made up of 144 drawings. The images were made after the request to "draw the national border the way you picture it". These, mainly colour pencil, drawings vary in artistic skill, but this is beyond our scope of interest. Some plots show

---

63 See Misha Mel'nichenko, Sovetskii anekdot, Ukazatel' syuzhetov, Moscow: Novoe literaturnoe obozrenie, 2014.

64 For instance, the phrase "border guard on duty" was sometimes used metaphorically in contexts having little to do with politics, demonstrating the image was deep-seated in the minds of people representing a variety of social strata. They play with the multiple meanings of the Russian word 'post', which can denote i. e. 1) sentry post or being on duty; 2) religious fast(ing), i.e. abstinence from non-vegetarian food. Thus, both religious and non-religious people can use the phrase to explain the essence of an Orthodox fast: "to fast means to stand sentry", "to guard one's heart". The image was used to make explanations in education and medicine 'easier to understand'. For example, the topic of a school biology class was formulated as follows: "The skin, a man's 'sentry'", http://900igr.net, [Accessed: June 2014]. The same image found its way into a drug package leaflet: "biomolecule begins to act as a 'sentry at the border'. It is constantly on guard and responds immediately to any invasion of free radicals by destroying them" (Memo on antioxidant therapy approved by the Chairman of the Expert Council for the system of Voluntary certification of dietary supplements Yu.T. Kalinin on February 28, 2007. Author's personal archive). It is certainly only the art works and images with extensive and deep-rooted associations in the minds of people that can demonstrate such continuity.

65 See, e.g. Alla Sal'nikova / Dilyara Galiullina, Tatarskaya "Alfba": natsional'nyi bukvar' v multikul'turnom prostranstve (konets XIX – nachalo XX vv.), Moscow: NPB im. Ushinskogo, 2014, 222–223.

66 An indicative fact is that Raisa Torban's "Yeti", first published in 1938, was re-printed in Lipetsk in a volume of novelettes by this author and was recommended to schoolchildren for reading. See Didakticheskoe posobie dlya uchiteley kraevedeniya, Lipetsk: Lipetskiy institut razvitiya obrazovaniya, 2008, 37.

67 Author's personal archive.

much similarity, obviously indicating borrowings between schoolchildren within groups. On the other hand, the levels of generalization/detail in unraveling the topic vary. Pupils use different scopes of representation: from drawing the globe with continents or countries outlined on it to a particular incident at the border. Let us systematize the drawings by the level of generalization of the border image and try to identify the specific traits that distinguish 2015 pictures from those drawn five years earlier.

- The most generalized representation of the border in children's drawings is a *schematic map*. Not surprisingly, the central position in such an image would be occupied by a rough contour of Karelia or Russia. Among foreign countries, denoted by various means (inscription, flag, cultural symbols), the most frequent in drawings from 2010 was Karelia's neighbour Finland (a quarter of all drawings), whereas other countries were in the periphery of attention. Thus, Ukraine was 'present' in four cases, Kazakhstan and China in three, Mongolia and Japan were mentioned twice each, and there were singular references to Abkhazia, Azerbaijan, England, Byelorussia, Iran, Uzbekistan, the USA, Sweden.

  In 2015 the situation changed fundamentally: Ukraine was mentioned as frequently as Finland, and the previously absent Crimea appeared. The number of references to 'other countries' dropped drastically (Great Britain and Israel were mentioned once each). In some pictures Russia appears as an epitome of amicability, opposed to 'the rest of the world'. The USA was 'upgraded' from an 'outsider' to a frequently mentioned country. The symbolic border between Russia and the USA usually separates a stereotypic set of items, with vodka, balalaika and ear-flapped hat on the one side, and coca-cola, hamburger, iPhone, etc. on the other. Sometimes the USA is marked by monster images, pictured as the 'antiworld'.
- An average level of generalization is found in pictures with a *panorama, a border landscape*. The main highlights there are the borderline and checkpoint (or gate) guarded as a rule by armed people. A substantial part of the drawings reveals children's familiarity with border crossing infrastructure (passport control, customs, gas station, café). In some of these drawings the border is rather conventional, with uniform space on both sides: e. g. covered in flowers or filled with images of trees, woods. Territories are labeled either by the names of countries written on them, or by a drawing of the national flag. A trait typical of 2010 drawings is symbolic images portraying Russia as a traditional agrarian country as opposed to urban markings of Finland. There are log frame houses, horses in meadows, girl with plait over shoulder ('Russian beauty'), woman with shoulder yoke on one side of the border; and tall buildings, modern cars, stylish girls on the other. The signs of connection are a road running across the border, sometimes migrating birds, reunion of friends at the border. In a substantial part of materials from 2015, Russia as a peace zone is opposed to Ukraine as a war zone.
- The highest level of detail is found in pictures of a *border crossing checkpoint*. Text (sometimes in Finnish) proves drawings from 2010 most often depicted a checkpoint on the Finnish border. In some drawings one can see "Welcome" signs in Russian, English and Finnish. In many drawings, even from 2010, the focus is on the dividing and prohibitive signs: boom barrier, "STOP" sign,

> barbed wire fence, armed guards, dog. Yet, five years ago military machines at the border were depicted very rarely, mainly by 7–8-year-olds.

In 2015, most drawings portrayed a very different frame of mind. Widely present is the war topic, which is clearly a projection from TV screen. The border in that case separates the peaceful and peace-loving Russia from war-ridden foreign land. A phenomenon to observe is that compared to 2010 the number of drawings with fantasy plots or those inspired by computer games has increased, indicating the children's desire to stay in the 'world of childhood'. This fact can also be interpreted as a reaction to the war theme, which is hard for children to take, as their psychological protest against confrontation, disturbance of the habitual world order.

Conclusions

During the Soviet and post-Soviet time, the discourse concerning the border which was either targeted at children or somehow reached the children's audience has undergone changes which generally matched the alteration of 'internationalism' and 'patriotism' periods in the national ideology. Various theories may describe cultural model shifts as alteration of openness and closeness of the society, "spreading out" (decentralization) and 'solidification', "building of a vertical structure" (centralization). These opposite tendencies reflect the periodic change of cycles, where new and less steady forms of culture give way to archaic and steady ones, and vice versa.[68]

An obvious turning point was the beginning of the 1930s, when early Soviet internationalist targets were replaced by a growing patriotic discourse. Stalin's death and the Thaw period pushed the pendulum in the opposite direction. When Brezhnev came to power, it went back and froze in 'stagnation' to swing with a renewed momentum towards unprecedented openness to the world during 'perestroika' and the post-Soviet decade.

Naturally, Soviet propagandist texts meant for an adult audience and those for children followed the same vector. Not only weren't children kept away from Soviet propaganda, but they were one of its 'target groups'. Primers and other elementary school textbooks, teacher's manuals contained images and symbols of the national border, and reflected some realities of Soviet borderlands. A distinctive feature of a majority of texts about the border written for children is a child character, who, finding oneself in the force field of opposition between good and evil, would always made an ideologically 'correct' choice. A similar indoctrination was fulfilled by games. Game action, as a ritual equivalent of a myth, established and maintained the officially approved world model, where images of ideological relevance were getting integrated into the system of mental universals.

For a great cause, a fictional child hero or player in a game devised by adults could depart from the norms of behaviour: deceive a suspicious stranger, eavesdrop on adults, betray the favourite toy and, finally, easily accept violence as the solution for the suspect problem. Didactic ideals were often sacrificed to political-

68 See Vladimir Papernyi, Kultura Dva, Moscow: Novoe literaturnoe obozrenie, 1996, 194; 215.

ideological causes, and simplification and sketching of situations when described to children served to unmask and highlight the 'true objectives' of politicians. Heroic feat for the sake of the Homeland justified the inversion of behavioural norm, which in the late 1930s one tried to squeeze into the Soviet pedagogic frame of reference. How did these contradictions influence the young personality and the choice of the behavioural model by individual children? Many of the people who spent their childhood at the border in the 1930s recollected that in spite of the propaganda they were governed by the family precept that one should avoid difficult situations or contacts with authorities. On the other hand, the formulas and plots of propagandist texts about the border have been implanted into the memories, rendering the memorates somewhat hybridized and diglossic, using both the public and the private description languages[69], indicating a gap between words and deeds, between the official and the 'domestic' discourse.

The Soviet canon of representing the border remained constant, and its most noticeable alterations are associated with a humorous rendition of old plots and an ironical take on characters. During the Thaw period, the spy image in literature and art, including those targeted at children, was gradually remoulded from a diabolical into a comical figure. Nevertheless, the border guard figure, portrayed as a noble sentinel, persisted in primaries, i. e. books that speak the language of power, up until the end of the 20th century. In the context of the 1990s this fact reflected the opposition and intertwining of the Soviet border discourse with the post-Soviet one, oriented at erasing borders and building 'cultural bridges'.

Contemporary Russian media representation of the border open to both adults and children is free of former unidimensional and obtrusive images, but filled with new political figures and symbols, which are being rapidly integrated into a myth matrix, re-creating a black-and-white world. One of the indicators of the new Russian mythology built up around the border theme is children's drawings. Pictures contain manifestations of children's daily realities, dreams and fears. Where in 2010 drawings revealed the childhood dream and the childhood reality, and the world in the pictures appeared diverse, colourful, filled with bright and subtle tones, in 2015 the world is displayed as a field of confrontation between good and evil, there are signs of children fearing war or trying to retreat to 'another reality' – a fantasy, a computer game. A picture from TV, understood and transformed in their own way, is in the core of what most children think of the border.

Abstract

This paper deals with the children-targeted version of the myth about Soviet borders generated through texts of various genres, the techniques of impressing it upon children. The lingo and implications of the governmental and pedagogical discourses on the subject are exposed. An attempt is made, relying on texts published both in editions for children and in those meant for school teachers, youth organization leaders, day-care teachers, to iden-

69 For details see Olga Ilyukha, The Sociocultural Landscape of the Soviet-Finnish Borderland of the 1930s as Seen through Autobiographic Childhood Stories, in: Katarzyna Stokłosa / Gerhard Besier (eds.), European Border Regions in Comparison. Overcoming Nationalistic Aspects or Re-Nationalization?, New York-London: Routledge Studies in Modern European History, 2014, 221–235.

tify the characteristics of the Soviet canon for representing the border and its later modifications. The paper describes how the notion of the border was explained to children in the Soviet time. It also demonstrates how games were used as a tool to shape a mythologized worldview in Soviet schoolchildren.

The lines of post-Soviet border-related reflections are outlined, and the opposition and intertwining of the Soviet discourse with the post-Soviet one, targeted at erasing borders and building 'cultural bridges', are shown. The author used her own collection of children's drawings on the subject to disclose the notions of the border maintained by contemporary children, the surviving stereotypes and the new trends.

Making Space for the Future?

Reconstructing Spatial Identities after Armed Conflict

Dorte Jagetić Andersen

Introduction

What happens to a place influenced by a recent armed conflict when its symbolic significance is appropriated by the larger national community in a nation-building process? Rebuilding the physical environment after a violent conflict is hard enough. However, if nation-building prevents reconstruction because, for symbolic reasons the place is preserved as it was just after the conflicts, this becomes an almost impossible task.

This chapter problematizes the way in which war heritage solidifies an image of the Croatian town Vukovar as national symbol, affecting the town-scape and its populations. Vukovar, situated by the Danube in the region Slavonia bordering Serbia, in 1991 experienced an 87 days' siege, known as the battle of Vukovar. Before the conflicts, the area was a strategic part of the Yugoslav development setup at the Danube but after the partitions and integration into the independent Croatian state, its inhabitants did not return and its buildings and industrial sites were not restored to any great extent.

In this landscape of decay, the national and local authorities have decided to erect several monuments to commemorate the Homeland War, the Croatian name for the country's participation in the breakdown of Yugoslavia. The article focuses on these post-war initiatives developing new heritage infrastructures and disseminating narratives of belonging into identity-formation at everyday level. It mobilizes the concepts of spatial identity, particularly the national, and war heritage, showing how the town has frozen in time because of its task to represent the ultimate sacrifice for the nation.

The article begins with a brief introduction to the context of partition and national identity-construction in post-conflict Croatia. To analyse the tangible and intangible remains of war in Vukovar, it introduces the concept of war heritage and its relation to nation-building. Following this, the reader is taken on a tour through Vukovar and surroundings, directing the focus towards the remaining presence of war and conflict in the town-scape and the often very emotional responses to these material remains. Through the exemplary case of Vukovar, the article contributes to research investigating relations between nation-building and heritage by showing how the use of war to solidify national identity prevents restoration and, not the least, over-coming ethnic tension.

Reconstructing spatial identities

Aggressive nationalisms and partition of ethnic groups reflect the nature and consequences of the conflicts experienced in the 1990s in the former Yugoslavia.[1] The conflicts were directly linked to violent and separatist nationalist political ideologies influencing mainly Serbia and Croatia. Partly responsible for the escalation of the conflicts[2] was thus an 'ethno-nationalism', defining the national community in terms of its monoethnic origins with an in-born right to authority over the political, economic and social affairs in a territory.[3] The ideal world is territorially divided into ethnically homogenous states and based on the belief that people with a specific identity present in a certain geographical area has more right to power than others.

The conflicts spurred a general distrust towards 'the ethnic other',[4] distrust which was not just utilized at state level to legitimize ethnic cleansing but became an integral part of civil society and thus the very existence of people in the regions affected by the conflicts.[5] These challenges have, paradoxically, been combatted with the very same logic causing the problems in the first place; partition has been the tool most widely used by national and international communities to solve conflicts in the area, best exemplified by the German state's recognition of Croatia and Slovenia's status as independent republics very soon after the conflicts broke out.[6]

Partition obviously challenged the Yugoslav idea: "The peak of Yugoslavia's multifaceted crisis reveals that its identity can no longer be defined through the ideology of the post-war communist era. All that this kind of unity has left behind it are differences: cultural, linguistic, religious, economic."[7] When a state containing multiple identities disintegrates, partition can be implemented to keep differences territorially separate and provide each difference with its own

1 John R. Lampe, Yugoslavia as History – twice there was a country. Cambridge 2000; Mary Kaldor, New and Old Wars. Organised Violence in a Global Era. Cambridge 2007.

2 Whereas internal dynamics such as nationalism explains much about the root causes of the conflicts, external influences must be taken into consideration if we want to explain their escalation and the destabilization of the entire region (cf. Susan L. Woodward, Balkan Tragedy: Chaos and Dissolution after the Cold War. Washington DC 1995).

3 Walker Connor, Ethnonationalism: The Quest for Understanding. New Jersey 1993.

4 Ethnicity remains a highly problematic concept to apply practically because its meaning is so contested (cf. Richard Jenkins, Rethinking Ethnicity: Arguments and Explorations. London 1997).

5 Jaume Castan Pinos / Dorte Jagetić Andersen, 'Challenging the post-Yugoslavian borders: The enclaves of Sastavci and Dubrovnik' in: Janczak / Osiewicz (ed.), European Enclaves in the Process of De-bordering and Re-bordering. Berlin 2015, 81–98 (Thematicon, Bind 18); See Kaldor, New and Old, Loc. Cit. (Note 1).

6 See Lampe, Yugoslavia, Loc. Cit. (Note 1).

7 M Bakić-Hayden / Robert M. Hayden,'Orientalist Variations on the Theme 'Balkans', in: Symbolic Geography in Recent Yugoslav Cultural Politics' Slavic Review 51 1 (1992), 15–32; here: 5.

space of power. The aim is to thereby reduce the risk of further combat and ethnic cleansing.[8] After the break-up of Yugoslavia, differences were thus sorted out by confining them geographically but also in terms of loyalty and belonging. As regard the latter, the belief in the area has largely been that nation-building is the way to do the sorting.

Unlike the five other independent republics, nation-building in Croatia began already during the conflicts. The first president of the republic, Franjo Tudjman, who headed the country during the conflicts, with his proclamation of the "one-thousand-year-old-dream of independence" explicitly emphasized nation-building as part of his party, HDZ's political program.[9] Nation-building in Croatia was in other words a governmentally directed project uniting a story of origins with the struggle for independence: "The nation-building strategies of the new Croatian elites in the 1990s regarding historical narratives were twofold: to reach deep into the past to re-create the almost mythical emergence of the Croatian nation and its state-building efforts, and to de-legitimize any kind of 'Yugoslavia'."[10]

As regard the de-legitimization of the Yugoslav legacy, the story told in the years during and following the conflicts emphasized a Croatian freedom fight against Serbian aggressors. The Serbs, also called Serbo-chetniks, were not only portrayed as nationalists but also as defenders of the Yugoslav project, which had in effect always been an attempt to create a greater Serbia. Hence, the Croatian constitution's article 142 stipulates that it is forbidden to enter associations which could lead to a renewal of the Yugoslav state: "Any procedure for the association of the Republic of Croatia into alliances with other states, if such association leads, or may lead, to a renewal of a South Slavic state union or to any form of consolidated Balkan state is hereby prohibited."[11]

War heritage

Emphasis in Croatian nation-building narratives is on war and they draw on emotions, including heroism and martyrdom, thus forging the national unity as one of brotherhood in arms. The defence of Dubrovnik in 1991, the battle of Vukovar in 1991, and the military operations Flash and Storm have achieved the status of milestones in the narratives. As Winland argues, pain and suffering caused by warfare unite Croats not only in the homeland but in the entire world.[12] Croatia is an extreme case when it comes to images of war becoming an integral and legitimate part of everyday life. As Pavlaković states: "The reproduction of

8 Cf. Chaim Kaufmann, 'Possible and Impossible solutions to ethnic civil wars', in: International Security 20 4 (1996), 137.

9 Vjeran Pavlaković, 'Fulfilling the Thousand-Year-Old-Dream: Strategies of Symbolic Nation-Building in Croatia', in: Kolstø (ed.), Strategies of Symbolic Nation-building in South Eastern Europe, London 2014.

10 See Pavlaković, Fulfilling, Loc. Cit. (Note 9), 22.

11 Croatian Parliament, 'The Constitution of Croatia (consolidated text): International Provisions' http://www.sabor.hr/Default.aspx?art=2412 [Accessed: 30.09.2018].

12 Dahpne N. Winland, We are Now a nation: Croats Between 'home' and 'homeland'. Toronto 2007, 22.

war narratives and nation-building discourses as part of everyday nationhood (Fox and Miller-Idriss 2008) are prevalent in the media, at sporting events, in consumer advertising, in novels and films (Crnkovic 2012) and in the music industry (Baker 2010)."[13]

Wars are thus not necessarily resolved because the violent conflicts are. In their aftermath, wars exist as physical records, tangible remains, and memories many years after they have been fought and the reasons why the wars were fought are remembered. Significantly so, wars reiterate in heritage-making, and as time passes it is mostly through heritage that people encounter and remember war. Heritage objects which seem to be of the past are not passive but become active partners in a material/non-material dialogue with the present; war heritage make sense of and act upon the present, and it informs strategies for future developments.[14]

Research shows that these processes are deeply complex.[15] Heritage is received by many different groups and perceived in different ways by them: "Values are placed upon artefacts or activities by people who, when they view heritage, do so through a whole series of lenses, the most obvious of which are: nationality; religion; ethnicity; class; wealth; gender; personal history; and that strange lens known as 'insideness'."[16] It is therefore hard to intentionally control the significance and meaning of a heritage product. Nevertheless, heritage has proven to unite people by stirring their memories and it is active in constructing identity - or even better, heritage is always already involved in identity-forming processes with an impact on public and collective memories and sense-making.

War heritage sites and the selection of what is remembered and what is forgotten form part of collective and personal identities.[17] It is not just the legacy of the past but when erected it is also lived and practiced and it is always referring to a canon, that is, a specific representation of the past. Hence, heritage is used by some and for specific reasons.[18] Moreover, the choice of which heritage to present seemingly involves ongoing selection processes through which some aspects of a war become highlighted, moving into the public realm, and others disappear from public consciousness. Through such processes war becomes communicated as owned by particularly well-defined communities irrespective of how they were affected by the war. The selection is tainted by power and dominance, both in the aim at gaining power and portraying who is in power. As stated by McDowell: "[…] heritage is a highly political process, malleable to the needs of power and often subject to contestation, […]"[19]

---

13 See Pavlaković, Fulfilling, Loc. Cit. (Note 9), 20.

14 Laurajane Smith, The Uses of Heritage. London 2006.

15 Cf. Iain J.M. Robertson (ed.), Heritage From Below. Aldershot 2012; CRIC, 'Identity and Conflict. Cultural heritage and the reconstruction of identities after conflicts', http://www.cric.arch.cam.ac.uk/index.php 2013 [Accessed: 20.09.2018].

16 Brian J Graham / Peter Howard, Ashgate Research Companion to Heritage and Identity. Aldershot 2008, 2.

17 Jeffrey K Olick / Joyce Robbins,'Social Memory Studies, in: "Collective Memory" to the Historical Sociology of Mnemonic Practices' Annual Review of Sociology 24 (1998), 105–140.

18 See Smith, Heritage, Loc. Cit. (Note 14).

19 See Graham and Howard, Heritage and Identity, Loc. Cit. (Note 16), 37.

Heritage plays a key role in nationalism being a highly effective tool for political elites in their nation-building projects: "There is however, another dimension to this, which is that heritage and identity arguably continue to privilege the national at the expense of other scales. While Amin (2004) may argue for an equal and empowered multiple public with no myth of origin or destination identified only by its commitment to plural demos, 'it is the nation which ultimately and inevitably returns as the backdrop to the liberal fantasy' (Mitchell, 2004, 648) and 'remains a potent rallying cry in Europe' (Peckham, 2003, 2) and worldwide."[20] War heritage is unique in this regard because is cuts to the chase, so to speak, representing the clear-cut difference between those who belong to the nation and the others, represented as the enemy: "In a state of war, ethno-national identities are explicitly displayed in ways not possible during peacetime, since the difference between one's group and the 'Other' – the enemy – becomes a question of survival."[21] When nation-building is done through war narratives, war remains and memories do not fade and lose relevance in the public realm. Rather, war takes presence making it possible for individuals and groups to position themselves in terms of public claims on the war, something, which affects identity constructions.

For past historical events like a war to continue to be part of the present, they need to gain other form, forms that influence the meanings associated with them. History gets re-cast within meaning-scapes that often take material form.[22] War heritage would normally be present at specific sites; at museums, where the war is re-enacted through exhibitions providing the audience with knowledge about the war; monuments, which is a very usual way of paying tribute to victims and heroes of war; architecture, buildings and in other visible images such as photography, graffiti, etc. However, war heritage is also present as events and happenings and often personified in names of those whose deeds are remembered.

It is thus often in tangible form that a war becomes part of the present, recognizable, potentially even shared by the larger society. Simple messages, as well as their repetition and imitation are at the core of these narratives, as are the selection processes through which they become repeated and imitated. The remaining part of this article highlight narratives through which the history and memories of the battle of Vukovar became national property in Croatia, thus illuminating some of the material, practical and emotional consequences of these narratives. The article therefore takes the reader on a tour to the most important sites of the narration, sites, which have become symbolic for the remembrance of war. The tour takes us from Vukovar town-scape with its buildings and monuments, to museums, events and happenings, thereby illustrating how the Croatian presence in the Yugoslav conflicts is recast. Each site is connected to Croatian nation-building, not just through the narratives told but also vis-à-vis emotions among locals and the national population thereby functioning as identity markers.[23]

20 See Graham and Howard, Heritage and Identity, Loc. Cit. (Note 16), 8.
21 See Pavlaković, Fulfilling, Loc. Cit. (Note 9), 25.
22 Bjørnar Olsen, In Defense of Things: Archaeology and the Ontology of Objects. Plymouth 2013.
23 Emotions are central to the function of nation-building narratives as identity markers (cf. Jonathan Heaney, 'Emotions and Nationalism: A Reappraisal', in: N. Demertzis (ed.), Emotions in Politics: The Affect Dimension in Political Tension. Hampshire 2013).

The tour taken in the article mimics a tour the author took in the Autumn and Winter of 2015–2016 where she conducted ethnographic fieldwork in Vukovar. Consequently, the tour is a very condensed and more intense version of what the author experienced during her stay. To offer legitimacy to the author's experiences, there is ongoing dialogue with other texts throughout the tour. As such the work is somewhat autoethnographic[24] but following a dialogical/performative narrative method[25] where the author stages both events and dialogue to underline how war heritage is brought into play in spatial identity-formation.

A town in mourning

In 1999, the Croatian Parliament adopted a decision proclaiming 18 November the Vukovar Memorial Day. An annual march takes place in Vukovar on this day where 50,000 Croats travel to Vukovar to march the streets. In 1991, Vukovar became the site of a battle between the Yugoslav People's army (JNA) and the so-called Croatian 204th Vukovar brigade. Officially the conflicts in East Slavonia began in August 1990 with the killing of 12 policemen in Borovo, an industrial site located outside Vukovar. Unlike many other places in the region, people in Vukovar chose not to surrender and were held under siege by the Serbian paramilitary forces backed by the JNA for 87 days until 18 November after which the town fell under the occupation of Serbian forces occupying most of this Croatian border region and deporting a large amount of its citizens, before it was taken over by Croatia in operation Storm in 1995. During the siege, the town was defended by approximately 1,800 members of the National Guard Corps, police, and volunteers organized as the 204th Vukovar Brigade. The siege destroyed the town almost completely. The population decreased significantly having approximately 80,000 inhabitants including the surrounding villages, at the time of the siege and today approximately 33,000, mostly Croats and Serbs.

When measured in numbers and size, the Vukovar battle cannot be compared to battles such as Antietam or Stalingrad. However, if it was possible to measure its significance for the nation and national identity in Croatia, Vukovar stands out. Its significance relates to the aggressors being very strong, remembering that the JNA had the third biggest army in the world at the time of the conflicts, and the destruction being so incomprehensible. Hence, part of the story about Vukovar concerns the size of the place and its populations; it is a story about the small standing up to the great aggressors. As it says on a tourist site introducing the town: "Hard is the story of Vukovar – the hero city, the symbol of Croatian freedom, but this is a story of victory and indomitability of human spirit that shall live forever."[26]

---

24 Carolyn Ellis, The ethnographic I: A methodological novel about autoethnography. Walnut Creek (CA) 2004.

25 Susan E. Chase, 'Narrative Inquiry: Multiple Lenses, Approaches, Voices', in: Denzin / Guba (eds.), The Sage Handbook of Qualitative Research. Thousand Oaks 2005.

26 Danubiumtours 2013. http://danubiumtours.hr/en/articles/news/paths-of-defenders-of-vukovar-144/Graham [Accessed: 21.09.2018].

Entering Vukovar

Visiting Vukovar, it is striking how the town-scape confronts you head on with images of war and devastation: It is literally every forth building, which is left empty and full of bullet holes, even today, 25 years after the conflicts: "Although Vukovar has been rebuilt to a great extent, at first glance any passer-by can see that something terrible took place in these streets. Buildings hit by shelling, some with bullet holes pock-marking the brickwork, remain unrepaired in the town center."[27] Inhabitants who fled Vukovar during the siege and the years under Serbian authority received support from the US and EU to rebuild their houses in the years following the conflicts. Nevertheless, many families chose to leave the town behind forever, thus also leaving the town-scape with a ghostlike appearance. Even houses in the town centre are abandoned and left as they were just after the siege (figure 4.1).

Figure 4.1: Street upon entering the centre of Vukovar. Photo: Dorte Jagetić Andersen

Accordingly, Vukovar's water tower might be the best-known building of the town. It rises high to the eye of the spectator with a message of unimaginable destruction: "I walked around town for an hour before finding the water tower. It was cone-shaped, the bottom half grey concrete and the top a band of burnt red.

27 Barbara Matejcić,'Vukovar Still Imprisoned by its Bloody Past', the Balkan Fellowship for Journalistic Excellence website, http://fellowship.birn.eu.com/en/alumni-initiative/alumni-initiative-articles-vukovar-still-imprisoned-by-its-bloody-past 2012 [Accessed: 30.09.2018].

A Croatian flag flew on top of it. I walked around it, careful not to step on broken shards of beer bottles. The tower was 50 meters high and too enormous to fully take in. Patches of blue sky shone through the giant bomb holes all over it that had been left as a reminder of what happened here. It was the symbol of a city that was symbolic for the rest of the country."[28]

For those who still live in or own houses in the town, their reconstruction attain significance, sending a message of not wanting to submit to aggressors who destroyed the town as well as to those who want the town to be left devastated. The Vukovar pension where I stayed for three weeks late October and early November 2015, located at the Danube river bed, was hit by a missile, leaving the building demolished. When the town was under siege, the Yugoslav army fired missiles across the Danube, a stretch of river approximately 20 meters broad, hitting residential areas. The pension owner, a young couple with three small children, were proud to have repaired it and to now be able to use it for business purposes. At the entrance to the pension, they showed pictures exhibiting how the house looked just after the siege in 1991 compared to how it looked when restored in 2014. Most houses surrounding the pension were damaged, though. The couple had also chosen not to live in Vukovar themselves but in the nearby Vinkovci, which was, according to them, a much better place for the children to grow up. When asked, they seemed to find it hard to explain to me exactly why they did not want to live in Vukovar.

Another striking aspect to the streets of Vukovar are the many tourist busses on the parking lots and the many school classes wondering around town in lines, moving from monument to monument. Particularly the white cross, a commemoration of the victims of the Homeland War is a popular venue (see figure 4.2 on the next page). The white cross close links Croatian national pride to the Catholic faith, making Vukovar a town of national heroes and catholic believers. Something similar is at play in the less spectacular monument, also located by the Danube, made up of gravestones rising from the ground, symbolizing the fall and resurrection of the town and its people.

The monuments commemorating the Homeland War and those who fought against the Yugoslav aggressors, help narrate the stories of heroes struggling for independence, making the town a symbol of these struggles fought through faith and sacrifice, and won in the end despite of long years of suffering under foreign occupation. Unlike Dubrovnik, an international tourist destination rebuilt to its former glory, Vukovar remains the living proof of Serbian atrocities and the struggles against them. The monuments underline the significance of a town, which is itself a monument. In line with the narrative, the school classes visiting town are accommodated in what was the 204th Vukovar Brigade Barracks, now Hostel Dubrovnik. The hostel's primary purpose is to accommodate the 8th graders visiting Vukovar as a part of the school-project, Eighth-graders Visit Vukovar. Monuments are powerful when communicating past events to future generations: "Monuments, for examples, "[m]ark the great pinnacles of human achievement selected from the past, they give an edifying sense that greatness

28 Andrea MacDonald, 'Rediscovery: Traveling to Vukovar', Road Junky website http://www.roadjunky.com/1599/rediscovery-travelling-to-vukovar/ 2008 [Accessed: 25.09.2018].

Figure 4.2: White Cross where the Vuka meets the Danube. On the cross, it says: Vukovar a miraculous town, Vukovar is pride, Vukovar is defiance, It's a tear in one's eye, Sorrow at one's heart … and a smile on one's lips, Vukovar is both past and future. Photo: Dorte Jagetić Andersen

was once possible, and it still is possible. They provide present generations with inspiration." (Leerssen, 2001, 207)."[29] Monuments teach the young Croats to be proud of their nation, happy that they are free to enjoy it, and respectful of those who fought to liberate them. As a Croatian member of the World Youth Alliance formulated it: "It is today, when we, young people listen to the stories of the Homeland war, and some of us remember their young father with a gun on his shoulder, going to defend his people, it is today that I wish to remind the young people from Croatia and the whole world to strive for good, which has the same value for the state and the individual, but also that they don't forget that it is more divine to achieve this freedom for peoples and the states, as says Aristotle. Whatever the conditions we live in might be, we shall never give up on freedom

29 See Graham and Howard, Heritage and Identity, Loc. Cit. (Note 16), 45.

for excellence, on what is good, true and beautiful, so that our dignity can be realized in all its potential which strives to excellence."[30]

War in place

Vukovar has become a memory container gathering the nation to mourn its victims and celebrate its heroes: "The story of Vukovar, a "town which symbolizes Croatian homeland War and suffering," is one of the main episodes of the Homeland War narrative. It is a milestone of the master narrative of the Croatian identity and of the entire nation-building process … the town of Vukovar holds a central place in Croatian victimhood … it is "a special symbolic place of Croatian suffering in the war and its striving for independence."[31]

A place, which is symbolic for the town and its destiny, is Vukovar hospital. If you search hard enough, you will find a reconstruction of the life of several hundred wounded and hospital staff who were captured in Vukovar hospital during the occupation of the city, including a multimedia presentation of wartime events (figure 4.3).

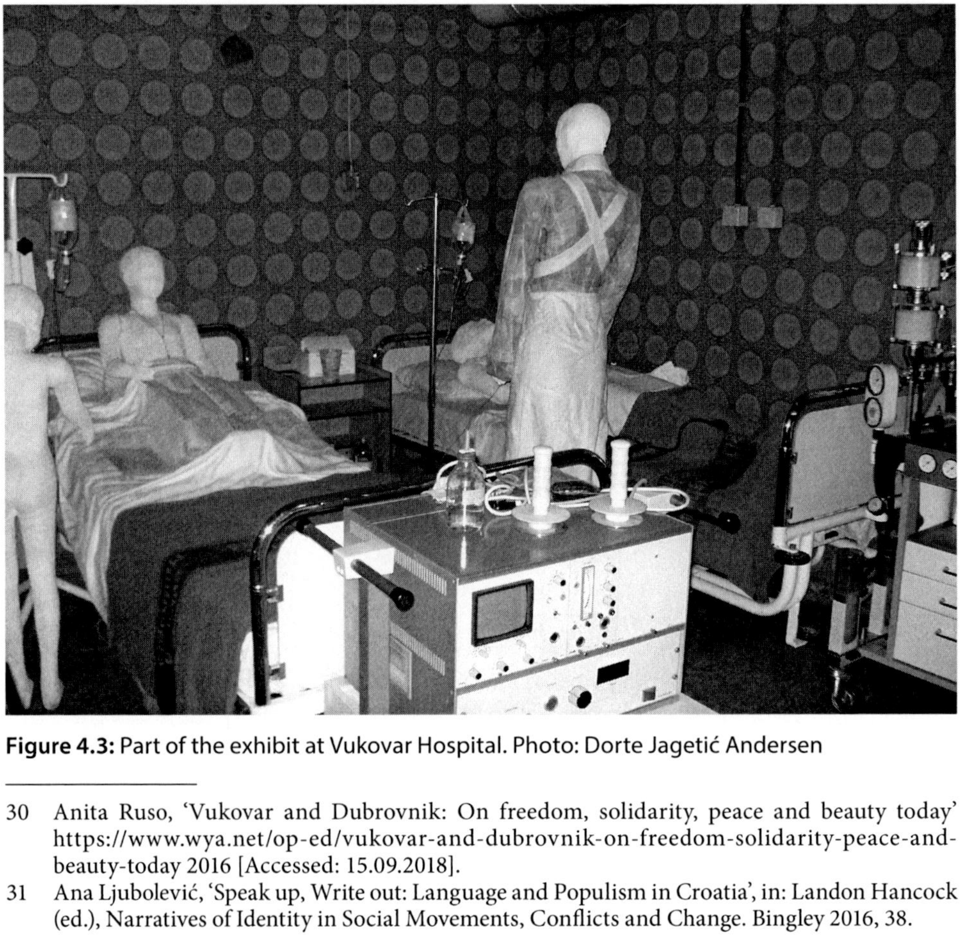

Figure 4.3: Part of the exhibit at Vukovar Hospital. Photo: Dorte Jagetić Andersen

30 Anita Ruso, 'Vukovar and Dubrovnik: On freedom, solidarity, peace and beauty today' https://www.wya.net/op-ed/vukovar-and-dubrovnik-on-freedom-solidarity-peace-and-beauty-today 2016 [Accessed: 15.09.2018].

31 Ana Ljubolević, 'Speak up, Write out: Language and Populism in Croatia', in: Landon Hancock (ed.), Narratives of Identity in Social Movements, Conflicts and Change. Bingley 2016, 38.

The exhibit is in the basement of the still functioning Vukovar Hospital, and the visitors are moving around the corridors together with doctors and nurses. JNA bombed the hospital despite international law stating that such locations should not be the target of military attacks and to prevent the patients from being harmed, they were hidden in the basement. The basement is left as it was at the time of the siege with holes in the ceiling where rain now enters the building.

Despite its significance, it is hard for visitors to find the exhibition. No signs show the way, only in a basement driveway at the back of the hospital you will find banners indicating that you have found the place. Considering the importance of the place for the story of Vukovar, its hidden location tells the additional tale of being preserved for those who know; the Croats themselves.

I was guided around the exhibition by the vice director of the hospital. He was the only English speaking person present at the time of my visit and he found it important to tell the story of the hospital because, as he said, it may contribute to preventing similar things from happening again. He said the exhibition was among the most visited in Croatia, which came as a surprise to me, not only because of the difficulties I had finding the place but also because I was the only actual visitor in the exhibition. Apart from the two of us, the national Croatian television was there with three witnesses of the events, making a program celebrating the 25th anniversary of the day where the organization Doctors without Borders evacuated 111 patients from the hospital, which was also the last time anyone tried to help the people in Vukovar.

The patients who were left in the hospital when the town was taken over by Serbs, were killed outside town, an event known as the Ovčara massacre. As my guide said, he did not understand why no one helped these patients just as he could not understand why no one was helping people in Kobane in Syria, occupied by IS at the time where I visited the exhibition. In Croatia, it is not uncommon to refer to what happened in Vukovar as did my host in the hospital, namely in the same way as the Holocaust is appropriated; asking why no one did anything and portraying events to future generations to prevent them from happening again. Not only does this speak into an internationally accepted way of referring to war in terms of absolute victimization; it also raises the people of Vukovar to a level even higher than they would otherwise be.

War in person

On a field outside town, in-between a huge pig farm and herds of cats and dogs, I found the mass grave site where the remaining hospital patients had been taken and killed. Apart from a monument on-site, a memorial hall, the Ovčara Memorial Centre, was opened in 2006 in the hangar where the patients spent the last hours of their lives. The memorial hall is rather artistically made, articulating the events foremost through the names of the victims of the massacre; names are exhibited on the walls of the place, being lightened up individually in the otherwise dark room.

Often victims who died and people who fought in Vukovar are mentioned by name, either as part of the monuments or as names on displays. On the one hand, this signals how every single person participating in the events is a martyr and national hero whose deeds should be remembered. On the other hand, a few individuals clearly stand out as incarnations of how the battle should be remembered. One is Siniša Glavašević, a Vukovar citizen and war reporter, who sacrificed his life radio broadcasting to the nation every day during the battle. In the book *Stories from Vukovar*, Glavašević last report on 18. November is published ending with these words: "The picture of Vukovar at the 22nd hour of the 87th day [of the siege] will remain forever in the memory of the witnesses of this time. There are infinite spooky sights, and you can smell the burning. We walk over bodies, building material, glass, detritus and the gruesome silence. [...] We hope that the torments of Vukovar are over."[32] My guide at Vukovar hospital also mentioned the French volunteer, Jean-Michel Nicollier who died in Ovčara even when a French television team, who interviewed him in the hospital, had offered to bring him home. According to my guide, Nicollier did not want to leave because: "He had his worst moments and his happiest moments in Vukovar." 2012 his mother was given a medal of honour for what he did for the Croatians. The foreigner participating in liberation struggles for nations who are not their own is a known figure 20th century European history.[33]

Despite the memorial hall being very artistic, its caretakers looked as if they also worked at the pig farm. They had a little souvenir shop in a room connected to the hall selling nationalist stickers and the Catholic merchandize you find at most Croatian graveyards. The shop keeper was quick to find everything available in English for me and I was nice enough to buy most of it off him, one of the only ways I could communicate a little with him to get an impression of the place and its visitors. Clearly it catered mostly for the Croatian public, with limited interest in a broader audience. Despite of this and even when I was the only one there at the time, the shopkeeper said they were visited by a large amount of people. He seemed to be right; I had a look in the visitor book where many comments were entered every day, mostly thanking the victims for their deeds.

Two additional destinations where these tourists would go, are the Homeland War Memorial Cemetery and the Memorial Hall for Croatian Defenders. The cemetery is erected at a mass grave site and it consists of a field with 938 white crosses commemorating the 938 bodies found on site as well as a proper cemetery with the graves of and names of those identified. In the middle of the graves there is a monument of copper with a burning flame. Even when I was alone at the cemetery the three times I visited, there was always many flowers left by the monument (figure 4.4).

The Memorial Hall for Croatian Defenders locates on the other side of town in what used to be a post office used as a command building in 1991 for this part of the town. The hall is a monument constructed in the shape of a tightly clenched fist, which symbolizes the strength needed to defend Vukovar from the Yugoslav aggression. The centre of the hall features a chasm with a cupola of a destroyed JNA tank and the names of the members of the 204th Vukovar Brigade who died

32 'Vukovar' on the Diaspora Diaries website https://dgrbesic.wordpress.com/tag/sinisa-glavasevic/ [Accessed: 10.09.2018].

33 See for instance George Orwell, Homage to Catalonia, London 1962.

Figure 4.4: Homeland War memorial. Photo: Dorte Jagetić Andersen

written around it. The 12 video displays in the walls show photographs and video recordings from the war, and you hear war reports as well as information about every member of the brigade who died. Placed outside the building is an "enemy tank", again to illustrate the strength of the aggressor and the courage of the defensive forces.

Celebrating (with) the boys

The 204th Vukovar Brigade has become a symbol of the liberation of the Croatian nation and the fulfilment of the thousand-year-old-dream. In the nation-building carried out by the Tudjman government in the 1990s, the fact of having belonged to the brigade became monumental. Not only were the survivors and the widows of dead members of the brigade rewarded with lifelong pensions. Especially the male population in Croatia now lived the dream "if only I had been part of the 204th brigade", deprived of an important experience if this was not the case. The deeds of the brigade are exemplary for Croatian men, who willingly sacrifice their lives for the nation.

Hence, our tour around Vukovar heritage sites must go to the Vojarna Vukovar Muzej, a war museum dedicated to "the boys", the members of the brigade, and the military achievements of the Homeland War. Most of the museum is open air and you walk among tanks and military airplanes, missile launchers and bunkers. A lonely exhibit building, shows mostly military maps, flags from the 204th brigade and pictures of the soldiers and their names. When I wanted to see the exhibition, I passed a fence through which I could see the exhibition but the gate into the facility was closed and no one seemed to be in the exhibition. I walked further to find another entrance but ended up at the Velepromet camp. Velepromet was used by the JNA as a detention camp opened early November 1991 and existing until March 1992.

Walking back to the Vojarna, a police van pulled up to the gate I passed before and six policemen jumped out. A man in military clothes noticed them from inside the museum and he came to the gate. I could tell from their conversation that the policemen were searching for the museum entrance, as was I. Lurking in the background, the policemen noticed my interest and asked if I wanted to drive with them to the entrance.

They were from Zagreb and stationed temporarily in Vukovar to patrol the border because of the problems experienced at the border between Croatia and Serbia in the autumn of 2015, where Europe was at the peak of a so-called refugee crisis. Busses with refugees were driven across the Serbian border through Vukovar and to a camp just outside town and at this specific point in time, Vukovar was therefore populated with officials, like the policemen, controlling the refugee flows, voluntary aid workers from all over Europe and journalists on their own mission to inform the wider public about events. This parallel scenario seemed surreal because of the devastation of the place but also very appropriate considering the significance of the town-scape as regard war and conflict.

The policemen had some time off and wanted to use this to see the exhibition. "It concerned an important piece of Croatian history," as one of them told me. We were let in to the museum by the gates to park inside the facilities (other visitors had to park outside) and we were pretty much alone on the premises, only a few more visitors were wondering around among the tanks and airplanes. The policemen were shown around by a woman in military clothes, who spoke very fast making it much too hard for me to understand what she said. I was still lurking in the background, however. To visit the exhibition together with six men and a woman dressed in uniform borrowed a sense of authenticity that I would not miss for the world; here were the defenders of the nation, the most precious the nation had to offer and I was finally among them in their live versions. Then and there I felt I had arrived in Vukovar.

Upon which past should the future dwell?

The spatial identity of a place is linked to the narratives told about the place; when Croatians think of Vukovar, they think of war and devastation, victory and liberation. However, this article shows we can go further than that; the collective memory of a place does something to the community. Even when the construction of heritage is usually not done for the sake of the locals (it is the nation that is celebrated), people living in the specific places come to understand themselves through the lens of the way their heritage is presented. Even when it is well known that events were not like their reconstructed version in heritage-making

– to the extent of lying about actual events – it is hard for locals not to become part of the constructions.

Vukovar's status in the national narrative underlines ethnic divisions in the town and its surroundings. Serbs, of whom there is still a considerable number, and Croats live separately, having each their own institutions and cafés. Post-war Vukovar is a town captured in a post-conflict trauma, doomed to either repeat the violence of ethnic division or to practice resistance through forgetting. Here cultural identities are cast in stone and for those living in and appreciating the town, hope seem scarce; Vukovar moan a future that will never come. One sense a certain chill in the town. Locals look at you with suspicion if they do not know you and to which of the ethnically separated groups you belong: "If looks could kill, there would be many dead people every day in Vukovar. This is still a divided place[.]"[34]

War narratives may attract tourists but they do nothing to overcome ethnic tensions. In Vukovar, several heritage institutions therefore work to change the town's status in the social memory by focusing on the distant past and the history of cultures immigrating to areas around the Danube, uniting the people living on either side of the Danube. Thus, the iron bird of the Vinkovci culture is today the official symbol of Vukovar town. There is also a heated discussion in Croatia if the area should have double language road signs (Latin and Cyrillic), a wish from the Serbian minority and a way for the two sides to reconcile. The Slavonia region could be the first to follow Istria's example where Italian and Croatian are both recognised official languages. These initiatives indicate how it might be silence about the conflicts, which is the best option for the town to make space for the future.

However, these remain delicate matters because of the town's past and status in the national narrative. It remains hard to avoid the memories of conflict when most visitors to the place, like myself, search to experience real time what was told about the conflicts in school and on television. Outsiders almost demand of people in Vukovar that they relive the atrocities and, somewhat paradoxically, their ability to do so becomes the way the town is kept alive, even when it appears rather respiratory. Leaving Vukovar, one is also left wondering how many years it will take until the Serbs remaining in Vukovar will also take to the streets on 18 November.

Abstract

The article problematizes the way in which war heritage is used to solidify the image of the Croatian town Vukovar as a national symbol and how this affects the town-scape and its population. Focus is on post-war initiatives to develop new heritage infrastructures, disseminating narratives of national identity at everyday level. The author mobilizes the concepts of spatial identity, particularly the national, and war heritage, showing how the town has frozen in time because of its task to represent the ultimate sacrifice for the nation. Despite of attempts at reinventing the town's image differently it is left devastated. Through the exemplary case of Vukovar, the article contributes to research investigating relations between nation-building and heritage by showing how the use of war to solidify national identity prevents restoration and, not the least, over-coming ethnic conflicts.

---

34 See Matejcić, Vukovar, Loc. Cit. (Note 27).

Trieste and Chernivtsi

Prologues on urban monument policy

Steffen Höhne

1. Introductory remarks

When considering the era of social upheaval, both Trieste (Trieste/Trst) and Chernivtsi (Černivci/Cernăuţi) were, respectively, largely peripheral Italian and Ukrainian cities. An important cultural significance is, nevertheless, attributed to both. Furthermore, the modern perspective assigns them the status of being central, Habsburg-oriented cultural cities on the basis of and with reference to their diverse multilingual literary development, especially in the late 19th and early 20th centuries.[1] In the case of Trieste, one need only mention James Joyce, Italo Svevo and Umberto Saba as representatives of this urban culture and, similarly, Mihai Eminescu, Iwan Franko, Karl Emil Franzos and Paul Celan in the case of Chernivtsi. With reference to Chernivtsi, it is also important to note its attribution as a mythical city, which similarly points to the city's exceptional nature.[2]

This article deals with more than simply a literary or cultural-historical reconstruction of the respective cities' history;[3] it also seeks to analyse the cultural practices of memory. With the help of these practices, we can reconstruct the processes of cultural appropriation and demarcation that have been in effect through the various historical disruptions in each city to the present day. These practices can be understood as relatively autonomous and permanent measures in the sense of the city's interdependent effect on the inhabitants and the inhabit-

1 On the Cultural Studies Debate on Central European, (Cultural) Cities see Moritz Csáky, Das Gedächtnis der Städte. Kulturelle Verflechtungen – Wien und die urbanen Milieus in Zentraleuropa, Wien-Köln-Weimar 2010.

2 For example see Deutsches Kulturforum östliches Europa, Mythos Czernowitz (ed.), Eine Stadt im Spiegel ihrer Nationalitäten, Potsdam 2008; critical to the Chernivtsi Myth see Winfried Menninghaus, 'Czernowitz/Bukowina' als Topos deutsch-jüdischer Geschichte und Literatur, in: Merkur 53 3 4 (1999), 345–357.

3 For Trieste see Claudio Magris / Angelo Ara, Triest. Eine literarische Hauptstadt in Mitteleuropa, München 2007; Neil Kent, Trieste, Adriatic Emporium and Gateway to the Heart of Europa, London 2011; for Chernivtsi see Harald Heppner (ed.), Czernowitz. Die Geschichte einer ungewöhnlichen Stadt, Köln 2000; Helmut Braun (ed.), Czernowitz. Die Geschichte einer untergegangenen Kulturmetropole, Berlin 2005; Andrei Corbea-Hoisie, Czernowitzer Geschichten. Über eine städtische Kultur in Mittel(Ost)Europa, Wien-Köln-Weimar 2003.

ants' impact on the city.[4] If we also consider cities in the mode of Henri Lefèbvre,[5] as the result of actions in the past and of performative realizations or stagings; or as per Martina Löw, as a concept of stubborn development and a consequent structuring creative power; in this way, approaches of urban logic or city-habitus are reached. Urban logic ['Eigenlogik'] praxeologically includes the cities' hidden structures as mostly implicit pre-reflective processes of the "constitution of meaning" and its respective habitus, having been established on the spot.[6] Looking at the increasing social and ethnic differentiation in cities such as Chernivtsi and Trieste in the 19th century, urban living environments and the possibilities of political and cultural identification seem to constitute themselves along concepts of alienation and alterity. In this way, the urban habitus is characterised by ambiguities and different memories in rival cultural spaces, which are symptomatically expressed, among other things, in policies regarding monuments. As a result, the history of pluri-national Habsburg cities is always a history of successful, but also failed, attempts to negotiate intercultural differences and disagreements.[7]

2. Urban monument policy

The development of urban culture in Habsburg cities like Trieste and Chernivtsi was always related to the marking of territories and the drawing of borders by different national and social groups. In other words, related to the determination of what is one's own and what belongs to the foreigners, concepts which are frequently bound to borderland issues. The choice of a specific architectural style, the symbolic character of a particular building or place, or an urban planning redesign are examples of this development. These examples are often attributable not only to aesthetic or functional considerations, which can be seen in the names of streets or local suburbs, but can also be seen in the choice of a neo-Baroque Habsburg, a neo-Gothic German or a Czech neo-Renaissance style.[8] According to integrative reasoning, urban development measures are also about creating community, awakening an awareness of togetherness, and proposing modes of identification. In addition, they also reflect the exertion of pressure aimed at preventing the assimilation of individual groups from other countries. With regard to these two studied cities, Trieste and Chernivtsi, the aim is to understand the interdependencies between (cultural) political orientation and urban

4 Martyn Lee, Relocating Location. Cultural Geography, the Specificity of Place and the City Habitus, in: Jim McGuigan (Hg.), Cultural Methodologies, London-New Delhi 1997, 126–141.

5 Henri Lefèbvre, Writings on Cities, Cambridge-Oxford 1996, differentiates between spatial practice, spatial representation and representative spaces, 'cities' are thus understood as the result of past action and performative staging.

6 Martina Löw, Soziologie der Städte, Frankfurt am Main 2008, 76. [Eigenlogik erfasst praxeologisch die verborgenen Strukturen der Städte als vor Ort eingespielte, zumeist stillschweigend präreflexive Prozesse der Sinnkonstitution" und ihres jeweiligen Habitus]

7 See Renate Lunzer, Triest. Eine italienisch-österreichische Dialektik, Klagenfurt 2002, 13. According to Lunzer, Trieste functions as both amalgam and archipelago logos.

8 Michaela Marek demonstrates this in an exemplary study using Prague as an example: Kunst und Identitätspolitik. Architektur und Bildkünste im Prozess der tschechischen Nationsbildung, Köln-Weimar-Wien 2004.

representation, i.e. to discuss the processes of legitimisation, de-legitimisation and re-legitimisation in policy regarding monuments, based on several selected examples. More specifically, monuments in the narrower sense, which were specifically erected for the purpose of commemorating "events or personalities",[9] as symbols that were intentionally positioned in the public domain – in addition to buildings, squares, street names[10] or exhibitions on urban history – these monuments constitute deliberate visualizations and presentations of a desired, or normatively-prescribed, collective identity, or even a corresponding image that is connected with exclusive claims to ownership. As a visual element and as a historical-political medium, they are an expression of publicly binding identity politics. They materialize as artefacts of urban groups' underlying attitudes and ways of thinking; whereby deciphering their meaning also always brings to light multiple encodings and multiple claims.

Monuments as cultural artefacts are also effective indicators of differences between items that are not deemed to be worthy of preservation and items that are considered to be part of a foreign cultural heritage tradition. In this respect, these are always paradoxical phenomena, since monuments owe their creation to concrete social or political situations, but motivate the viewer to identify positively across different situations, even when they appear to ignore or suppress inherent contingency. Monuments form an elevated sphere of reality where the evidence of human activity is registered a second time, albeit not in terms of their utility value, but in terms of comparison with other cultures or the monuments representing them.[11] Like culture as a whole, they serve as instruments that indicate people's descriptions of themselves and of others. As national cultural artefacts, they are confronted with the problem of increasing contingency caused by modernisation processes. They seek to respond to this by creating a contingency-minimizing (collective) identity. Monuments, in particular, seek to resolve contingency by highlighting identity, minimizing insecurity and uncertainty, and by averting individual and collective marginalisation. Thus, periods of national-cultural revitalisation require monuments in order to stabilize norms of behaviour and attitudes in the name of cultural identity – by differentiating them from the 'foreign' with regard to the outside world and by promoting integration within their own society. The fact that monuments refer back to a highly precarious function of memory, and that they say little about the actual content of history, speaking instead to its fundamentally variable appropriation,[12] has been aptly summarised by Robert Musil:

> Denkmäler haben außer der Eigenschaft, daß man nicht weiß, ob man Denkmale oder Denkmäler sagen soll, noch allerhand Eigenheiten. Die wichtigste davon ist ein wenig widerspruchsvoll; das auffallendste an Denkmälern ist nämlich, dass

9 Lexikon der Kunst 1, Leipzig 1968, 519, in contrast, monuments represent in the broader sense every testimony to the cultural development of humanity that has a special artistic, historical, scientific significance and is, therefore, considered worthy of commemoration by society.

10 Nicole Eller / Stefan Hackl / Marek Ľupták (eds.), Namen und ihr Konfliktpotential im europäischen Kontext, Regensburg 2008.

11 Niklas Luhmann, Die Kunst der Gesellschaft, Frankfurt am Main 1997, 341.

12 Dietrich Erben, Denkmal, in: Handbuch der politischen Ikonographie 1, published by Uwe Fleckner / Martin Warnke / Hendrik Ziegler, München 2011, 235–243; here: 235.

man sie nicht bemerkt. Es gibt nichts auf der Welt, was so unsichtbar wäre wie Denkmäler. Sie werden doch zweifellos aufgestellt, um gesehen zu werden, ja geradezu um die Aufmerksamkeit zu erregen; aber gleichzeitig sind sie durch irgendetwas gegen Aufmerksamkeit imprägniert […].[13]

Aside from the reality that it is not clear whether they should be described as memorials or monuments, monuments also have all sorts of other features. The most important of these is actually somewhat contradictory; the most striking thing about monuments is the fact that you don't notice them. There is nothing in the world that tends to be as invisible as monuments. They are certainly constructed with the intention of being seen, even to attract attention; but, at the same time, they seem to contain some inherent element or other that prevents them from attracting attention […].

3. Trieste in the spotlight of monument policy

3.1. 'Habsburg' Trieste

During the 18th century, the Habsburg city of Trieste – a largely insignificant town that had been established in 1382 under Duke Leopold III – developed into an important port city. Emperor Charles VI is considered the founder of modern Trieste, having guaranteed safe passage of shipping with the patent of 2 June 1717, and granting Trieste and Fiume the status of a free port with the patent of 18 March 1719. Even though the port of Trieste was far from competitive in the 18th century,[14] Austria was able to take over the legacy of Venetian trade policy with the help of Trieste. Further infrastructure measures, such as the extension of the Semmering mountain pass in 1728 (commemorated by an obelisk on the Semmering Pass and a monument to Lorenz Fanolli in Piazza Unità in Trieste), and the expansion of the port and city (e.g. Borgo Teresiano between Piazza della libertá and Piazza della Borsa) were undertaken during the reign of Charles' daughter, Maria Theresa (see Fig. 5.1). This period also saw the establishment of the Chamber of Commerce, the stock exchange, construction of the Theresien-Molos and a new hospital.[15] During the reign of Joseph II, who visited Trieste several times, the Guiseppino district was expanded near to Piazza Giuseppina (now P. Venecia) and Via del Lazzaretto Vecchia. A notable characteristic of the reform era under Maria Theresa and Joseph II, however, was the antagonism between a modernising and centralising policy with the aim of creating a centralist-hierarchically organised and governed territorial state, on the one hand, and a conservative, regionally-oriented policy of urban autonomy based on the tradition of class-based rights, on the other.

13 Robert Musil, Denkmale, in: Prosa und Stücke. Kleine Prosa, Aphorismen, Autobiographisches, Essays und Reden, Kritik, Reinbek bei Hamburg 2000 [1927], 604–608; here: 604.

14 Horst Friedrich Mayer, Triest: Österreichs Tor zur Welt, in: Cornelia Szabó-Knotik (ed.), Wien-Triest um 1900. Zwei Städte – eine Kultur? (= Musikleben, 2), Wien 1993, 1–16.

15 There is no monument to Maria Theresa other than the name of the district. The exhibition Maria Theresa, Trieste e il porto (December 1980 – February 1981) was staged to mark the 200th anniversary of Maria Theresa's death. See Catalogue: Maria Teresia, Trieste e il Porto, published by the City of Trieste 1981.

Figure 5.1: Borgo Teresiano[16]

Described as an "archipelago of different cultures, whose individual groups each ignored one another",[17] a clear characteristic of the pre-national period of urban history in the first half of the 19th century was a generally liberal and tolerant climate, marked by tolerance towards ethnic minorities and domestic policies aligned to the multi-ethnic state. "Trieste was a veritable cultural melting pot."[18] Nonetheless, the Slovenian population faced very little opportunity for advancement within the urban society.

In the city, it is not difficult to find commemorations of Habsburg rule, including monuments of Charles VI, as the founder of modern Trieste, of Governor Maximilian and of Empress Elizabeth (Sissi). However, there is only a commemorative plaque commemorating Maria Theresa,[19] and a bust to Joseph II, which has since been removed. At the same time, there are markers relating to local identities and others representing the politics of historical monuments, such as

16 All Figures are privately owned (all date from 2016, except for figures 9 and 14 from 2009), I thank Marit Haferkamp and Kirsten Heyerhoff for making Fig. 15–18, Manfred Weinberg for making Fig. 19 and Sibylle Höhne for the others.

17 See Magris / Ara, Triest, Loc. Cit. (Note 3), 17.

18 Ibid. see Claudio Magris, Die Stadt aus Papier. Triest und seine Literatur, in: Triest – die Stadt zwischen den Welten. Ein literarisches Lesebuch, published by Helmut Eisendle, München-Zürich 1994, 207–220; here: 209.

19 Jože Pirjevec, Die Triest-Frage, in: Patrick Ostermann / Claudia Müller / Karl-Siegbert Rehberg (eds.), Der Grenzraum als Erinnerungsort. Über den Wandel zu einer postnationalen Erinnerungskultur in Europa, Bielefeld 2012, 135–152; here: 145.

the politician and patron Domenico Rossetti (1901), the historian Pietro Kandler or the Mayor, Mutius Joseph Spiritus Ritter von Tommasini, in the Trieste city park, and the Muzio-Tommasini-Park.

3.2. Trieste and the Risorgimento - the Italianità

For the period prior to 1848, Trieste Italianità, or the concept of belonging to Italy, can be seen as the citizens of Trieste wavering between municipal ideas ('nazione Triestina') – in the sense of maintaining an alliance with Austria (being 'citizens of Trieste, without actually being subservient to Austria') – and national Italian concepts (the journal La Favilla). The revolution of 1848/49 was reasonably quiet and moderate in Trieste, in contrast to other Italian Habsburg territories. The construction of the first European mountain railway in early 1854 over the Semmering Pass from Vienna to Trieste, following the plans of Carl Ritter von Ghega[20] and completed in 1857, stimulated the city's economic development significantly. The construction of the Suez Canal in 1869, the expansion of port facilities and the connection to the Westbahn (Trieste-Görz-Villach-Salzburg) train line brought further economic progress. Nevertheless, despite this economic integration, a national orientation towards Italy was emerging increasingly from the late 19th century.

The more liberal laws during the 1860s regarding associations and the press also initiated discussions about concepts of Italianità in Trieste. This was also the beginning of the constitutional period for the Habsburg Monarchy: The October Diploma of 20 October 1860, which regulated freedom of assembly; the February Patent of 26 February 1861, as the constitution of the Austrian Monarchy; and, the Association Law of 15 November 1867. From this time on, the "freedom of the individual citizen, guaranteed by fundamental rights, to form associations and to participate in their activities",[21] existed, albeit under state supervision. Associations subsequently aimed to achieve both national integration and exclusion, as well as political mobilisation, with respect to educational, cultural and sports clubs, academic associations and, explicitly, the category of defence associations (Schutzvereine).[22] The stabilisation of the Italian population in Trieste was nevertheless challenged by the national awakening of the Slovenes, which found its symbolic expression in the construction of a Narodni dom (1904).[23] In addition,

20 The Via C. Ghega in Borgo Teresiano commemorates him.

21 Peter Burian, Das Vereinswesen in den böhmischen Ländern, in: Ferdinand Seibt (ed.), Vereinswesen und Geschichtspflege in den böhmischen Ländern, München 1986, 39–51; here: 41; Branko Marušič, Die Vereinstätigkeit im österreichischen Küstenland, in: Politische Öffentlichkeit und Zivilgesellschaft 1, Vereine, Parteien und Interessenverbände als Träger der politischen Partizipation (= Die Habsburgermonarchie 1848–1918, VIII), Vienna 2006, 541–585; Re Trieste, see also Sacha Zala (ed.), Die Moderne und ihre Krisen. Studien von Marina Cattaruzza zur europäischen Geschichte des 19. und 20. Jahrhunderts, Göttingen 2012.

22 S. Peter Haslinger (ed.), Schutzvereine in Ostmitteleuropa. Vereinswesen, Sprachenkonflikte und Dynamiken nationaler Mobilisierung 1860–1939, Marburg 2009.

23 On the function of national houses (Nationalhäuser), see Peter Haslinger / Heidi Hein-Kircher / Rudolf Jaworski (eds.), Heimstätten der Nation. Ostmitteleuropäische Vereins- und Gesellschaftshäuser im transnationalen Vergleich, Marburg 2013.

it faced trialistic plans for the reconstruction of Habsburg, which also had a mobilizing effect with regard to national political orientation. The delegitimizing defeats of Habsburg in 1859 and 1866 and the foundation of the Kingdom of Italy (1861) also influenced the new urban orientation with respect to Italianità. After 1866, socialization patterns changed in the context of modern mass society, including compulsory school education and new forms of association. As a consequence, the city's relationship to the state changed, and reorientation began to take place among various urban groups. In the case of the nationally 'awakening' Slovenian community, however, social advancement from the late 19th century was no longer simply linked to their becoming fluent in a foreign language – Italian – and, consequently, assimilating into the local society.

Intellectual debate was shaped by the inherent contradiction between the ideology of Italianità, which only enjoyed the support of a relatively small group, and Trieste's economic dependence on Habsburg. It was essentially conflict between economic interests and irredentist desires, and this made Trieste an "extremely sensitive outpost" in the cultural crisis, as seen in the (disintegrative) crisis culture.[24] The conflict quickly intensified when the two groups, the Italians and the Slovenes, who each claimed Trieste as their 'natural capital',[25] made separate demands on the city. These demands led to permanent tensions, not only between the ethnic groups, but also between the domains of the culturally intellectual Italianità and those with an economically-determined Habsburg orientation.[26]

The intercultural dialogue of old national liberalism shifted to a holistic concept of being Italian, in which the mythology of national defence included a tendency towards dichotomization of ethnocentric images of others and of oneself. The sense of the Slavic threat became symptomatic of the concept of a bastion inhabited by Latin peoples for over a thousand years opposed to the double-headed eagle.[27]

---

24 See Magris / Ara, Triest, Loc. Cit. (Note 3), 20.

25 At the end of the 19th century, Trieste was the largest Slovenian-speaking city.

26 See Magris / Ara, Triest, Loc. Cit. (Note 3), 65–70. On this Trieste dialectic, or as an early expression of Triestinità, see Scipio Slataper: "Wir müssen uns davon überzeugen, daß Triest auf andere Art und Weise italienisch ist als die übrigen italienischen Städte. [...] Triest ist italienisch: aber die höhere Kultur muss es in Graz oder Wien aufstöbern. [...] Das ist Triest: ein Produkt der Tragödie [...] unser Dialekt ist verschieden von den übrigen italienischen Dialekten [...] Auch jetzt ist unsere Seele anders [...]. Triest hat einen Triestiner Typus: „es muss eine Triestiner Literatur wollen." See also the concept of the "double soul" [*doppelten Seele*] according to Slataper: "Zerrissen zwischen Italien und Österreich, geteilt zwischen Geist und Profit, scheint die Stadt einer permanenten Spannung unterworfen" (See Magris / Ara, Triest, Loc. Cit. (Note 3), 65).

27 See Lunzer, Dialekt, Loc. Cit. (Note 7), 26, differentiates between an economic austriacantismo and political-cultural Italianità in the bourgeoisie of Trieste, between slavophobia and integration of the Slavs into the production process and the conflict between supporters of utraquization, e.g. Angelo Vivante (Trieste as a connection of different ethnic and economic currents) and ultra-nationalist opponents such as Ruggero Timeus Fauro. According to Fauro, the "peaceful mediators between the different races" were decadent pimps (Lunzer, Loc. Cit. Note 7), 30, Vivante, who advocated a peaceful coexistence of nationalities, committed suicide after Italy entered the war.

Figure 5.2: Verdi-Monument 2016[28]

In terms of monument policy, Habsburg symbols gradually began to be superimposed towards the end of this period, which is particularly evident in the example of Giuseppe Verdi. Without going into specific detail about Verdi's role in the Risorgimento, we need only mention *Nabucco* with its choir of captured Hebrews *Va penisiero* as the unofficial second national anthem, as well as the use of the name Verdi as an acronym for Vittorio Emanuele Re d'Italia.[29] In its descriptions

28 For the Inauguration of the Verdi-Monument 1906 see the picture in Santi, Kulturen, Loc. Cit. (Note 16), 102.

29 In addition to Bellini's Norma with the choir *Guerra, guerra*! as the 'Marseillaise' of the Italian unification movement, Verdi was attributed central importance for the Risorgimento, see Birgit Pauls, Giuseppe Verdi und das Risorgimento. Ein politischer Mythos im Prozeß der Nationenbildung (= Politische Ideen, 4). Diss. Berlin, Akademie Verlag 1996; Dies.: Revolutionär wider Willen. Verdi, die Politik und die italienische Oper seiner Zeit, in: Udo Bermbach (ed.), Verdi-Theater. Stuttgart 1997, 1–21; On the role of national myths, see Klaus von See: Das Nibelungenlied – ein Nationalepos? in: Joachim Heinzle und Anneliese Waldschmidt (eds.), Die Nibelungen. Ein deutscher Wahn, ein deutscher Alptraum. Studien und Dokumente zur Rezeption des Nibelungenstoffs im 19. und 20. Jahrhundert, Frankfurt am Main

of the city, Trieste labels itself as the 'most Verdian' of all Italian cities.[30] This relates, on the one hand, to the composer's status within the Risorgimento but also, on the other hand, to post-1866 descriptions of Trieste as being part of the Irredenta.[31] Verdi's symbolic significance for Trieste, as part of a 'Giuseppine Trinity' (Garibaldi, Mazzini, Verdi), becomes clear in the history of Trieste's theatre and the significant change of the theatre's name from *Teatro San Pietro* to *Teatro Communale G. Verdi*. It is also demonstrated in the Trieste Verdi monument's history, through which the city's Italianità was to be symbolically asserted and increased in value. On January 31, 1901, immediately after Verdi's death, both the theatre and the square were named after Verdi (Piazza Verdi), and on February 4, 1901, a proposal was put forward to erect a monument "all'ultimo Grande della musica italiana" [*to the last great master of Italian music*].[32] This monument to Verdi, which was solemnly unveiled on 27 January, 1906, was erected near Piazza San Giovanni in close proximity to the recently built Trieste National Hall, or Narodni dom. In this way, it served as a symbolic marker of urban space, negatively targeting, in particular, the increasingly self-confident Slovenian minority, which was progressively demonstrating its reluctance – in contrast to earlier decades – to assimilate into the Italian community.[33] In the monument (see Fig. 5.2), Verdi himself appears to be a "peaceful and introspective person", who represents the "ideals of national consciousness and fatherland", but it is a purely Italian fatherland.[34] Significantly, Habsburg officials were not invited to the ceremonial unveiling.

The celebration of Verdi incorporated performances of his operas. On the evening of the unveiling, the theatre performed the overture from *Giovanna d'arco*, the romantic aria from *Luisa Miller*, the cavatina from *La Traviata* and the choir *Va pensiero*. After the interval the overture from *Aroldo* was followed by the aria *Pace mio Dio* from *Forza del Destino*, the cavatina from *Trovatore*, and the quartet from *Rigoletto*, as well as the choir from *Lombardi*. Through this unquestionably patriotic program, Trieste became "symbolically a part of the entire Italian-speaking area",[35] and Verdi evolved into a representative of the "late Trieste Risorgimento".[36] Following Italy's entry into the war in 1915, nationalists attacked the monument, and Verdi's nose was cut off. The government removed the monument, deeming it to represent irredentist politics. After the war, it was returned to its former location.

1991, 43–110; A national connotation of music is typical of the emerging national movements in the 19th century, see Bartók for Hungary, Grieg for Norway, Sibelius for Finland, Smetana for the Czech Republic, Richard Wagner for Germany.

30 See Santi, Kulturen, Loc. Cit. (Note 16), 53.

31 Irredentism (Irredenta = 'unredeemed Italy') is a battle term coined in 1877 by a national movement that emerged after the unification of Italy in 1861/66 and called for the extraction of 'unredeemed' areas, some of which were still Habsburg property, such as Trentino, Trieste, Istria, Dalmatia.

32 See Santi, Kulturen, Loc. Cit. (Note 16), 97.

33 For such occupation strategies, see Rudolf Jaworski / Peter Stachel (eds.), Die Besetzung des öffentlichen Raumes. Politische Codierungen von Plätzen, Denkmälern und Straßennamen im europäischen Vergleich, Innsbruck 2007.

34 See Santi, Kulturen, Loc. Cit. (Note 16), 103.

35 See Santi, Kulturen, Loc. Cit. (Note 16), 105.

36 Santi Loc. Cit. (Note 16), 111.

3.3. Politically-inspired monument installations post 1918

As far as Trieste was concerned, the year 1918, which saw the end of Central European ecumenism, was initially associated with a sense of growing disappointment. The long-desired Italianità came to be seen as an 'oppressive embrace' of Mother Italy, which mutated into a 'totalitarian stepmother'.[37] Reaction patterns included growing over-patriotism, which led to the emergence of fascism in the 1920s. At the same time, there were intense discussions with Central European modernity. Trieste held an avant-garde position in Italy; its authors (including Italo Svevo, Umberto Saba) and forms of analytical practice (Edoardo Weiss and psychoanalysis) challenged the classicist movements of Italian representative culture and hegemonic discourse from the margins.[38]

Initially, the desire for de-Austrianisation of the city and community, which was to be implemented through symbolic Italianisation in the manner of the Italianità, shaped municipal politics after 1918, as it did in other Crown lands. In terms of monument policy, this trend was manifest in the destruction of various monuments, including the removal of busts of Duke Leopold III, who had brought Trieste under the rule of the Habsburg in 1382. Likewise, the busts of Emperor Frederick III and Ferdinand III were removed from the loggia of the town hall,[39] as well as the Franz Joseph-statue (1916) and the monument to mark the 500th anniversary of Habsburg rule in Trieste (1382–1882) in front of the central station. Only the monuments of Charles VI and Leopold I were preserved. In historiography, Trieste's privileges were officially ignored under the guise of 'imperial immediacy', which continued until 1918; a pattern of interpretation was to be enforced that delegitimized Austria as an intruder on Italian territory.

In the Parco della rimembranza (Memorial Park), next to the Cathedral of San Giusto, monuments were erected to those who had 'fallen in all wars' (see Fig. 5.3), among them a monument by Attila Selva, dedicated to the volunteers killed in action fighting against Habsburg, depicting a group of naked soldiers carrying a fallen comrade (see Fig. 5.4). However, to the present day there is still no monument to the fallen of Trieste who fought, or had been compelled to fight, for Habsburg, even though these represent about 98 percent of the victims from Trieste in the First World War.

---

37 After Claudio Magris / Angelo Ara, Triest, Loc. Cit. (Note 3, 252 f.), this is the moment when the topos of Italianità is replaced by the Central European topos and, thus, the discovery of a cultural affiliation to Habsburg. Lunzer also mentions the first impulses for a historical revaluation of the Austrian inheritance. This experience of disappointment is related to the dichotomy between the past and the reality of a marginalized, peripheral city, Loc. Cit. (Note 7), 38; see, for example, Biagio Marin and his demand for autonomous consciousness: "Trieste has fallen ill with the Austrian disease of heteronomy, it does not stop being a government-approved plate licker; but it does not understand that the plates of Italian bureaucracy are lean and taste bitter. […] It must renounce the myth of Austrian Italy and accept Italian Italy […]. In short, Trieste must create a truly autonomous consciousness […]." (Cited according to Lunzer Loc. Cit. [Note 7, 38]).

38 See Lunzer, Dialekt, Loc. Cit. (Note 7), 15.

39 See Santi, Kulturen, Loc. Cit. (Note 16), 112.

Figures 5.3 and 5.4: Monument to the volunteers killed in action (Parco della rimembranza)

The monument to the national martyr Guglielmo Oberdan, officially Wilhelm Oberdank, assumes a special role in this semantic recoding. Oberdan had Italianised his name and planned an assassination attempt on Emperor Franz Joseph, for which he was executed. A bronze monument, flanked by two female figures announcing his posthumous fame, was erected at the site of his prison cell, which had since been converted into a massive crypt (see Fig. 5.5). Among other aspects, the Roman she-wolf with the abbreviation SPQR (Senatus Populusque Romanus) (see Fig. 5.6), refers to the traditional irredentist context harking back to Roman antiquity.

Accompanied by a portico with the coats of arms of Italian and Dalmatian cities, the cult of Oberdan, which emerged after 1918, symbolizes the return of Trieste to Italy. At the same time, a concept of irredentism as a precursor of fascism is underpinned and reconciliation between the monarchy and the Republican freedom movement is asserted.[40] As early as December 20, 1918, Mussolini held a speech at the *Sacrario Oberdan*, which is located at the entrance of the *City Museum of Risorgimento*.[41] The newly designed Piazza Oberdan is also an urban counterpoint to the classical Borgo Teresiano.

The politics of Italianità underwent a radicalization with the rise of fascism, which appeared to be a "ruthless de-nationalizer and centralizer.[42] The intention was to achieve an Italianization of the local population, and areas of conflict with the Slovenian population were reinforced through oppression and bans. Trieste's Slovenian population was confronted with the alternatives of assimilating or being expelled. Slovenian organisations and meetings were banned, the Slovenian language was suppressed in public life, and Slovenian surnames were arbitrarily

40 Rolf Wörsdorfer, Krisenherd Adria 1915–1955. Konstruktion und Artikulation des Nationalen im italienisch-jugoslawischen Grenzraum, Paderborn et al. 2004, 118.
41 See Wörsdorfer, Krisenherd, Loc. Cit., 113.
42 See Wörsdorfer, Krisenherd, Loc. Cit., 571.

Figures 5.5 and 5.6: Crypt for Guglielmo Oberdan(k)

Figures 5.7 and 5.8: Guglielmo Oberdan(k) prison cell with memorial plaques

Italianised, which subsequently led increasingly to Slovenian citizens emigrating or escaping to Yugoslavia. Violent clashes between Italians and Slovenes ultimately led to the fascist black shirts' arson attack on the Narodni dom on 13 July, 1920.[43]

On the site of Narodni dom, the Portici di Chioggio was built with a relief of naked men fighting each other and the inscription: "Fifty years ago, the battle against the foreigners took place on this site."[44]

The monuments refer to Trieste's Italianità, and the underlying patterns of argumentation are based on the typical dichotomies of national discourse. These include the prevalence of one's own distinct groups in contrast to rival groups, historical versus unhistorical nations, and historical lines of argument as opposed to ethnic modes of justification. However, the use of argumentative models – further evidence of the arbitrariness of linguistic or symbolic signs – may vary.

3.4. On the road to the Habsburg myth

In the years after 1945, reinforced by the uncertain phase of the UN mandate, there was a shift from the concept of Italianità, the attraction to belong to Italy, which had been discredited by fascism, to Triestinità, a longing to belong to Trieste.[45] This was also associated with the discovery of the city's unique character, its difference to other cities and the appeal of its specific Austrian heritage, an "underlying feeling of non-affiliation, in the uncertainty and indefinability of its identity.[46] Originating from a mythology of disappointment regarding Italy and the old Julian complex of supra-Italianism as the true Italian spirit, this road to neo-irredentism formed the basis for the revalorisation of Austrian character and heritage and the emergence of the myth of Austria and, thus, a new era of reflection on finis Austriae.[47]

In terms of monument policy, the post-1945 period is characterised by the cult of sacrifice and competition for laying down memories with a return to Habsburg and to Trieste's constitution as a location of world literature in the tradition of Triestinità, with rival cultures of memory manifesting themselves across the cityscape. In April 1941, the Slovenian culture was focused on the fascist occupation of the territory known at the time as Slovenia, as well as the policy of exterminating everything that was considered Slovenian with a targeted resettlement policy and 'racial structure'. Following the collapse of the 'Provincia di Lubiana', 6,000 people from the Slovenian side were registered as killed, over 200,000 inhabitants had been imprisoned and frequently were deported to the San Sabba concentration

43 For Narodni dom see Monika Pemić, Die eigene Präsenz manifestieren. Die Slowenen und ihr Zentrum in Triest, in: Haslinger / Hein-Kircher / Jaworski, Heimstätten, Loc. Cit. (Note 23), 161–182.

44 Pirjevec, Triest-Frage, Loc. Cit. (Note 19), 135–152; here: 146.

45 See Magris / Ara, Triest, Loc. Cit. (Note 3), 245.

46 See Magris / Ara, Triest, Loc. Cit. (Note 3), 255.

47 On the 'prehistory' of Magris and the concept of the Habsburg myth and the intellectual-historical context, see Renate Lunzer's illuminating study (Loc. Cit. Note 7). On the Habsburg myth itself, of course, Claudio Magris, Der habsburgische Mythos in der modernen österreichischen Literatur. Wien 2013.

camp (built in October 1943). The Italian culture of remembrance was oriented towards the Yugoslavian occupation of Trieste by Tito's troops (at the beginning of 1945). This was combined with arbitrary acts of violence against Italian citizens of Trieste, as well as the demand for long-term claims on Trieste and the denial of the city's Italian character. The focus here is on the mass murders and the so-called 'Foibe massacres', which claimed some 13,000–18,000 Italian victims.

After the Second World War, four levels were superimposed on the cityscape with respect to monuments. Initially, the city turned its face to events suffered in the period of fascism. On the Slovenian side, this included the Opicina Monument and the plaque dedicated to four members of TIGR executed in 1945. On the Italian side, the *Foibe di Basovizza* assumed this same role. Both groups identify closely with the *Risiera di San Sabba* as a monument, a compound that had been refunctioned by the German occupying forces as a concentration camp. Based initially on the interest of modern visitors, it is pertinent to conclude that the old irredentism was delegitimised in terms of memory culture, evidently overshadowed by events from more recent history. In 2009, the number of visitors to the *Civico musea della Risiera di San Sabba* exceeded 57,000, and 104,000 visited the *Foibe di Basovizza*. In contrast, the *Civico museo del Risorgimento – Sacrario Oberdan* 2009 attracted just over 300 visitors.[48]

A second level of memory policy relates to the lost areas of Istria, Fiume and Dalmatia (see Fig. 5.9; this monument is located near the railway station), and the *Parco della rimembranza* contains monuments to Italian victims of the expulsions (see Fig. 5.10).

The third level of monument policy, however, draws on the context of Habsburg traditions. In addition to the staging of exhibitions,[49] the city witnessed a reconstruction of previous monuments. In 1997, the Statue of Sissy, [*Elisabetta*] Empress Elizabeth of Austria was returned to its original location near the main railway station.[50]

In addition, the monument of the former governor, Massimiliano I. (see Fig. 5.11), which had been removed in 1920, was rebuilt in 2009. Until 2009, this monument had been located in the *Parco di Miramara* near 'his' castle, but it has now been returned to its original place, in the *Piazza Venezia*. The inscriptions are only in Italian. The monument was created by the sculptor Johannes Schilling, on the initiative and under the direction of Baron Pasquale Revoltella. A committee first installed the monument in 1875 by in the *Piazza Giuseppina*

48 Numbers from Francesco Fait, Triester Erinnerungen und Erinnerungsorte, in: Ostermann / Müller / Rehberg, Grenzraum, Loc. Cit. (Note 19), 171–183; here: 183, the author of this article managed to visit the *Civico museo del Risorgimento* on 13 July 2016. However, it was opened especially for him, and closed immediately afterwards! No further visitors were anticipated that week, according to the results from the demand.

49 In addition to the exhibition on Maria Theresa mentioned previously, an exhibition about Maximilan was staged in Miramar, see the catalogue by Laura Ruaro Loseri / Maximilian, Kaiser von Mexiko, Von Triest nach Mexiko, Triest 1986; in addition, the exhibition: *Dampfschiffahrt Gesellschaft des Österreichischen Lloyd. Postdienst zwischen Triest und Dalmatien* from 23.7.–1.10.2016 in *Civico Museo della Civiltà istriana fuimana dalmata*.

50 The statue built in 1912, removed in 1921. Rose-Marie Borngässer, Kaiserin Sisi kehrt nach Triest zurück, in: Die Welt (04.10.1997), The 'Sissi' monument created by Franz Seifert was a concession to the Slovenes in Trieste from Mayor Riccardo Illy, according to sources.

Figures 5.9 and 5.10: Memories of the lost areas of Istria, Fiume and Dalmatia

(now *Piazza Venezia*) in Trieste, and it was later moved to the park of Miramare Castle The bronze monument, over 9 metres high, displays Archduke Ferdinand Maximilian in vice-admiral uniform. His eyes and hand were directed towards Miramare Castle. The statue stands on a pedestal that is decorated with allegorical figures and reliefs. These symbolize the power of the House of Habsburg and Maximilian's philanthropy, as well as his interest in the sciences and art.

According to hypothesis, the Habsburg renaissance in Trieste is an expression of communal integration and the positioning of cultural tourism. It is a symbol of

Figure 5.11: Statue of the Governor Maximilian in Piazza Venezia (2016)

a modified Triestinità, the modern version of longing to belong to Trieste, even if the rediscovery of allegiance to Austria, in the sense of intercultural unity, is not entirely free of nostalgic implications. In the end, in the 19th century did not actually witness the emergence of an ethnically homogeneous Trieste (melting pot), but a sounding board as a prerequisite for cultural heterogeneity.[51] This is why the concept of Triestinità is ultimately more than an illusion or merely a utopian projection! In the final analysis, it is a question of ensuring an urban habitus that is not obvious, but is beyond linguistic, national and ideological attributions. Initially, Triestinità and the assigning of renewed importance to Austrian traditions are the result of the experiences of loss caused by the post-1918 economic and political crisis. These were expressed in an increased pressure to assimilate, mutual estrangement (Italy-Trieste) and, finally, in the de-legitimation of irredentism, with its Manichaean, over-simplified alternative (Italy or Habsburg), as well as the (fascist) extremist patriotism, through all of which the processes of cultural mediation were blocked. The second loss experience of 1945/1954 with its renewed marginalisation led to the new 'myth' – an inversion of the old dualism – moving away from economic Austria-centrism and cultural allegiance to Italy, with a view to cultural Austria-centrism and economic irredentism against Rome. These are important ingredients of the sense of loyalty to Trieste, of Triestinism.

The fourth cultural approach to memory involves a recourse to multilingual and multi-cultural Trieste. In this context, representatives of modernism, in particular, came to assume an important role in the plans for monuments (see Fig. 5.12–5.14, all by Nino Spagnoli). In addition to specific cultural institutions (James Joyce Literature Museum and the Italo Svevo Museum), specialised cultural-literary tourist walks have been newly designed and signposted throughout the city.

The importance of this cultural re-mapping becomes clear when considering the fate of the first Svevo monument, a bronze bust of Giovanni Meyer, which was unveiled on 26 April, 1931, in the presence of his family and city authorities in the town park, only to be overturned and defaced eight years later on 8 September, 1939.[52]

If we summarize urban development as it is reflected in the policy of monuments, we find a successful implementation of the aspiration to achieve a cultural monopolisation of the urban cultural space. Trieste as a supranational political entity needed to be recoded nationally. The Trieste monuments signpost shifts in the city's perception of itself, in which the image of the city changes from the 'Habsburg double-headed eagle' through Italianità to a sense of loyalty to Trieste itself, even though the Slovenian component still appears to have been marginalized. Reenactments of the Habsburg past and the recourse to literary modernity, however, not only point to (heterogeneous) concepts of the past and orientations towards the future, but also to the inherent contingency represented in monuments.

---

51 Roberto Bazlen, Interview über Triest, in: Triest – die Stadt zwischen den Welten. Ein literarisches Lesebuch, Helmut Eisendle (ed.), München-Zürich 1994, 11–18; here: 15f.

52 See the official homepage of Trieste, http://itinerari.comune.trieste.it/das-triest-von-italo-svevo/ [Accessed: 17.07.2017], where the reactions of the fascist newspapers are also mentioned. In Milan's Il Popolo d'Italia (The Italian People) on 09.09.1939 it said: "Un busto inutile eliminato" (An unnecessary bust eliminated). In *La Tribuna* from Rome: „Questa notte è stato deposto dal piedistallo il busto in bronzo di Italo Svevo, scrittore noto soltanto perché ebreo" (Tonight, the bronze bust of Italo Svevo, a writer known only for his Judaism, was removed from its pedestal).

Figure 5.12: Umberto Saba[53] at the intersection of Via Dante and Via San Nicolò

53 See also the flyer Trieste by Umberto Saba with walks from the birthplace on Via di Riborgo (approximately the present Via del Teatro Romano) in the old Jewish ghetto, which was renovated between 1934 and 1938, over the antique bookstore in Via San Nicolò to the practice of Edoardo Weiss (Via San Lazzaro).

Figure 5.13: Italo Svevo[54] in Piazza Hortis (2004)

Figure 5.14: James Joyce[55] in Via Roma to celebrate the centennial arrival in Trieste (2004)

4. Chernivtsi from the perspective of monuments

Chernivtsi is certainly worthy of a cursory view, as a city where regional patriotic Habsburg traditions also endured until 1918, only then to be overlaid by progressive Romanianisation, Sovietisation and Ukrainianisation in terms of monument policy. The process of urbanisation was also comparably delayed in Chernivtsi, primarily starting after the city was occupied by Habsburg troops in 1775 in the aftermath of the Russo-Turkish war. At this time, a "highly competitive poly-ethnic society" with free citizens began to emerge through the introduction of administrative and social modernisation measures, including the development of legislative and educational systems.[56] This process was associated with the wide-ranging implementation of tolerance in a form of 'westernisation', and provided the relevant precondition for the later myth of Chernivtsi and Bukovina. A rapidly develop-

54 See the flyer Trieste by Italo Svevo, with walks from the birthplace in Via dell'Acquedotto (today Viale XX. Settembre) over the Berlitz School in Via San Nicolò, where Svevo met James Joyce, to the Svevo Museum in Via Madonna del Mare.

55 See the flyer Trieste by James Joyce, with walks from Piazza della Stazione (today Piazza Libertà), where Joyce arrived on 20/10/1904 to the Joyce Museum in Via Madonna del Mare.

56 Emanuel Turczynski, Longue durée: Kulturen und Lebensformen in Czernowitz, in: Jahrbuch für Geschichte und Kultur Südosteuropas (JKGS), München 2002, 107–115; here: 107; see also Kurt Scharr, Die Landschaft Bukowina. Das Werden einer Region an der Peripherie

ing regional patriotism formed the basis for a "security community" with strong regional cohesion, in which the "conflict-economic coexistence was able to strike a balance despite the existence of different customs and faiths".[57] Prerequisites for this included the demographic balance of ethnic groups, balanced regulation of interdenominational relations, the specific sphere of freedom and justice, multilingualism in education and functional bilingualism (although not polyglotism)[58] as well as a political culture of compromise with limited pressure to assimilate.

Like in Lviv/Lwów, no national political monuments were created initially in Chernivtsi.[59] The Habsburg rule was demonstrated through the Karl Peckary's Austria statue, originally standing in the Austria-place (today Soborna Ploshcha), and erected in 1875 for the city's 100-year membership of and allegiance to the monarchy. The university also opened its doors in the same year. Furthermore, on occasion of the 40th anniversary of Franz Joseph I's reign, a monument (1888) was erected in front of the Schützenhaus [*meeting house of the riflemen*], which was demolished during the First World War. Also worth mentioning is the 'Kaiserfelsen' imperial rock with a portrait of Franz Joseph, which was constructed in 1908 to mark the 60th anniversary of his reign and located on the Habsburg Heights (Fedkovych Park) above the current main university building. The imperial rock was erected by the Association for the beautification of the City of Chernivtsi. During the occupation of the Bukovina in 1918, the Romanian administration removed the portrait and dedication plate. The Elisabeth Monument, erected in 1911, also disappeared, as did the statue of Austria, although the damaged torso of the Austria statue was rediscovered during canal works in 2003.[60] As recently as August 18, 1998, prior to the Orange Revolution, the Kaiserfelsen was restored, but ransacked and damaged once again during the night of March 4, 2001. A new monument to Franz Joseph has since been donated by Arseni Yatsenyuk (see Fig. 5.15).

National political monuments were primarily created after 1918 to symbolize and legitimize Romanian rule.[61] The Unirea monument deserves particular men-

---

1774–1918, Köln-Weimar-Wien 2010; Markus Winkler (ed.), Partizipation und Exklusion. Zur Habsburger Prägung von Sprache und Bildung in der Bukowina 1840–1918–1940, Regensburg 2015.

57 Emanuel Turczynski, Exogene und endogene Faktoren der Konsensbildung in der Bukowina, in: Friedrich Gottas (ed.), Südostdeutsches Archiv 38/39, München 1996, 97–116; here: 107. Critical to this besides Menninghaus Loc. Cit. (Note 2) also Trude Maurer, Eintracht der Nationalitäten in der Bukowina. Überprüfung eines Mythos, in: Geschichte in Wissenschaft und Unterricht 52 (2001), 180–191.

58 On bi- and multilingualism see Kazimierz Feleszko, Die einstige Bukowina – eine Kulturgemeinschaft. Gedanken über die Folgen der Verwendung ‚fremder' Sprachen, in: Friedrich Gottas (ed.), Südostdeutsches Archiv 40/41, München 1998, 162–183.

59 Grzegorz Rossoliński-Liebe, Der Raum der Stadt Lemberg in den Schichten seiner politischen Denkmäler. 2009, in: *kakanien revisited* www.kakanien.ac.at/beitr/fallstudie/ GRossolinski-liebe1.pdf.

60 Re the statue of Austria see http://austria-forum.org/af/Wissenssammlungen/Symbole/Austria_ Statue_Czernowitz [Accessed: 16.03.2017].

61 On the Romanianisation of Chernivtsi and Bucovina, see Mariana Hausleitner: Die Rumänisierung der Bukowina. Die Durchsetzung des nationalstaatlichen Anspruchs Großrumäniens 1918–1944. München 2001; see also Ibid., Fünf verschiedene Vereinshäuser in Czerno-

Figure 5.15: Emperor Franz Joseph (2009)

tion; erected in November 1924 at the Unirea Square (Central Square) on the occasion of the (re)annexation of Bukovina to Romania, the monument is a two-armed installation with scenes from Romanian history. At the rear, the Romanian aurochs crushes the Austrian double-headed eagle. Also located in Central Square, the statue of the Virgin Mary, created as a symbol of Habsburg Catholic rule, was replaced by a soldier bearing a Romanian flag.[62] The Schiller statue (built in 1907) was removed from the forecourt of the Drama Theatre in 1920, the pedestal is now situated in the courtyard of the German House (see Fig. 5.19) in what was previously called Herrengasse (now Kobylianskoy Street), but the marble statue has been lost.[63] Just as Trieste experienced the destruction of the Narodni dom,

witz und ihre Entwicklung bis 1914, in: Haslinger / Hein-Kircher / Jaworski, Heimstätten, Loc. Cit. (Note 23), 89–112.

62 The statue of Mary, erected in 1827, was moved by the Romanian Royal Administration to the courtyard of the Church of the Sacred Heart in 1923, and then demolished in 1944.

63 In 1963, a statue of Olga Kobylianska was erected in front of the theatre, to be replaced in 1980 by a modernised version.

Chernivtsi had to deal with nationalist attempts to occupy public space in the years after 1918 and with efforts to eradicate history.[64] In Chernivtsi, too, the 'assault of memorials' functioned as a victory gesture and was a part of a battle over the power to define and the power of interpretation of urban space.

In Soviet era, the Unirea monument was demolished and removed in three stages, in 1940, 1945 and in 1951. At first, a red star was erected on the pedestal as a sign of the Sovietization of northern Bukovina following the Hitler-Stalin Pact. The monument itself was dramatically toppled by Willy Pragher in 1941 in the aftermath of the invasion of Czernowitz by Romanian and German troops.

In 1945, an obelisk was erected in the place of the demolished monument in what was now called the 'Red Square', commemorating of the liberation of the city of Chernivtsi from the German-Romanian occupying forces.[65] The statue of a Romanian soldier erected in the place of the Marian column was also replaced in 1951 by a monument to Lenin, designed by M. Vronskyj and O. Olijnyk (subsequently removed in 1992). In turn, this was replaced in 1991 by a statue of Taras Ševčenko, designed by Petro Lemskij and Mykola Lysakiwskij (Fig. 16). The years inscribed on the monument indicate the period of time since its foundation.[66]

While it might not (yet) be appropriate to speak of being overrun by a 'flood of monuments', as was the case in Lviv,[67] Chernivtsi does demonstrate a striking ideological overlap with that city. Certainly, a developing sequence of monument politics seems to be taking place in Chernivtsi, parallel to the progressive Ukrainisation and re-Habsburgisation, and very similar to the activities in Trieste, signifying a clear intention to portray Chernivtsi as a metropolis of world literature. An early example of this movement is the statue of Paul Celan in the People's Park (see Fig. 5.17), others include the plaque at Rose Ausländer's birthplace (see Fig. 5.18), plaques for Celan at the 'false' birthplace (2011), for Elieser Steinbarg (in the street of the same name) and plaques dedicated to K. E. Franzos and Mihai Eminescu in front of the theatre at the former German School (1990).[68] In addition, Edward Turkiewitch's memorial stones deserve particular note: In 2007, a memorial stone was erected on the banks of the Prut for the Jewish victims of a mass shooting in 1941, and another in 2011, dedicated to the victims of the

64 During the Romanian period, monuments were created for the historian Dimitirie Onciul (1928) and the Prime Minister Ion I. C. Brătianu (1936), which were later moved to a Bucharest museum in 1940.

65 Other Soviet monuments included a monument of a tank, commemorating the victory of the Soviet Union, a monument to the heroes of the Soviet Union and one to the heroes of the Red Army (all in 1946), plus a monument to Kalinin (1956), which replaced the monument erected in 1897 of Tomaszczuk, the founder of the university.

66 Further monuments were erected in the context of Ukrainianisation and regionalisation of the poet and composer Sydir Vorobkovych (1992), of Osip Yuri Fedkovych (1995), Ivan Franko and of the first Metropolitan of Bukovina, Eugen Hackmann (2006). See also the digital portal *Digitale Bukowina*, which is currently under construction. For Ševčenkos' role in the process of Ukrainian nation building, see Jenny Alwart, Mit Taras Ševčenko Staat machen. Erinnerungskultur und Geschichtspolitik in der Ukraine vor und nach 1991, Köln-Weimar-Wien 2012.

67 Rossoliński-Liebe, Raum, Loc. Cit. (Note 59).

68 For Eminescu, a monument by Dmytro Horshkowskyj was also erected in 2000.

Figure 5.16: Taras Ševčenko (erected 1999)

Figure 5.17: Celan (erected 1992)

Figure 5.18: Rose Ausländer (erected 2001)

ghetto – which should be seen, at the very least, as noteworthy attempts to remember the fate of the city's Jewish inhabitants.

It remains to be seen whether an increased re-nationalization is actually forthcoming, in addition to an urban-historical, monumental-political localisation and regionalisation, as might be indicated by the representation of Bukovina with allegorical figures in the Central Square, or whether the series of sculptures assist the path to a peaceful Twin City partnership with Salt Lake City. Without a doubt, there are a number of taboo-breaking monuments that substantiate a deep-seated break with the Soviet era in Chernivtsi.[69] However, it would appear that Chernivtsi also wants to reach out to and engage in its multinational past, certainly in a far more conscious manner than the parallel city of Lviv.[70]

Figure 5.19: The Schiller pedestal

5. Conclusion

In the examples examined here, urban monument policy obviously refers to the constitution of collectively binding spatial concepts and images, which are intended to have a group-stabilizing effect via inherent relationships of hierarchy,

69 References to the Soviet phase include the memorial to the heroes of Bukovina (1995), which commemorates the fallen from the two world wars, and the memorial to fallen soldiers from Bukovina (1999) in the war in Afghanistan.

70 Harald Binder, Stadt, Urbanisierung und Nationsbildung in der Ukraine, in: Andreas Kappeler (ed.), Die Ukraine. Prozesse der Nationsbildung, Köln-Weimar-Wien, 175–189; here: 180.

demarcation, and concepts of proximity and distance. This work on urban space has aimed to recognise all endeavours to establish a demarcated national territory as a unit of reference.[71] Spatial units are certainly always the product of both political decisions and economic developments, but they are also the result of communicative processes. These manifest themselves in forms of demarcation, inner hierarchisation, and opportunities for inclusion and participation. Throughout the 19th century, local references and living environments were broken up in both Trieste and ('belatedly') in Chernivtsi, initially discursively in the media, as well as in new social institutions such as associations. In this way, new, nationally exclusive behaviour patterns and attitudes became not only plausible, but also acceptable. Primarily, the reorganisation of the centre and the periphery also changes the hierarchical relationships within the space, leading to new forms of spatial concepts. In this respect, it seems reasonable that Musil's assessment should be contradicted, as the various overlays prove anything but an 'invisibility' of monuments. After all, this is only to be enforced in comparison with the respective precursor monuments. Whether this succeeds depends on the respective local conditions with regard to memory-cultural work in the urban space, which, for its part, never comes to an end, and yet also remains contingent.[72]

Abstract

Based on case studies examining Trieste and Chernivtsi, this article explores different cities' policies regarding monuments and memorials, looking back to the 19th century and through to the present-day. In the process, it is revealed how, in the first instance, local references and living environments were increasingly replaced by selected national monuments in Trieste and (somewhat belatedly) in Chernivtsi over the course of the 19th century, leading to the domination of nationalist and ideologically-based monument policies, especially in the aftermath of 1918. It is not until that critical year of change, 1989 and subsequently, that a heightened recourse in monumental policy starts to emerge, looking back to the Habsburg era, as well as to those cities' multi-national and multi-lingual traditions.

71 Peter Haslinger, Die 'Arbeit am nationalen Raum'. Kommunikation und Territorium im Prozess der Nationsbildung, in: Komparativ. Leipziger Beiträge zur Universalgeschichte und vergleichenden Gesellschaftsforschung 15/2: Arbeit am nationalen Raum. Deutsche und polnische Rand- und Grenzregionen im Nationalisierungsprozess, Leipzig 2005, 9–20.

72 Published in German, in: Andrei Corbea-Hoişie / Ion Lihaciu (eds.), 'Toposforschung (…) im Lichte der U-topie'. Literarische Er-örterungen in/aus MittelOsteuropa (= Jassyer Beiträge zur Germanistik, XXI), Iaşi-Konstanz 2017, 149–175.

Ukrainian-Russian Border after Euromaidan

Regional Perspective*

Volodymyr Kravchenko

Introduction

The history of independent Ukraine is too short to be summarized from a *longue durée* perspective. The present form of the Ukrainian state is historically unprecedented, as are its current borders. These facts create many difficulties for those attempting to understand, describe, and explain what is going on in Ukraine today. As is well known, recent events in Ukraine have taken many observers by surprise. Western specialists have only recently discovered and begun exploring contemporary Ukraine as a coherent phenomenon, which may compel them to challenge some deeply rooted dogmas in East European, Soviet, and Russian studies.

Historically, Ukraine can be understood only in the broad context of transnational histories and nested geographies. Ukrainian-Russian relations are the central axis of that context, both defining and reflecting the processes of self-identification and symbolic mapping of the two countries and nations.[1] Those relations are multi-layered, comprising a broad spectrum of distinct identities with their respective spaces, symbols, and articulations. At the same time, Ukrainian-Russian relations have been shaped very considerably by the evolution of nation-state building throughout the post-Soviet space. History, very often in the form of imagined historical mythology, constitutes the main foundation of those relations.[2] It is an important part of everyday life and present-day politics.

---

* I am deeply grateful to Myroslav Yurkevich for his editing of the manuscript of this article.

1 Taras Kuzio, Russia-Ukraine Crisis: The Blame Game, Geopolitics and National Identity, in: Europe-Asia Studies 70 3 (2018), 462–473; Agnieszka Pikulicka-Wilczewska / Richard Sakwa (eds.), Ukraine and Russia: People, Politics, Propaganda and Perspectives, E-International Relations (Bristol, UK) 2015; Serhii Plokhy, Ukraine and Russia: Representations of the Past, University of Toronto Press 2008.

2 Heorhii Kasianov, Past Continuous: Istorychna polityka 1980–2000: Ukraina ta susidy, Kyiv 2018; Iryna Vushko, Historians at War: History, Politics and Memory in Ukraine, in: Contemporary European History 27 1 (2018), 112–124; David Marples, Russia's perceptions of Ukraine: Euromaidan and historical conflicts, in: European Politics and Society 17 4 (2016), 424–437; Alexei Miller / Paul W. Wert, The "Ukrainian Crisis" and Its Multiple Histories, in: Kritika: Explorations in Russian and Eurasian History 16 1 (2015), 145–148; Volodymyr

In the course of the last few centuries, a huge interactive Ukrainian-Russian cultural borderland has come into existence.[3] This was not a demarcated, consolidated, or even clearly articulated space. On the contrary, it was heterogeneous, dotted with many enclaves created by military conflict, modernization, or sociocultural identification. Several historical regions appeared and disappeared in the borderland: Malorossiia (literally "Little Russia"), Novorossiia (literally "New Russia"), the Donbas (Donets Basin), and Sloboda Ukraine. During and after the dissolution of the Soviet Union, these historical names acquired new political meanings.

In this article I deal with discourses, not with "real" historical regions located in the Ukrainian-Russian borderland. As a historian, I am not convinced that regional particularities or even identities can be traced far back into the pre-Soviet period. Recent regional discourses are in fact new social constructs created in the process of nation-state building in Ukraine and Russia. Most of them are products of the decomposition and further nationalization of the Soviet symbolic space. It is in this capacity that they became instrumental in what may be defined as "regional geopolitics."[4]

In what follows, I shall attempt to describe the main features of developing regional historical discourses in Ukraine and their function in the context of the Ukrainian-Russian conflict during and after the Euromaidan and the Russian annexation of the Crimea in 2014. I begin with a brief description of Ukrainian-Russian relations after the dissolution of the Soviet Union and proceed with a consideration of recent Ukrainian regionalism and its role in the symbolic reconfiguration of the Ukrainian-Russian borderland. This process is still evolving, with consequences that can hardly be predicted. I believe, however, that the process can be understood in historical context.

Kravchenko, Fighting Soviet Myths: The Ukrainian Experience, in: Serhii Plokhy (ed.), The Future of the Past: New Perspectives on Ukrainian History, Cambridge (MA) 2016, 437–474; Idem, Ukraine faces its Soviet past: history vs. policy vs. memory, in: Jie-Hyun Lim / Barbara Walker / Peter Lambert (eds.), Mass Dictatorship and Memory as Ever Present Past, Palgrave Macmillan 2014, 87–119.

3 Volodymyr Kravchenko, Ukraine: History Confronts Geography, in: Ilkka Liikanen / James W. Scott / Tiina Sotkasiira (eds.),The EU's Eastern Neighbourhood: Migration, Borders and Regional Stability (BASEES/Routledge Series on Russian and East European Studies), Routledge 2016, 36–49; Vladimir Kravchenko / Olga Filippova / Aleksei Musiezdov, in: Predstavlenia o "Pogranichie" i praktiki ikh ispol'zovaniia, Vilnius 2012; Vladimir Kravchenko, Kharkov / Kharkiv: stolitca pogranichia, Vilnius 2010.

4 Valentin Mihaylov / Stanislaw Sala, Subnational identities in the context of the changing internal geopolitics. The case of post-revolutionary Ukraine, in: Bulletin of Geography. Socio-economic Series 39 (2018), 79–96; Gearóid ÓTuathail, Localizing geopolitics: Disaggregating violence and return in conflict regions, in: Political Geography 29 (2010), 256–265; Il'in Mikhail, Etapy stanovleniya vnutrennei geopolitiki Rossii i Ukrainy, in: Polis 3 (1998), 82–94; Yurii Shevtsov, Regional'naia geopolitika Ukrainy v usloviakh mirovogo krizisa, http://www.trust.ua/news/2489.html [Accessed: 11.11.2018].

Ukrainian-Russian relations

Ukrainian-Russian relations during and after the breakup of the Soviet Union have been informed by the process of nation-state building in both countries. Neither Ukraine nor Russia enjoyed full-fledged statehood in the Soviet Union. Both inherited a very particular and limited idea of modern nationhood, as well as truncated state institutions and porous, almost invisible administrative borders. Even though Ukraine and Russia claim ancient historical legacies, they are in fact new countries with new identities and borders. The building of their respective nation-states has involved the rethinking, reshaping, and redivision of common or overlapping legacies of symbolic space and time. The nature and dynamics of that process, however, have differed in the two countries.

Russia has not decided whether it is an empire or a nation-state, while Ukraine wavers between territorial and ethnic models of national consolidation. Russia is coming to terms with a history of Orthodox imperialism, while Ukraine is struggling to attain ethnocultural integrity. Russia has proclaimed its non-European status, while Ukraine is trying to join the European project. Both countries have been constantly changing and renegotiating their national and geopolitical identities. Ukrainian-Russian relations are asymmetrical because Russia has advanced much further toward national consolidation than Ukraine, which was unable to establish its national priorities for about twenty years. As a result, Russian policy toward Ukraine has been proactive, while Ukrainian policy remains reactive.

When the Soviet Union ceased to exist as a politico-administrative unit, all its institutions, including established borders, began to lose political legitimacy. Reverting to its imagined imperial past, Russia ended up discarding its Leninist nationality policy. That decision led Russian elites to deny the very existence of Ukrainian statehood and even of a distinct Ukrainian nationality, denouncing them as artificial constructs elaborated by enemies of Russia.[5] "Dissolution of the USSR did not take place immediately and came to an end in December 1991. This process of dissolution stretches from the times of Perestroika until now."[6] This explains the recent roots of the current Ukrainian-Russian conflict, which was hardly imaginable even a few years ago.

The Russian neoimperial renaissance has been accompanied by intensive mythmaking. Thus, the mystical concept of a "Russian World" has become the new basis of post-Soviet Russian geopolitical and cultural identification.[7] President Vladimir Putin is promoting the notion of "Russia" as a spiritual condition rather than a "normal" state.[8] As Boris Dubin puts it, the phenomenon of Russian

5 Yuri Teper, Official Russian identity discourse in light of the annexation of Crimea: national or imperial?, in: Post-Soviet Affairs 32 4 (2016), 378–396.

6 Sergii Glebov, Separatism and Disputed Territories (the Case of Ukraine), in: Richard Q. Turcsányi / Maryna Vorotnyuk (eds.), Theorising Security in the Eastern European Neighbourhood: Issues and Approaches. Bratislava-Kyiv 2018, 28–40; here 33.

7 Jardan Østbø, The New Third Rome. Readings of a Russian Nationalist Myth, Stuttgart 2016; Mikhail Suslov, 'Holy Rus': The Geopolitical Imagination in the Contemporary Russian Orthodox Church, in: Russian Politics & Law 52 3 (2014), 67–86.

8 Timothy Snyder, The Road to Unfreedom: Russia, Europe, America, New York 2018,137.

national exclusivity, "to which many Russians apparently subscribe, is actually a succinct expression for a sense of not belonging to the world at large. It encapsulates the irrational particularity of the Russian collective (the 'we') which resists translation into a set of ready-made formulations. In other words, the 'way' is open-ended, indeterminate."[9] The focus of official Russian identity discourse has thus shifted from the state to the nation.[10]

Since a reimagined Ukraine was included in the concept of the "Russian World" as an "organic" element of Russian civilization, Russo-Ukrainian relations also entered the mystical realm. As Fedor Lukianov, editor in chief of the English-language Russian journal *Russia in Global Politics*, noted in 2008, those relations are "more relevant to the field of unconsciousness-collective and individual, than to the sphere of rational analysis."[11] In the Russian national narrative, Ukraine figures as a conglomerate of historical regions such as Malorossiia, Novorossiia, Volhynia, Galicia, and so on rather than as a nation-state with internationally recognized borders. Russians speak of places or events *na Ukraine* rather than *v Ukraine,* referring to Ukraine as a region or territory instead of a country. Consequently, Russian policy toward Ukraine has been formulated in terms of historical identity (i. e., Ukraine conceived as a region of Russia) rather than geopolitics.[12] This helps to explain the irreconcilable opposition of "Malorossian" and "Ukrainian" discourses in the Russian national narrative.

Post-Soviet regionalism

In the new Russian national narrative, Soviet Ukraine has been reimagined as the traditional Malorossiia.[13] This revival of "Malorossian" rhetoric, as well as the corresponding discourse in Russian public space, is associated with the increasing influence of prerevolutionary and émigré literature in Russian society. "Malorossiia" appears as a synonym of "Ukraine" in Aleksandr Solzhenitsyn's tract of 1990, *Kak nam obustroit' Rossiiu?* (published in English translation as *Rebuilding Russia*). Subsequently, "Malorossiia" began to squeeze "Ukraine" out of public space owing to the republication of works by such Russian nationalists as Sergei Shchegolev, Nikolai Ulianov, and their present-day followers. Generally speaking, the only contribution of these latter-day writers to the question is their acknowledgment that the western oblasts of today's Ukraine, and they alone – most notably historical Galicia, centered in Lviv – have a "Ukrainian" character.

In post-Soviet Ukrainian national discourse, by contrast, "Malorossiia" has been marginalized by "Ukraine." Mykola Riabchuk's essay collections *From Mal-*

9 Boris Dubin, The symbolics of the border in post-Soviet political mythology, Intellectual News 9 1 (2001), 45–49; here 46.

10 See Teper, Russian identity, Loc. Cit. (Note 5), 378–379.

11 See Glebov, Disputed territories, Loc. Cit. (Note 6), 32.

12 An alternative point of view see: Elias Gotz, It's Geopolitics, Stupid: Explaining Russia's Ukraine Policy, in: Global Affairs 1 (2015), 3–10.

13 On the differences between these two definitions of national identity see: Ivan Lysiak-Rudnytsky, Essays in Modern Ukrainian History, Edmonton 1987, 123–143.

orossiia to Ukraine: Paradoxes of Belated Nation-Building[14] and *Two Ukraines: Real Boundaries, Virtual Games*, published in the early 2000s, perhaps best exemplify this tendency. Riabchuk's "Malorossiia" exists not only on the spiritual plane but also in geographic terms: its boundaries on the Ukrainian electoral map are those of the eastern and southern oblasts, which are considered pro-Russian. The "two Ukraines" dichotomy took on a civilizational dimension during and after the Orange Revolution of 2004 in Ukraine. Admittedly, the "Malorossian" discourse is not limited to political rhetoric but has also acquired academic respectability. Even so, support for such discourse is limited among the population, probably for purely semantic reasons.

"Malorossian" discourse was the only one that functioned on both a regional and a national level in opposition to "Ukrainian" national discourse. Other regional discourses were (re)constructed by local post-Soviet elites seeking new ways to legitimize their bid for local resources and political power. The idea of a special regional identity was also a byproduct of the search for a new national identity. The shuffling and reshuffling of national, imperial, Soviet and local symbols and historical memories reflected the struggle between Ukrainian and Russian national mythologies for the reinterpretation of national space.

Thus, the "Novorossian" regional discourse was a combination of Russian imperial mythology, Odesa multiculturalism, and Ukrainian national renaissance mythology. In addition to these, the "Sloboda Ukraine" discourse promoted the "first capital of Ukraine" mythology and the idea of Ukrainian-Russian transborder cooperation. The "Donbas" discourse combined Russian imperial and Soviet mythologies of industrial modernization along with the "friendship of peoples" paradigm, and so on. As the Russian and Ukrainian nation-state building projects continued to diverge, Ukrainian regionalism became more pronounced than its Russian counterpart.

Ukrainian regionalism became visibly political and even took on a civilizational dimension during the presidential elections of 2004 and the Orange Revolution that ensued. A bid to proclaim "Southeastern autonomy" may be seen as the first attempt at political consolidation of the Ukrainian border regions. A conference of people's deputies representing Ukraine's southern and eastern oblasts as well as the Autonomous Republic of Crimea, intended to legitimize their political autonomy, was held in the peripheral town of Severodonetsk in Luhansk oblast on November 28, 2004. This was followed by attempts to endow the would-be autonomous part of Ukraine with an overarching symbolic identity. The Russian nationalist historian Oleg Nemensky came up with the idea of "Malorossiia" as opposed to "Ukraine."[15] In tandem with this, "some not entirely academic quarters in Moscow played with the idea of a major geopolitical redesign of the northern Black Sea area, under which southern Ukraine, from the Crimea to Odessa, would secede from Kiev and form a Moscow-friendly buffer

14 Mykola Riabchuk, Vid Ukrainy do Malorosii: paradoksy zapizniloho natciotvorennia, Kyiv 2000.

15 Oleg Nemenskii, 'Nedoukraintcy' ili novyii narod? Al'ternativy samoopredelenia Yugo-Vostoka Ukrainy, in: Russkii Zhurnal, 29 Dekabria (2004), http://old.russ.ru/culture/20041229_nem-pr.html [Accessed: 11.11.18].

state, "Novorossiia" – New Russia."[16] None of these variants gained substantial support from abroad or from the local population.

The Euromaidan of 2014 and its aftermath: the regional dimension

There is every indication that 2014 marks a watershed in the recent history of Ukrainian-Russian relations. In that year the two countries entered a period of open confrontation accompanied by a new round of mutual reidentification and national consolidation.[17] As the dramatic developments of Russia's armed aggression and the separatist movement in the Donbas claimed attention, not all observers took note that those developments began not with "Novorossian" but with "Malorossian" symbolic discourse. As early as January 2014, Russian civic organizations in Sevastopol raised the prospect of abandoning the Ukrainian legal framework, creating self-defense units led by reserve officers and, most important, establishing a "federative state of Malorossiia oriented toward Russia" on the basis of the southeastern and central oblasts of Ukraine.[18] Speaking at a meeting of the Liberal Democratic Party of Russia in Moscow on February 23, 2014, Vladimir Zhirinovsky called for the formation of a new Malorossian state in the eastern oblasts of Ukraine, with its capital in Kharkiv, and its subsequent absorption into the Russian state.[19] On the same occasion he announced that the first units of Russian "volunteers" were already prepared for dispatch to Kharkiv. In other words, Russian nationalists in the Crimea and Zhirinovsky based themselves on the premise that only the eastern and southern oblasts of Ukraine would be "Malorossianized" and detached from the rest of the country. They seemed oblivious of the fact that such a limited regional version of "Malorossiia" was bound to find itself in opposition to other regional discourses and mythologies.

After the Euromaidan, Kharkiv was groomed to assume the functions of an alternative capital of Ukraine. On February 22, 2014, more than three thousand lawmakers at all levels of government gathered in Kharkiv from the southern and eastern oblasts of Ukraine, including the Autonomous Republic of Crimea, to legitimize open confrontation with Kyiv. They were joined by numerous representatives of the Russian political elite from Moscow and the Russian oblasts bordering Ukraine. The oblast governor, Mykhailo Dobkin, declared the establishment of a National

16 Dmitrii Trenin, Post-imperium: a Eurasian Story, Carnegie Endowment for International Peace 2011, 100.

17 Kapitolina Synytsina, The Construction of the Image of Ukraine as the Other in Russian Media. Diss., Tartu Ülikool 2018; Lev Gudkov, Faktor vraga: Chto Rossiane dumajut ob Ukraintcakh, Novoye Vremya, 19 January (2018), https://nv.ua/opinion/gudkov/faktor-vraha-chto-rossijane-dumajut-ob-ukraintsakh-2446062.html [Accessed: 11.11.2018]; Andrea Chandler , Какая это дружба/what kind of friendship is this? Russia's 'Crimean Syndrome', in: European Security 27 (2018), 201–223; Gerhard Besier / Katarzyna Stokłosa (eds.), Neighbourhood Perceptions of the Ukraine Crisis: From the Soviet Union Into Eurasia?, New York 2017; Agnieszka Pikulicka-Wilczewska / Richard Sakwa (eds.), Ukraine and Russia: People, Politics, Propaganda and Perspectives, Bristol 2015.

18 Dmitrii Volokitin, Sevastopol'tsy zagovorili o sozdanii Malorossii, in: Rabochaia gazeta, 17, January 30 (2014), 1.

19 https://www.youtube.com/watch?v=NBGFdnyYZoU [Accessed: 11.11.2018].

Guard-type armed unit drawn from local and Russian members of various Cossack, veterans', paramilitary, and sports formations. They all expected President Viktor Yanukovych and his allies to start the battle for Ukraine. Seen from outside, these developments appeared to portend the new "Pereiaslav Agreement" already announced by Zhirinovsky, but no such scenario actually materialized.

The Kharkiv gathering did not accept the "Malorossian" idea as its ideological and political platform. The "Great Patriotic War" mythology of the Soviet period, with its attendant rhetoric, was activated instead. It is worth noting that the backers of this movement operated with pan-Ukrainian categories, not in terms of regional autonomy. The march to "liberate" Ukraine and Kyiv from the "fascists" was to proceed under the banner of the "Ukrainian Front," evoking associations with the Ukrainian Front of the Red Army in 1943. For reasons that remain unclear – a last-minute decision by Yanukovych, Putin's distraction by the special operation in the Crimea, or lack of support from the local establishment – no such march ensued. Very soon, the gathering of "southeastern" representatives dispersed in all directions. The political initiative shifted briefly to radical Russian nationalists, who were effectively neutralized by the Ukrainian Special Forces.

The Soviet-style rhetoric of the "Ukrainian Front," implicitly associated with the traditional Soviet paradigm of the "friendship of peoples" and the "march of liberation" from the north to the south and west, appeared to be only partly congruent with the regional discourse of "Sloboda Ukraine" in its various versions. It proved even more irrelevant when the Putin regime employed Russian nationalist rhetoric and symbolism in the Crimea. With Yanukovych gone, the Kremlin no longer counted on local "Malorossian" collaborators, abandoned the notion of assimilating Ukraine as a whole, and sought instead to grab anything available. Even the Soviet-era rhetoric of the Great Patriotic War gave way to the motifs of imperial military glory and sacralization of national space that accompanied the Russian annexation of the Crimea.

After the "Crimean gambit," the "Novorossian" geopolitical project appeared to be the next step toward the further destabilization and fragmentation of Ukraine.[20] It is important to note that this project was based on the political geography of the "Southeastern" autonomy of 2004 rather than on the region of imperial New Russia created in the eighteenth century. Speaking on a direct line to a Russian audience on April 17, 2014, President Putin first articulated the idea that the Ukrainian "Southeast" was in fact the Russian "Novorossiia." "... The question is to ensure the legal rights of Russian and Russian-speaking citizens of the Southeast of Ukraine. I would like to remind you that, using the terminology of tsarist days, it is Novorossiia – Kharkov, Lugansk, Donetsk, Kherson, Nikolaev, and Odessa – they were not part of Ukraine back then. These territories were

20 Mikhail Minakov, Development and Dystopia, Studies in post-Soviet Ukraine and Eastern Europe, Stuttgart 2018, 264–292; Mikhail Suslov, The Production of 'Novorossiya': A Territorial Brand in Public Debates, in: Europe-Asia Studies 69 2 (2017), 202–221; John O'Loughlin / Gerard Toal / Vladimir Kolosov: The rise and fall of "Novorossiya": examining support for a separatist geopolitical imaginary in southeast Ukraine, in: Post-Soviet Affairs 33 2 (2016), 124–144; Marlene Laruelle, The three colors of Novorossiya, or the Russian nationalist myth-making of the Ukrainian crisis, in: Post-Soviet Affairs 32 1 (2016), 55–74; Fedir Turchenko / Halyna Turchenko, Proekt 'Novorossiia' i novitnia rosiis'ko-ukrains'ka vijna, Kyiv 2015.

transferred to Ukraine in the 1920s by the Soviet government. Why they did so, God knows… The center of that territory was Novorossiisk, so the region is called 'Novorossiia.'[21] It is hard to say how Putin came up with this new conception of 'Novorossiia,' since it has very little to do with history.[22] Whether it was an improvisation or a political provocation remains an open question.

What seems more important is that Putin's "Novorossiia" actually tended to reimagine the former "Southeast" of Ukraine in national rather than geographic terms. Russian historians made haste to create a new "Novorossian" narrative designed to manifest the coherence of the region and legitimize its claim to political autonomy.[23] So far, however, their efforts to (re)construct a particular "New Russian" or "South Russian" regional identity seem poorly conceptualized.[24] Marlene Laruelle indicates the composite and contradictory nature of "Novorossia geopolitical adventurism" based on "three underlying ideological paradigms – 'red' (Soviet), 'white' (Orthodox), and 'brown' (Fascist)."[25] Even Russian nationalist historians have found themselves constrained to admit that the southern and eastern oblasts of Ukraine "have no particular self-awareness, no national thinking, and no local patriotic elites. They are simply territories insufficiently involved in the process of building a united Ukrainian nation."[26]

The Donbas seemed destined to become the base for the deployment of the "Novorossian" political project in Ukraine and "carry the torch" to other oblasts, but even these relatively small fragments of Ukrainian territory failed to establish a political union. The "Confederation of Novorossiia," solemnly proclaimed in 2014, was quietly dissolved in the following year. It soon became apparent even to politically committed Russian authors working on the construction of a "Novorossian" political identity that the fragmentation of the "Southeast" was hardly to be avoided.[27] Analysts currently note the fiasco of the "Novorossian" geopolitical project, from which the main centers of the Ukrainian-Russian borderland, including Kharkiv, Dnipro (formerly Dnipropetrovsk), and Odesa, have turned away.[28]

Russia's annexation of the Crimea and the armed conflict have turned the Donbas into the nucleus of Moscow's projected "Novorossiia." In 2014 the Don-

---

21 This quote is an officially adopted version of Putin's direct line (http://en.kremlin.ru/events/president/news/20796) slightly corrected stylistically according to video record of his oral speech (https://www.youtube.com/watch?v=Lz1B8o9p0Ts) [Accessed: 11.11.2018].

22 Patricia Herlihy, What Vladimir Putin chooses not to know about Russian history, in: Los Angeles Times, 1 May (2014), http://www.latimes.com/opinion/op-ed/la-oe-herlihy-russia-ukraine-odessa-20140501-story.html [Accessed: 11.11.2018].

23 Alexander Shubin, Istoriya Novorossii. Moscow 2015; Compare to: Valerii Smolii (ed.), Skhid i Pivden' Ukrainy: tchas, prostir, sotcium: u 2 tomah, Kyiv 2014.

24 See Mihaylov / Sala, Subnational identities, Loc. Cit. (Note 4), 90.

25 See Laruelle, Three colors, Loc. Cit. (Note 20), 55–74.

26 Oleg Nemenskiy, Modeli yuzhnorusskogo natsionalizma na Ukraine. Voprosy natsionalizma 2 18 (2014), 21.

27 Andrey Baranov, Politicheskaya identichnost' Novorossii: sostoyaniye i resursy konstruirovaniya, in: Kaspiyskiy region: politika, ekonomika, kul'tura 43 (2015), 98–106.

28 O'Loughlin / Toal / Kolosov, Rise and fall, Loc. Cit. (Note 20); Andrei Kolesnikov, Why the Kremlin Is Shutting Down the 'Novorossiya Project', May 29 (2015), https://carnegie.ru/commentary/60249 [Accessed: 11.11.2018].

bas unexpectedly found itself the leading center of the Ukrainian borderland and an outpost of the "Russian World," charged with the mission of returning Ukraine to the "all-Russian civilizational space."[29] But the Donbas elites were unprepared to play such a role: up to that point they had been involved in the construction of a regional identity capable of strengthening their economic status and guaranteeing their monopoly on political representation. To that end, they had fostered an eclectic amalgamation of elements of the "Russian World" with Soviet identity. As a result, the Russian language, Orthodoxy, the historical mythology of the Russian Empire, and even a "Russified" Khazar khaganate were bound together with the mythology of the Donetsk-Kryvyi Rih Soviet Republic, the Great Patriotic War, and the Brezhnev era of Soviet history.

The differentiation of the Donbas from Ukraine, initiated by the Euromaidan and the outbreak of armed conflict with local separatists supported by Russia, imparted new dynamism to the search for a regional identity distinct from that of Ukraine.[30] That search could now be sustained by institutions inherited from the USSR and the Ukrainian SSR. "Soviet-era symbols, monuments, and place-names are still very visible, if not dominant"; they are supplemented with newly erected monuments to Lenin, Stalin, and the Great Patriotic War.[31] The continuing armed conflict has endowed that process with a particular character.[32] Its effect has been to consolidate the population of the Donbas behind the front line and provide it with a new mythology of heroic struggle and victimization.[33] From an outsider's viewpoint, local identity politics look very similar to those of Transnistria over the past twenty-five years.[34] For the time being, Soviet historical mythology and the narrative of the "Grand Victory" remain the most salient elements in the construction of local identity.

The termination of the "Novorossian project" and the Kremlin's obvious unwillingness to incorporate the Donbas into Russia have forced the leaders of the Donbas separatists to assume the mantle of "Malorossian" identity in order to substantiate their "mission" in Ukrainian discourse. On July 18, 2017 Oleksandr Zakharchenko, the recently deceased leader of the self-proclaimed Donetsk People's Republic (DNR in Ukrainian), caused general surprise with his proclamation

---

29 Gubarev: Missiia Donbassa- vernut' Ukraine russkuiu identichnost', http://nahnews.org/417379-gubarev-missiya-donbassa-vernut-ukraine-russkuyu-identichnost/ [Accessed: 11.11.2018].

30 Sergii Pakhomenko / Kateryna Tryma / J'moul A. Francis, The Russian-Ukrainian War in Donbas: Historical Memory as an Instrument of Information Warfare, in: Sayapin, Sergey / Evhen, Tsybulenko (eds.), The Use of Force against Ukraine and International Law: Jus Ad Bellum, Jus In Bello, and Jus Post Bellum, The Hague 2018, 297–312; Alexandr Osipian, Historical Myths, Enemy Images and Regional Identity in the Donbass Insurgency, in: Journal of Soviet and Post-Soviet Politics and Society 1 1 (2015), 109–140; Victor Holovko, 'Tiahar postardians'koi ludyny': istoriohrafichnyj obraz donets'koi identychnosti, in: Istoriohtrafichni doslidzhennia v Ukraini 24 (2014), 38–50.

31 Roman Slyvka / Liubov Slyvka / Yaroslava Atamaniuk, Transformacje krajobrazu kulturowego Donbasu w czasie konfliktu zbrojnego w latach 2015–2017, Studia z Geografii Politycznej i Historycznej 6 (2017), 305–326; here 319–321.

32 Gwendolyn Sasse / Alice Lackner, War and identity: the case of the Donbas in Ukraine, in: Post-Soviet Affairs 34 2–3 (2018), 139–157.

33 See Slyvka / Slyvka /Atamaniuk, Transformacje, Loc. Cit. (Note 31).

34 Ibid, 320.

of a new federal state, Malorossiia, intended to replace the "discredited" Ukraine and become its "legitimate" successor.[35] This time it was Donetsk, not Kharkiv, that was to become the new political center of "Malorossiia." The motive force behind the proclamation remains unclear, as Zakharchenko disavowed his statement about "Malorossiia" within hours of its broadcast.

This curious episode is very telling. It reflects, on the one hand, the Russian regime's determination to treat the Donbas as an alternative "Ukraine." It is in this capacity that the region can be reintegrated into Ukrainian legal political and public life rather than being incorporated into the Russian Federation. "If Moscow manages to achieve the reintegration of the Donbas by political means into a common space with Kyiv on fundamentally new conditions, as a full-fledged subject of a decentralized state, then it will in fact obtain a new Ukraine…"[36] On the other hand, the "Malorossian" episode demonstrates that the Kremlin and its proxies dispose of very limited symbolic resources to support the political "mission" of the Donbas. Indeed, the notion of turning the Donbas into "Malorossiia" generated open mockery in the mass media.[37]

The reconfiguration of the borderland

The Euromaidan Revolution of 2014, the Russian annexation of the Crimea, and the "hybrid war" in the Donbas gave a great impetus to Ukrainian nation-state building. The very idea of the "Ukrainian nation" and its representative symbols has acquired new meaning.[38] The further "nationalization" of post-Soviet Ukraine is now in progress. Its main vectors are clearly making themselves apparent in the geopolitical orientations of Ukrainian citizens and their changing attitude to the recent Soviet past.

---

35 Adam Taylor, Ukrainian separatists claim to have created a new country: Malorossiya, or 'Little Russia', in: The Washington Post, July 19, 2017, https://www.washingtonpost.com/news/worldviews/wp/2017/07/19/ukrainian-separatists-claim-to-have-created-a-new-country-malorossiya-or-little-russia/?utm_term=.fc9b39185448 [Accessed: 11.11.2018].

36 Alexander Vershinin, Ukrainskaia politika Rossii: mezhdu miahkoi i zhestkoi salami, in: Problemnyi analiz i gosudarstvenno-upravlencheskoe proektirovanie: Teoria, praktika, metodologia, 47 3 (2016), 38–74; see also: Andrey Babitckii, Gorizonty Malorossii, "Life.ru", 6 August (2017), https://life.ru/t/percentD0 percentBC percentD0 percentBD percentD0 percentB5 percentD0 percentBD percentD0 percentB8 percentD1 percent8F/1033114/ghorizonty_malorossii [Accessed: 11.11.2018].

37 Aleksei Kaftan, Nostalgia po Malorossii. Zachem Zakharchenko podalsia v usluzhenie necromantam, in: Delovaia Stolitca, 18 July (2017), http://www.dsnews.ua/world/nostalgiya-po-malorossii-zachem-zaharchenko-podalsya-v-usluzhenie-18072017172900 [Accessed: 07.11.2018]; Elena Snigir', Novye malorossy. Kogda Zakharchenko vyriaditsia v sharovary Khmelnitskogo, Delovaia Stolitca, 24 July (2017), http://www.dsnews.ua/world/novye-malorossy-pochemu-flag-hmelnitskogo-ne-nuzhen-dnr-23072017220000 [Accessed: 11.11.2018].

38 Volodymyr Kulyk, Shedding Russianness, recasting Ukrainianness: the post-Euromaidan dynamics of ethnonational identifications in Ukraine, in: Post-Soviet Affairs 34 2–3 (2018), 119–138, Idem, National identity in Ukraine: Impact of Euromaidan and the war, in: Europe-Asia Studies, 68 4 (2016), 588–608; Olga Onuch / Henry E. Hale / Gwendolyn Sasse, Studying identity in Ukraine, in: Post-Soviet Affairs 34 2–3 (2018), 79–83; Marco Puleri, Hybridity Reconsidered: Ukrainian Border Crossing after the "Crisis," Ab Imperio, 2 (2017), 257–286.

The European vector of Ukraine's development is displacing the Russian one. A survey carried out by the sociological service of the Razumkov Center between September 9 and 14, 2016 showed that 45.8 % of Ukrainian citizens considered relations with the European Union to be their country's main foreign-policy priority; 12.6 % of respondents prioritized contacts with Russia, and 6.9 %those with other countries of the Commonwealth of Independent States.[39] Nevertheless, the farther east one goes, the greater the number of people for whom the European orientation is not the only one. The population of eastern Ukraine is almost evenly divided between the European and Russian orientations, with most opposing Ukraine's accession to the European Union.[40]

The Ukrainian-Russian border inherited by both countries from the Soviet period and recognized throughout the world is now undergoing deep institutional and symbolic reconstruction.[41] The process of its bilateral demarcation has been stalled since 2014, and in general the Ukrainian-Russian borderland looks much more fragmented than it did before that date. The border exists de facto, but its legal status has been steadily deteriorating, especially since the Ukrainian authorities' recent decision not to extend the "grand" Treaty of Friendship, Cooperation and Partnership concluded between Ukraine and Russia in 1997. According to Marek Menkiszak, the uncontrolled part of the Ukrainian border with Russia, including its maritime component in the Azov and Black Seas, constitutes 730 km or 35 % of its former total length.[42] The border of the separatist Donetsk and Luhansk "people's republics" with the rest of Ukraine has turned into a military frontier or "grey zone." Some scholars consider that the so-called faultline between "Eastern" and "Western" Ukraine has now been replaced by one between the Donbas and the rest of Ukraine.[43]

In 2014 the president of Ukraine, Petro Poroshenko, initiated the unilateral demarcation of the Ukrainian border with Russia. Accordingly, the government of Ukraine has adopted a project known as "The Wall," imagined in terms of civilizational difference as the "European bulwark," which is intended to create

39 Zovnishniopolitychni orientatcii hromadian Ukrainy. Rezul'taty sotciolohichnoho doslidzhennia, z 9 po 14 veresnia 2016 roku, http://razumkov.org.ua/napryamki/sotsiolohichni-doslidzhennia/rezultaty-sotsiolohichnoho-doslidzhennia-tsentru-razumkova-zovnishno-politychni-oriientatsii-hromadian-ukrainy [Accessed: 11.11.2018].

40 Ibid.

41 Vladimir Kolosov, Radical shifts in Russian-Ukrainian relations and geopolitics of neighbourhood, in: Journal of Geography, Politics and Society 8 2 (2018), 7–15; Vladimir A. Kolosov, Transformatsiia transgranichnykh vzaimodeistvii na rossiisko-ukrainskom pogranich'e posle 2014 goda (Transformation of Cross-Border Interactions on the Russian-Ukrainian Borderland after 2014), in: Comparative Politics Russia 2 (2018), 41–61; Gelinada Grinchenko / Oksana Mikheieva, From contact zone to battlefield area. (Un)real borders of (un)declared war in Eastern Ukraine, 2014–2016, in: Jussi Laine / Ilkka Liikanen / James W. Scott (eds.), Post-Cold War Borders: Reframing Political Space in Eastern Europe (2018); Marek Menkiszak, Borders in Flux: Ukraine as a Case Study of Russia's Approach to its Borders, in: Eurasia Border Review 6 1 (2016), 83–102; Mikhail Krylov / Alexander Gritsenko, Regional Identities in Russia and Ukraine: Examples of Research Practice, in: Valentin Mihaylov (ed.), Territories and Identities in Central, Eastern and Southeastern Europe, Częstochowa 2014, 297–315.

42 Menkiszak, borders, Loc. Cit. (Note 41), 90.

43 Anna Fournier, From Frozen Conflict to Mobile Boundary: Youth Perceptions of Territoriality in War-Time Ukraine, in: East European Politics and Societies 32 1 (2018), 23–55; here 38.

a dividing line between "Europe" and Russia.[44] The project provides for the construction of sophisticated features of civil and military engineering, including fences, trenches, ramparts, and the like. Recently Ukraine's hard border with Russia began to take on a symbolic dimension when the Orthodox ecumenical patriarch in Istanbul granted a *tomos* of autocephaly to the Ukrainian Orthodox Church (Kyiv Patriarchate), thereby reducing the authority of the Orthodox "Russian World." Nevertheless, the construction of the "real" Ukrainian-Russian border is far from completion.

The Ukrainian-Russian borderland still reflects the asymmetrical nature of Ukrainian-Russian relations. The findings of Russian scholars indicate the "underdeveloped ethnonational identity of the residents of Ukrainian border regions and their dependence on Russia in Russia-Ukraine communication."[45] Even after the annexation of the Crimea and part of the Donbas, a considerable number of residents of the Ukrainian-Russian borderland are opposed to severing or further reducing ties with Russia. Recent Ukrainian polls even suggest a slight increase in positive Ukrainian attitudes toward Russia, while corresponding data for Russian citizens indicate stability.[46]

The policy of decommunization, officially adopted in 2015, was intended to sever all connections between contemporary Ukraine and its previous Soviet incarnation and to consolidate Ukrainian national time and space. It treats communism and Nazism as *equivalent totalitarian regimes* and forbids all Soviet symbols, including monuments and toponyms. Its implementation radically changed the cultural landscape of Ukraine: hundreds of streets and some 1,000 cities bearing the names of communist activists have been renamed.[47] However, the policy of decommunization drew considerable criticism from Ukrainian and Western scholars.[48]

The same may be said about Ukrainian society. Thus, according to a sociological survey carried out in 2018 by the Kalmius Group in partnership with the GfK Ukraine Company, only half (49 %) of the population completely or partly supports decommunization in Ukraine, while a third (34 %) does not support

---

44 Menkiszak, borders, Loc. Cit. (Note 41), 91.

45 Valentin Babintsev, at all, Impact of the Russia-Ukraine crisis on ethno-national stereotypes of the residents of Russian/Ukrainian border regions, in: Man in India 96 10 (2016), 3429–3439; here 3429. See also: Valentin Babintsev, and all, Russian-Ukrainian Border Region: Negative Cultural and Civilizational Risks of Integration, in: International Journal of Environmental and Science Education 11 17 (2016), 10057–10069.

46 V Ukraintciv trokhy pokrashchylosia stavlennia do Rosii – opytuvannia, in: Ukrainska Pravda, 10 zhovtnia (2018), https://www.pravda.com.ua/news/2018/10/10/7194715/ [Accessed: 11.11.2018].

47 List of Ukrainian toponyms that were changed as part of decommunization in 2016, https://en.wikipedia.org/wiki/List_of_Ukrainian_toponyms_that_were_changed_as_part_of_decommunization_in_2016) [Accessed: 11.11.2018].

48 See polemics in: Krytyka, May 2015, https://krytyka.com/en/solutions/opinions/decommunization-identity-and-legislating-history-slightly-different-angle; https://krytyka.com/en/solutions/opinions/volodymyr-viatrovych-and-ukraines-decommunization-laws; https://krytyka.com/en/solutions/opinions/decommunization-and-academic-discussion [Accessed: 11.11.2018]; Kasianov, Past Continuous, Loc. Cit. (Note 2), 308–3321.

it.[49] On the territory of the Ukrainian Donbas, most citizens (46 %) do not support the policy. The same applies even to Poltava oblast, located in the center of the country.[50] Protests against official identity policy manifest themselves from time to time in acts of vandalism against new sites of memory and monuments symbolizing the heroic national narrative from the beginning of the twentieth century to the beginning of the twenty-first.

Ukrainians appear to have become even more divided rather than consolidated in their attitude toward the Soviet past. As of 2018, the number of those nostalgic for the Soviet Union in southeastern Ukraine has remained stable for the last few years – approximately 40 %, which is about four times more than in western Ukraine.[51] Although the cohort of those nostalgic for the Soviet past is steadily shrinking, 49 % of respondents in southern Ukraine, 39 % in the east, and 25 % in the central regions regret the breakup of the Soviet Union.[52] More than half of those interviewed in the southern and eastern oblasts are convinced that Soviet life was better than that in present-day Ukraine.[53]

Regional reconfiguration

After Russia's annexation of the Crimea, the eastern and southern regions of Ukraine underwent yet another political reconfiguration. The trend in those regions toward political consolidation within the framework of Ukraine was halted by the annexation of the Crimea and the de facto secession of part of the Donbas. The disappearance of the Party of Regions deprived the political elite of a political platform for joint action.[54] Finally, none of the ideological models of regional autonomism offered to the Ukrainian borderland elites by Russian political technologists proved viable in practice.

The basically ethnonational "Malorossian" idea migrated from one Ukrainian megalopolis to another but found support in none of them, since it does not have a regional character. It is associated not with Kharkiv, Donetsk or, even less, with Sevastopol but with Kyiv; that is, not with the border regions but with the

49 Sotciolohy rozpovily, de v Ukraini naibil'she sumuiut' za SSSR, Ukrainska Pravda, 10 veresnia (2018), https://www.pravda.com.ua/news/2018/09/10/7191628/ [Accessed: 11.11.2018].

50 Lyshe tretyna poltavtciv pidtrymuiut' zakony pro 'dekomunizatciu', in: http://poltava.to/news/33398/ [Accessed 11.11.2018]; Absolutna bil'shist' Dnipropetrovs'ka vystupyla proty pereimenuvannia mista, in: http://112.ua/statji/dnepropetrovsk-i-dneprodzerzhinsk-chto-v-imeni-tvoem-312473.html [Accessed: 11.11.2018]; Mykola Mykhailutsa, Decommunization/Renaming in Odessa Region: Historical Comparison, Methods and Results, in: Danubius, 3 (2017), 109–116.

51 "Who wants the USSR back in Ukraine?" in: Euromaidan Press, 13 kvitnia (2018), http://euromaidanpress.com/2018/04/11/soviet-people-in-ukraine-why-do-they-miss-it-and-what-danger-does-this-pose-for-ukraine/ [Accessed: 11.11.2018].

52 Dynamika nostalgii za SRSR, in: 8 zhovtnia (2015), http://ratinggroup.ua/research/ukraine/dinamika_nostalgii_po_sssr.html [Accessed: 11.11.2018].

53 See Loc. Cit. (Note 49), https://www.pravda.com.ua/news/2018/09/10/7191628/ [Accessed: 11.11.2018].

54 Taras Kuzio, Rise and Fall of the Party of Regions Political Machine, in: Problems of Post-Communism 62 3 (2015),174–186.

center of Ukraine. Kyiv might be "Malorossianized" only from Moscow, but that could hardly be accomplished without a real war instead of a "hybrid" one. That is why Russian propagandists pin their hopes on counterposing "Malorossian" to Ukrainian identity, given the subversive role of the former in the politics and culture of Ukraine.

The discourse of Russian "Novorossiia" was even less well suited to the consolidation of the border regions than the relatively neutral discourse of the "Southeast." Russian-speaking residents of the Ukrainian borderland might respond to appeals for modernization but showed no enthusiasm for militant rallying cries of anti-Western clerical nationalism. "Novorossiia" was "new" precisely because it lacked the sacral significance that lingered in such tropes of Russian nationalist discourse as, for example, an imagined "Russian" Crimea or a "Malorossian" Kyiv. Finally, it must be borne in mind that the notion of a Putinesque "Novorossiia" lacked roots not only in historical New Russia but also in "Malorossiia" and other regional discourses of the "Sloboda Ukraine" or "Donbas" variety.

After the fiasco of the "Malorossian" and "Novorossian" autonomist scenarios, some analysts remarked on the disappearance not only of the "Southeast" but also of "Eastern Ukraine" as common denominations of the borderland.[55] By contrast, a new "Central Ukraine" began to take shape between the eastern and western border regions. As Natalia Pohorila suggests, "Central Ukraine has an identity of its own, circumvented by its history, complex and known by early attempts at state building."[56] Finally, the city of Dnipro was hastily proclaimed a symbol of Ukrainian loyalty and even a new "heart of Ukraine."[57] To be sure, all such assertions by interested observers should be evaluated in the context of the ongoing symbolic struggle for the borderland. Regional discourses are continuing features of its political and cultural landscape.

Since the assassination of Oleksandr Zakharchenko in August 2018 and the removal of his lieutenants from power, Donetsk has been engaged in the creation of its regional identity in the framework of the "Russian World." Zakharchenko's successor, Denis Pushilin, who openly opposed the "Malorossian" identity for the Donbas, has proclaimed his intention to integrate the region into Russia. But another Russian policymaker, Konstantin Zatulin, a hardliner with regard to Ukraine, announced that Russia would be prepared to recognize DNR "independence" on the models of South Ossetia and Abkhazia rather than incorporate

55 Maxim Vikhrov, Tri mifa ob ukrainskom yugo-vostoke, Максим Вихров, Три мифа об украинском юго-востоке, 28 april (2014), https://republic.ru/world/tri_mifa_ob_ukrainskom_yugo_vostoke-1091432.xhtml [Accessed: 11.11.2018]; Olexander Demchenko, Pivdennoho Skhodu bil'she nemaie, in: Ukrainska Pravda, 22 kvitnia (2014), http://www.pravda.com.ua/articles/2014/04/22/7023182/ [Accessed: 11.11.2018].

56 Nataliia Pohorila, Political and National Identity in Ukraine's Regions: Where Does the Center Fit? in: Polish Political Science Review 4 1 (2016), 18–32. However, other researchers suggest that "In the central part of Ukraine sub-ethnic identity is relatively weak" (Anatoliy Melnychuck / Oleksiy Gnatiuk / Mariia Rastvorova, Use of territorial identity markers in geographical researches, Scientific Annals of "Alexandru Ioan Cuza" University of Iaşi, Geography series, LX.1 (2014), 157–184; here 166.

57 Andriy Portnov, Kak natchinalas' voyna na vostoke Ukrainy ili potchemu Khar'kov i Dnepropetrovsk ne stali Donetskom i Luganskom? in: Gefter 22 01 (2016), http://gefter.ru/archive/17295 [Accessed: 11.10.2018].

it.[58] In any case, the Donbas is drifting away from Ukraine. Some Ukrainian observers already consider it a lost territory.[59] Others, no doubt, would appreciate such a scenario.

It would appear that the former role of Donetsk as the Ukrainian regional center most opposed to official Kyiv has passed not to Kharkiv but to Odesa. A good many observers have noted the activity of anti-Ukrainian forces in the city. Memory of the death by fire of many opponents of the Euromaidan in May 2014, as well as the failure of attempts at modernization and the extensive influence of the criminal element create a climate favorable to the cultivation of such attitudes.[60] It is too early to say whether Odesans opposed to Kyiv are reverting to the discourse of the historical New Russia, which was centered on Odesa in pre-Soviet times, or whether the idea of an "Odesa People's Republic" will come out on top. For the time being, both tendencies are monopolized by forces associated with the clerical version of the "Russian World."

As for Kharkiv, it now finds itself in an indeterminate zone somewhere between Dnipro and Odesa. For lack of political leadership, Kharkiv is no longer considered the capital of the Ukrainian-Russian borderland. Like Odesa, however, Kharkiv retains its political potential as a center of opposition to Kyiv.[61] Once armed conflict broke out in the East, the "Sloboda Ukraine" regional discourse returned to its former role as a symbol of cross-border cooperation or even a metaphor of a "Euroregion" incapable of national mobilization. To be sure, even in this modest guise the regional discourse of "Sloboda Ukraine," adopted by local communists to promote their cause, has been effectively suppressed by local Ukrainian radicals.

Preliminary conclusions

Mykola Riabchuk's question about the end of Ukrainian ambivalence remains difficult to answer.[62] Many of us still remember the purely rhetorical "end of history" metaphor, which bears no relation to reality. The division and (re)distri-

58 Yurii Butusov, Deputat Gosdumy Zatulin: "Donetsk i Lugansk nado vernut' v Ukrainu. Nasha oshibka – my ostanovilis' v sentiabre 14 v Mariupole", in: Censor.Net, 10.09. (2018), https://censor.net.ua/resonance/3085410/deputat_gosdumy_zatulin_donetsk_i_lugansk_nado_vernut_v_ukrainu_nasha_oshibka_my_ostanovilis_v_sentyabre [Accessed: 11.10.2018].

59 Yaroslava Vermenych, Fenomen pohranychia: Krym i Donbas v doli Ukrainy, Kyiv 2018, 325.

60 Henry E. Hale / Oxana Shevel / Olga Onuch, Believing Facts in the Fog of War: Identity, Media and Hot Cognition in Ukraine's 2014 Odesa Tragedy, in: Geopolitics (2018), 1–31 DOI: 10.1080/14650045.2018.1465044; Oleksii Bratushchak, "Urky": Iak Odesa peretvoriuet'sia na 'kryminal'nu respubliku', in: Ukrainska Pravda, 18 zhovtnia (2018), https://www.pravda.com.ua/articles/2018/10/18/7195471/ [Accessed: 11.11.2018]; Tomasz Piechal, Odessa Oblast: Governor Saakashvili's superficial changes, in: OSW/Commentary, Centre for Eastern Studies,196 (2016), URL: https://www.ceeol.com/search/gray-literature-detail?id=563545 [Accessed: 20.11.2018].

61 Partia 'Za Zhyttia' obognala 'Oppoblok' v Kharkove i Odesse – sortcopros, in: Apostrophe, 17 avgusta (2018), https://apostrophe.ua/news/politics/political-parties/2018-08-17/partiya-za-jittya-obognala-oppoblok-v-harove-i-odesse---sotsopros/138704 [Accessed: 11.11.2018].

62 Mykola Riabchuk, Two Ukraines' Reconsidered: The End of Ukrainian Ambivalence? in: Studies in Ethnicity and Nationalism 15 1 (2015), 138–156.

bution of the joint Ukrainian-Russian inheritance is progressing differently on opposite sides of the political border between the two countries. On the Russian side, the borderland looks more consolidated and dependent on the political center than it does on the Ukrainian side. The space of Ukrainian identity remains highly heterogeneous at all points, and even its near future looks murky. Every presidential election in Ukraine, including the impending one of 2019, has been overloaded with existential questions.[63]

The very heterogeneity of Ukrainian identity space allows for a variety of collective identities, including local and regional ones. In Kharkiv and Odesa local identities overshadow the national one.[64] Local differences may be more apparent at opposite ends of the East-West system of symbolic coordinates, but inhabitants of the rest of Ukrainian territory are united by their dependence on tradition and avoidance of all political extremes that might jeopardize their personal safety. The national poll conducted by the Razumkov Center at the end of June 2018 shows that most Ukrainian citizens, no matter where they live, are centrists as regards their ideological and political preferences, which they cannot or do not want to articulate clearly.[65] The same may be said about sub-ethnic and sub-regional identities, which seem more pronounced at opposite ends of the East-West axis but more muted in the rest of Ukraine.[66]

The perplexing fact that many inhabitants of the Ukrainian-Russian borderland manage to combine Ukrainian patriotism with support for pro-Russian political parties[67] is not to be explained by habit or attachment to tradition. The most advanced eastern and southern oblasts are steadily losing their economic and cultural potential. The Ukrainian elites cannot offer them real rather than mythical future prospects or guarantee their rights and personal safety. Ukrainian national discourse in its current version is unable to come to terms with the historical legacy of imperial and Soviet modernization. The southern and eastern lands of Ukraine have not been properly incorporated into the national historical narrative.[68]

Ukrainian regional projects, for their part, are replete with political limitations and intellectual weaknesses. During the political crisis of 2014 they were effectively marginalized by the competing Ukrainian and Russian national discourses. It is hard to imagine the local borderland elites summoning the strength for regional political mobilization on the scale achieved in 2004: they lack the

---

63 Yaroslav Hrytsak, Samyi Bolshoi strakh, in: Novoe Vremya, 10 November (2018), https://nv.ua/opinion/grytsak/samyj-bolshoj-strakh-2495849.html [Accessed: 11.11.2018].

64 Hromads'ka dumka u mistakh-milionnykakh: elektoral'ni orientatcii ta nastroi naperedodni Dnia Nezalezhnosti Ukrainy. Rezul'taty doslidzhennia, in: Ukrinform, 17 serpnia (2018), https://www.ukrinform.ua/rubric-presshall/2518531-elektoralni-orientacii-ta-nastroi-naperedodni-dna-nezaleznosti-ukraini-rezultati-doslidzenna.html [Accessed: 20.11.2018].

65 Pres-reliz Tcentru Razumkova 'Ideolohichni orientatcii hromadian Ukrainy', in: http://razumkov.org.ua/napryamki/sotsiolohichni-doslidzhennia/presreliz-tsentru-razumkova-ideolohichni-oriientatsii-hromadian-ukrainy [Accessed: 11.11.2018].

66 See Mihaylov, and Sala, Subnational identities, Loc. Cit. (Note 4).

67 See Loc. Cit. (Note 61), https://apostrophe.ua/news/politics/political-parties/2018-08-17/partiya-za-jittya-obognala-oppoblok-v-harove-i-odesse---sotsopros/138704 [Accessed: 11.11.2018].

68 Olexander Halenko, Pivden' nahadue, shcho istoriu Ukrainy tchas perepysaty, in: Valerii Smolii (ed.), Skhid I Pivden' Ukrainy: tchas, prostir, sotcium: u 2 tomah, Kyiv 2014, 54–75.

requisite political leadership, ideology, and even organizational machinery. There is, however, a basis for regional alternatives to the national project, as shown by responses to the implementation of the newly adopted Ukrainian law on education in compact settlements of ethnic minorities.

The recent tragic events in the Ukrainian-Russian borderland demonstrate the serious methodological limitations of traditional Ukrainian regional and border studies. To my mind, the categories of gradient, transitional zone, and borderland are better suited to the description and analysis of Ukrainian-Russian nested geographies and histories than the regional approach.[69] So far, Ukrainian regional discourses look more like byproducts of political technology than expressions of viable historical entities with clearly articulated identities. Historians seeking to trace the latter back to times out of mind often yield to the temptation to produce new mythologies, as if historical maps of Eastern Europe and the USSR were reliable guides to making sense of the electoral map of present-day Ukraine. In my opinion, local differences in the political and cultural orientations of Ukrainian citizens can be better explained by insufficient and inconsistent reforms of the Soviet legacy than by the imagined historical legacies of Hetman Borodavka, Empress Catherine the Great, or the anarchist Nestor Makhno.

Abstract

The Euromaidan revolution of 2014 followed by the Russian annexation of the Crimea and a military conflict on Donbas is a watershed in the history of Ukraine and Ukrainian-Russian relations. Both of these countries are going on the road of "nationalization" of the former Soviet nation and its symbolic space. Russia has advanced far beyond Ukraine in this direction. The erosion of Soviet space and clash of the Russian neo-imperialist with Ukrainian ethnic-cultural doctrines contributed to symbolic heterogenization of Ukrainian border territory and emergence of regional discourses. They played an important role in the process of re-bordering and transformation of Ukrainian-Russian borderland. At the same time, Ukrainian regional discourses were marginalized by the Ukrainian and Russian national projects. The interplay between regional, national, and border discourses on Ukrainian-Russian borderland can contribute to the updating of methodological arsenal of respective disciplines.

69 Serii Plokhy, The Gates of Europe: A History of Ukraine, New York 2015, 352; Alexander Gritsenko, Ethnocultural gradient and regional identity along the Russian-Ukrainian-Belarussian Borderlands, in: Regional Research of Russia, 1 4 (2011), 351–362; Georgiy Kasianov / Philipp Ther (eds.), A Laboratory of Transnational History: Ukraine and Recent Ukrainian Historiography, Budapest-New York 2009.

"So close and yet so far"?

Experiences from the Polish-Russian and Ukrainian-Russian border regions

Gerhard Besier

When looking for reasons behind the serious problems in Polish-Russian and Ukrainian-Russian cross border co-operation and regional integration, it is not sufficient simply to refer to the historical tensions that have existed over centuries between these countries.[1] The "close relationship" is rooted in common habits, values and norms, including specific behaviours in connection with "the other".[2] Notions of honour, pride, masculinity and other traits, learned by generations during processes of socialization, stand in the face of practical compromises and a strategy of forgetting in the light of new-beginnings. Legends and myths about "the other", as well as our "cultural memory", are used to reinforce these traditional attitudes. If we are to dispense with the stereotypes and prejudices that hinder fruitful co-operation, we need to shed light on social-psychological processes, acknowledging the "neighbour" as "them" and the "family" as "we", which only deepens the gap between both sides. Even though Russia and Ukraine, for instance, are so close with regard to their feelings, both countries remain so far apart. Within their own restricted perception, people are only really aware of their differences, not their closeness, provoking a sense of mutual foreignness. This contribution aims to explain how emotional anthropological factors are actually working to limit cross-border co-operation. And using an interdisciplinary approach, it is essential that we identify how we need to change our own minds in order to recognize the neighbour as a member of the family.

Typically, empires show a clear tendency of minimizing their internal borders, while reinforcing their external borders. Ethnic, linguistic and cultural distinctions within the empire are marginalized as much as is reasonably possible. In contrast, the culture of "the others" outside of their own sphere of influence are represented as being foreign and incompatible. Endeavours such as these cer-

1 Cf., for instance, Gerhard Besier / Katarzyna Stokłosa (eds.), Neighbourhood Perceptions of the Ukraine Crisis. From the Soviet Union into Eurasia?, London-New York 2017.

2 Cf. Gerhard Besier, Neither Good Nor Bad. Why Human Beings Behave How They Do, Newcastle upon Tyne: CSP 2014, 73 ff.

tainly existed within the Habsburg Monarchy,[3] as well as in the Tsarist Empire. Following the collapse of both empires, the path trodden by each of these regions could hardly have been more different. While the Habsburg Empire was broken up into numerous small nation states after 1918, which each evolved quite individually and distinctly, the Soviet Union initially only condoned any form of separation on the marginal edges. During the course of its ongoing development, the Soviet Empire sought to put these early weaknesses right once again. The system, which was labelled as socialist ideology, was intended to level out all individual differences within the empire and the satellite states – for instance, where the part of the world designated as the "Bloc" was incited to join the international "fight for peace". The proclamation of national independence declared during the Khrushchev era ultimately proved to be little more than lip-service.

After the collapse of the Soviet Union, with all the associated signs of disintegration, it has been Putin's policy from the beginning of this century to pursue a restitution of the Russian Empire. In the process, he made free use of all the archaic human behaviours and traditional myths and legends, which were certainly not unfamiliar to the general population and which formed, in point of fact, a key component of their folk, or popular, culture across the generations.[4]

It was from this repertoire of myths and legends that the idea of a common Slavdom originates, together with the religious concept of the "Holy Rus", which was to forge together Russia, Ukraine and Belarus under higher portent, as it were, for eternity in the form of the Russian Orthodox Church (ROC). Together with the ROC, which pursued very similar demands, Putin relied on this ideology in particular to justify the annexation of the Crimea and all other military interventions for the preservation of the territory that was deemed to be holy. The very genuine fear on the part of former Soviet republics can, therefore, be clearly understood, concerned as they are that they will likewise be integrated into this involuntary community.

Equally, after centuries of shared cultural history, it is extremely difficult for Ukraine, as well as for Poland and other countries that had previously been parts of Russia's dominions, to establish the sense of their country being completely different. In almost all areas, an attempt is being made to place clear and evident emphasis on their own traditions and habits and to reconstruct a history that is completely separate from Russia.

For this purpose, they make use of old myths and archaic notions of an imagined "other one", concepts of a stranger that have been extensively researched in the fields of Anthropology and Social Psychology.[5] In this setting of essentially forced perspectives of segregation, a revival of the sense of "the other" is hap-

---

3 Cf. Konrad Canis, Die bedrängte Großmacht. Österreich-Ungarn und das europäische Mächtesystem 1866/67–1914, Paderborn, 2016; Andrea Komlosy, Grenzen: Räumliche und soziale Trennlinien im Zeitenlauf, Wien 2018, esp. 48 ff.

4 Cf. Gerhard Besier, Mental Borders Create Limited Minds. How to Overcome Prejudices, Stereotypes and Concepts of an "Enemy" in the Second Decade of the 21st Century, in: Birte Wassenberg (ed.), Castle-talks on Cross-Border Cooperation. Fear of Integration? The Pertinence of the Border, Stuttgart 2018, 265–280.

5 Cf. Benedict Anderson, Imagined Communities: Reflections on the Origin and Spread of Nationalism, London-New York rev. ed. 2016.

pily celebrated through stereotypes, prejudices and concepts of the enemy. Negative stories of how completely different the others are, of their evil brutality and primitiveness, as well as their ugliness and lack of culture are freely circulated. These defensive stories are promulgated by means of stories emphasising "us", where "our own" is represented as being better, more attractive, more noble and civilised. Among other things, these stories assume the role of reinforcing the sense of belonging among the group of "us" in stark contrast to the foreign outsiders. These tales of "us" and "the others" are fundamentally legends that have accompanied and shaped humanity for centuries.

In a mood of enlightened optimism at the end of the 20th century there was, nevertheless, a general belief that we had finally risen above these irrational stereotypes once and for all. As has since been shown, however, it would appear not to be very difficult at all to revive these natural stories and to exploit them politically.

In order to underscore the inherent difference between Ukraine and Russia, the Ukrainian orthodoxy implemented a deliberate break from the Moscow Patriarchate and, thus, shattered the spiritual grip that the Kremlin had utilised so effectively in the past for their own political purposes.[6] In mid-December, 2018, a special "Council of Unification" in Kiev established a new Orthodox Church, which is independent of Moscow. The Synod's aim was to bring together the three existing, rival Orthodox Churches in Ukraine and to found an independent, autocephalous Orthodox Patriarchate in Kiev. This act was presented to the Ukrainian population as an act of spiritual liberation from Moscow, and it was supported by the Ecumenical Patriarch of Constantinople, Bartholomew I, who is recognised as *primus inter pares*, "First among Equals", by all Orthodox Church leaders across the world. In contrast, the Patriarch of Moscow, Kirill I, deemed this declaration of independence as a schism, and broke off all contact to Bartholomew I. On both the Russian and on the Ukrainian sides, politics was heavily involved in the course of these events. While Russian politics roundly condemned the secession, the Ukrainian President, Petro Poroshenko, and the Ukrainian Parliament actively promoted the establishment of this new Church.

Similarly, in Poland, it is not unusual to identify various events and catastrophes being exploited to denote a very clear demarcation from Russia. Among the horror stories circulating about strange and foreign others, accounts surrounding the crash of the Polish Air Force government aircraft at Smolensk in mid-April 2010 truly belong among the ranks of stories that would be considered barely plausible other than within the national-conservative circles of Poland.[7] Notwithstanding careful and thorough investigations on the part of both Russia and Poland, stubborn rumours persist that the accident could well have actually involved a Russian assassination of President Kaczyński. Speculation was rife that the Russians had tampered in some way or other with the navigation system, or that the plane crash had somehow been caused by laser beams or an electromagnetic pulse. Among supporters of the Polish political party "Law and

---

6 Cf. Osteuropa 68 8–9 (2018); Religion & Gesellschaft in Ost und West 46 (11/2018).

7 Cf. Deutsches Polen-Institut Darmstadt (ed.), Jahrbuch Polen 2018 29: Mythen, Wiesbaden: Harrassowitz 2018, 16–19.

Justice" (PiS) and their affiliated circles, a firm belief persists to the present day that the plane was deliberately destroyed. Other attack theories freely exploit the plane crash for domestic political gains, claiming that the liberal opposition is undoubtedly responsible for the accident.

This story also reflects how difficult it can be to dispel tales of conspiracy and other various accusations. People want to believe in them because they possess a certain discharge function and they create a context of justification that is both emotionally believable and compatible with their expectations. It would seem to be part of modern people's nature to be constantly searching for causes for and reasons behind any and every event. Gross negligence, an exaggerated opinion of oneself or a predilection for risk-taking no longer seem to be enough for modern individuals. They far prefer to explore deeper and more obvious explanations. Political tensions, such as the antagonistic feelings of hostility between Poland and Russia, mean that any explanation of a genuine accident would come across as too simplistic and too mundane; such an account simply does not gratify the modern thirst for conspiracy. It becomes entirely reasonable to attribute any evil event to "the Russians", and so why not specifically blame them for the crash of an aircraft in which the bearer of Poland's national hopes and aspirations – their President Lech Kaczyński – tragically perished? Furthermore, this version of the story perfectly matches the guiding myth encompassing so much of Polish history, of being the Christ of nations and, thus, always to be the victim.

Because myths essentially deal with emotionally authenticated "messages of truth", it is extremely difficult to put a stop to them by means of rational arguments. Ultimately, protracted enlightened psycho-education is needed if these highly charged emotional tales are to be banished from people's minds in order to assert rational arguments as action-guiding criteria in their place.

Time and again, phenomena such as these asserting the need for mental separation are also used to justify the existence of borders. This is particularly the case when the feeling of an impending economic or political crisis determines how people think. In these situations, there is a clear and present desire to close ranks and to mark out a clear difference to the "others" in the belief that they have the potential to represent a danger to "us". The previously intended creation, even though mutually perceived as having open borders, suddenly loses all sense of value, collapses and gives way to a return to "one's own". In order to defend this new entity, people revert to and rely on traditional borders and effective border protection, even if this means resorting to military defence.

It is possibly difficult to find a better example than the plane crash at Smolensk to raise the question why such absurd and delusional constructs can resonate so effectively within the political field. We frequently experience remarkably robust communities of political belief based on irrationality, whose proclamations – regardless of their empirical dubiousness – have absolutely no impact on the shared commitment to that which is fictional. In fact, their pronouncements are actually far more likely to strengthen the sense of cohesion among the social group of "true believers". Anthropologists and religious scholars offer an answer to this mystery regarding the manifest success of these empirically incorrect and intrinsically implausible events. They argue that people have always benefitted from shared fictions; in the history of mankind, belief in the unbelievable has created powerful communities. Commitment to that which is fundamentally a fiction requires considerable effort, especially when so-called unbelievers vehemently contradict what is openly stated. As a consequence, it is not easy to remain undaunted and continue preaching the absurd message in the face of disagreement and contradiction. If believers remain committed to their message regardless, this sends out a strong signal to their fellow believers – irrespective of the scorn and derision being poured upon them, that they need to hold fast to their belief and, thus, demonstrate their reliability and trustworthiness. As proof of their loyalty, they offer up the sacrifice of their reason.

As the anthropologist Richard Sosis demonstrated, the costlier this dedication proves to be, as the belief demands steadily greater paradoxes from its believers, then it will simply prove itself to be all the stronger.[8] In this sense, strong, challenging communities of faith are said to be particularly successful and long-lived. At the same time, it is relatively unimportant what form of impositions are required from the people. What is important is that the believers openly and publicly show how far they are prepared to go for the sake and benefit of their community. The demonstration of costly dedication creates a strong sense of cohesion. It enables strangers from the same mythical community to be able to meet one another with trust and confidence. In addition, it keeps freeloaders and copycats at bay, those who are not really genuinely serious and are quick to bail in critical and exceptional circumstances. In circumstances such as those described here, committed, dedicated groups, with the fiction shared among them, can become a historical authority and power, as demonstrated by the so-called world religions.

Especially among radical groups – political sects – the transfer of these insights into the political field appears to be readily feasible and straightforward. Their preparedness to maintain a stance in the face of all logical evidence represents a tamper-proof signal of dedication. Bizarre stories simply attract increasing attention among followers and are easily spread like wildfire. Amazement at the unbelievable leads to an emotionally-based memory and is more easily remembered in perpetuity. All the same, one key requirement is that the story must still remain consistent and within the bounds of possibility.

Neurobiologists, anthropologists and religious scholars have also presented research results on this theme.[9] According to them, "successful" religions are based on a very few ontological categories and a highly-restricted catalogue of supernatural patterns.[10] Thus, the category "person" can be represented with the following non-intuitive models: a specific physical characteristic (gods), special biological characteristics (gods do not die), and other special characteristics (the

8 Cf. Richard Sosis / Candace Alcorta, Signaling, Solidarity, and the Sacred: The Evolution of Religious Behavior, in: Evolutionary Anthropology 12 (2003), 264–274; Richard Sosis / Eric Bressler, Cooperation and commune longevity: A test of the costly signaling theory of religion, in: Cross-Cultural Research 37 (2003), 211–239.

9 Cf. Pascal Boyer, Religion explained: The evolutionary origins of religious thought, New York 2001.

10 See against this Andrew Shtulman, Variation in the Anthropomorphization of Supernatural Beings and Its Implications for Cognitive Theories of Religion, in: Journal of Experimental Psychology 34 (2008), 1123–1138.

ability to hear, see, and know everything). Animals and objects, e.g. bleeding statues, can also have such patterns attributed to them.

Studies have shown that listeners remember stories that transcend customary ontology due to their surprising nature.[11] For instance, the story of Mary provides the best possible combination of cognitive markers – a woman bore a child without any prior sexual experience. Such a striking, yet simple form of ontological transgression explains our readiness to pray to her. Multiple breaches of the laws of physics would overstep the mark and place the doctrine beyond the bounds of credulity.

The teachings of institutionalized religion, such as those regarding God, tend to diverge from popular conceptions. A study by Justin Barret found that, when questioned, people provided a response, which, although conforming to mainstream religious teaching that God was able to do many things simultaneously, contradicted their own personal expectations. When recounting two episodes in which God had provided assistance, they provided the episode with a diachronic structure – God performed the first act before attending to the second.[12] Their non-dogmatic version of events streamed God into a very human pattern, making him conform to their intuitive expectations. "When the task allows for conscious monitoring, we get the theological version; when the task requires fast access, we get the anthropomorphic version."[13]

Empirical documents and indicators aiming to debunk counter-intuitive events and occurrences are dismissed – in both religion and in politics – as illusion or deception. It is inspiring, liberating even, no longer to have to adhere to what are often complex facts, putting forward instead simplistic explanations that, moreover, can be found in a sub-culture of their own on the downhill slope of a preferred concoction of prejudices. This is the case with the Smolensk plane crash just as much as with the myth of the "Holy Rus". In this case – contrary to all facts and clear evidence – there is a desire to highlight yet again the concept of the enemy in the form of the evil Russian spectre by means of an accident that was most likely caused by simple negligence. Even though the occurrence is ultimately unsuitable for this treatment, it is easily re-interpreted in a counter-intuitive manner, finding countless supporters along the way.

In the second case, a sense of fellowship and community between two countries is conceived that runs counter to the interests of the smaller country – namely Ukraine – simply because it no longer wants to be dominated by the stronger country – Russia. In order to emphasise the divergence of the two countries and to sanction the separation from Moscow, the Ukrainian bishop, Epiphanius, was elected "Metropolitan of Kiev and All Ukraine", even though there are no inherent religious differences between Moscow and Kiev. The dissociation of Ukraine from the Russian Orthodox Church after 300 years of Moscow church sovereignty followed the theologically somewhat questionable logic that church

11 See Pascal Boyer, Religion Explained, Loc. Cit. (Note 9), 80 f.

12 See Justin L. Barret, Exploring the Natural Foundations of Religion, in: Trends in Cognitive Science 4 (2000), 29–34. See also idem, Born Believers: The Science of Children's Religious Belief, New York 2012.

13 Boyer, Religion Explained, Loc. Cit. (Note 9), 89.

borders should be oriented in line with national borders. These measures count on the assumption that counterfactual aspects will gradually become reality over time in the consciousness of the people and, thus, supersede the former reality. This involves an act of liberation from enforced adaptation to restricting and correcting facts. If these are challenged, new freedoms open up for particular groups in the never-ending universe of ideological delusion.

The approval and acceptance of the extent of madness shared within the group serves as an indicator for what can be expressed within a movement. Frequently, dedicated groups will initially attempt to pursue their goals through small deviations from established facts, only to steadily increase their misinformation to the point of breathtaking absurdity.[14] Every phony or sham that is successfully launched becomes an open invitation to the next fake to surpass the previous deceit. With every escalation to new levels of counterfactual reality, together with its authentication by the social group, a return to reality becomes increasingly difficult.

With respect to the question of whether neighbours feel pulled further apart or drawn closer together, this means that there is virtually no common factual basis for such perceptions; at the most, there are "matters of belief" to which one can choose to adhere, or maybe not to observe. Nonetheless, the respective emotions and cognition are not left up to the individual. On the contrary, the relevant thought leaders seek to influence the general public to follow a direction that is opportune first and foremost for those very thought leaders. In 1951, Hannah Arendt wrote that the leaders of the masses' contempt for facts is freely expressed through the conviction "that facts are only dependent on those who have the power to entrench them."[15] The techniques involved in mass propaganda have most certainly been honed and refined over the past 70 years and have also become more comprehensive and omnipresent. This changes nothing from Hannah Arendt's fundamental belief that by acknowledging and accepting absurd fakes, people are effectively also seeking to escape the realities of fate and chance that are inherent in all reality.[16] Among large parts of the Polish population it is believed that it couldn't have been an unhappy coincidence – in fact, it most certainly was an unfortunate coincidence – that, of all places, the President of Poland and leading members of his government met their demise in Russia.

Abstract

Which factors trigger a feeling of togetherness and which one of separateness? Phrases like "So close and yet so far" and "So far and yet so close" can have a similar impact – dependent on our perceptions of communality. This cognition of similarities is mostly based on lifestyles, professions and a sense of mutual understanding. Factors need not be realistic but are perceived as genuine. If the reason why your counterpart seems like-

14 Cf. Neil Garret / Stephanie C. Lazzaro / Dan Ariely / Tali Sharot, The brain adapts to dishonesty, in: Nature Neuroscience 19 (2016), 1727–1732.

15 Hannah Arendt, Elemente und Ursprünge totaler Herrschaft. Antisemitismus, Imperialismus, Totalitarismus, München-Zürich 2003, 742.

16 Ibid., 745.

able is unclear, you will be keen to look for reasonable justification of your opinion, thus fostering your sympathy. In such cases, you will be able to ignore or bridge obvious objections and gaps between your mental state and theirs. Remember, for instance, the baffling friendship between the former German Chancellor, Gerhard Schröder, and the Russian President, Vladimir Putin. Furthermore: Felt closeness, as well as strangeness, can be both attractive and repellent. Your mood can easily change from the one to the other. In this respect, propaganda and selective disinformation, which denies or disputes fundamental facts, likewise play a central role like people's constant willingness to believe in the most absurd of constructs. So what? I am going to analyse some of the arguments in the field of social sciences in favour of a good and friendly neighbourhood or, alternately, an adverse demarcation and will base my analysis on the examples of Polish-Russian and Ukrainian-Russian cross border co-operation.

Euroregion, governance, community

Analysis of functional interdependence on the example of the Euroregion Spree-Neisse-Bober

Joanna Frątczak-Müller and Anna Mielczarek-Żejmo

Governance is understood as the interaction of people and institutions, on the basis of the relevant standards, to promote political or economic unit and the achievement of its objectives. In the European Union it takes the form of a multi level governance based on a partnership of public authority with the social subjects, representing the interests of citizens (such as non-governmental organizations, professional or economic associations, business and media). Public governance (instead of government) is a reaction to increasing problems with a quick and adequate response to social changes which results from the overload of modern institutions and a progressive procedural delegitimation and a hierarchical way of coordinating collective activities.[1] In the social reality getting so complex it is seen as an appropriate way of dealing with (1) increasing interdependence of issues and institutions in the public sphere, (2) fragmentation of public management mechanisms, (3) a progressive specialization in the area of public affairs, and (4) a deficit of trust to authorities along with increasing citizens' expectations towards them.[2] From this perspective, the regional issues indicate the growing importance of euroregions for meeting the needs of citizens and solve social problems.

The aim of the article is to analyze how the rules of euroregional institutions' co-governance are implemented. The subject of the presented study is the effective aspect of the European regions' functioning in terms of management. It is particularly important here to search for symptoms of their functional interdependencies with the supported communities. The subject of the presented analyses is the activity of the Euroregion Spree-Neisse-Bober (Euroregion, SNBE). We are looking for answers to three basic questions directly connected with the de-

---

1 Stanisław Mazur, Współzarządzanie a administracja publiczna [Governance and public administration], in: Stanisław Mazur (ed.), Współzarządzanie publiczne [Public governance], Warszawa 2015, 17–37.

2 A. Georges L. Romme / Jan Broekgaarden / Carien Huijzer /Annewiek Reijmer / Rob van der Eyden, From Competition and Collusion to Consent-Based Collaboration: A Case Study of Local Democracy, International Journal of Public Administration 41 3 (2018), 246–255, https://doi.org/10.1080/01900692.2016.1263206, [Accessed: 03.06.2018]. Claus Offe, Governance: An "Empty Signifier"? Constellations, 16 (2009), 550–562.

fined objectives of the carried analyses. They relate to (1) spheres of functioning of local communities which are the subject of the Euroregional activities (support), (2) the territorial coverage of these activities, and (3) the role played by the representatives of the different sectors in setting objectives and determining the conditions for cross-border cooperation within SNBE.

The conducted analyses refer to three explanatory perspectives: concerning regionalization and soft spaces, theory of governance and the concept of multi level governance. In the literature, regions are referred as territories determined by familiarity and regional identity or as a construct formulated by elite.[3] They make changes in the cultural sphere by removing social barriers and initiating cross-border contacts with representatives of all their parts, leading to an increase in trust between neighbors and to implementation of common interests.[4] They are established in order to create a community based on a bond, which would meet the needs of their participants and inhabitants of the borderland.[5] Despite efforts to increase social cohesion and initiate changes in the sphere of culture, in Poland they are identified rather as structural funds management entities. In the public governance model, emphasis is put on the central importance of interactions between the actors of different status. It should apply to the process of consulting, reconciliation and making decisions on common matters.[6] The approach, specific to public governance, requires the central entities' need for the use of multi-level governance, with its manifestations at least in three basic dimensions: (1) the involvement of entities of different statuses, purposes and functions, formally autonomic, but operationally interdependent, (2) the use of different mechanisms for decision reconciliation and implementation instruments (negotiations, deliberations, tenders, agreement, rarely unanimity), (3) the capacity to integrate the resources of the participants, serving both the public objectives as well as the particular objectives of the participants in decision-making processes.[7] Euroregions are part of multi-level governance in the EU. Multi

3 Martin Klatt, Mobile Regions: Copetitive Regional Concepts (not only) in the Danish-German Border Region, in: Dorte Jagetic Andersen / Martin Klatt / Marie Sandberg (eds.), The Border Multiple: The Practicing of Borders between Public Policy and Everyday Life in a Rescaling Europe, Ashgate 2012.

4 Joanna Frątczak-Müller / Anna Mielczarek-Żejmo, Cross-border partnerships – the impact of institutions on creating the borderland communities (the case of Spree-Neisse-Bober Euroregion), Innovation, The European Journal of Social Science Research 29 1 (2016), 77–97.

5 Phil Allmendinger / Graham Haughton / Jőrg Knieling / Frank Othengrafen (eds.), Soft Spaces in Europe: Re-negotiating Governance, Boundaries and Borders, London – New York 2015; Anssi Passi, The institutionalization of regions: A theoretical framework for understanding the emergence of regions and the constitution of regional identity, Fennia – International Journal of Geography 164 (1886), 105–146.

6 Stanisław Mazur, Ewolucja sfery publicznej i mechanizmów zarządzania publicznego w kontekście wytwarzania "wiedzy uwspólnionej" [The Evolution of the Public Sphere and Public Management Mechanisms in the Context of the Creation of "Shared Knowledge"], Rocznik Lubuski [Lubuski Yearbook] 34 2 (2017), 9–24.

7 Gary Marks, Structural policy and Multi-level governance in the EC, in: Alan Cafruny/Glenda Rosenthal (eds.), The State of the European Community: The Maastricht Debate and Beyond, New York 1993, 391–410; Simona Piattoni, Multi-level Governance: a Historical and Conceptual Analysis, European Integration 31 2 (2009), 163–180. Arjan Schakel / Liesbet Hooghe / Gary Marks, Multilevel Governance and the State, in: Stephan Leibfried / Evelyne Huber / Matthew Lange / Johan Levy / Frank Nullmeier / John Stephens (eds.), Oxford Handbook

level governance is seen as a challenge to reformulate the operation of national structures to ensure representation and political coordination as it overcomes the horizontal divisions and conflicts between regional political or administrative bodies or within them for involving partners from all sectors, as well as reduces the distance and lack of trust in the vertical relationships between the two levels of governance: national and supranational.[8] Their primary importance is the ability to enable non-public entities operating in their environment, in public projects and the potential to network control of social and economic systems, in a way that is beneficial to the public.[9]

Based on the presented theoretical considerations, we formulate the idea of functional interdependencies barriers between the activities of Euroregions and their local communities. This article presents the analyses of the three dimensions of this interdependence: subjective (issue of actions taken), territorial (distribution of partnerships and a range of functional interdependence), structural (representatives of each sector in the activities of the Euroregion).

The aim's implementation begins with the presentation of the empirical sources of the carried analyses. Then Polish-German borderland and determinants of the development of cross-border cooperation are characterized and the analysis of phenomena occurring in three, key for this article, dimensions (subjective, territorial and structural) of functional interdependence at the SNBE is presented.

Sourcing Foundation of the Analysis

The presented analysis base on results of research conducted in SNBE in 2013–2017 with the application of three methods: content analysis, survey and unstructured interviews.[10] The content analysis covered the official SNBE web pages (Polish and German) and the documents connected with the number and kind of projects being implemented. As a result, we obtained the information referring to the origins of SNBE, the process of its development, quantitative and qualitative data of the created partnerships and implemented projects and the resources employed, the documents essential for the cross-border cooperation and the functioning of the institution being analyzed.

The survey research was conducted with the application of structured questionnaires. The quota sample was constructed on the basis of the demographic

on the Transformation of the State, 2015, http://garymarks.web.unc.edu/files/2016/12/2014-schakel-marks-hooghe-Multilevel_Governance_and_the_State.pdf [Accessed: 30.09.2018].

8 Janusz Ruszkowski, Struktura wielopoziomowego zarządzania w Unii Europejskiej [The Structure of Multi-level Governance in the European Union], in: Janusz Ruszkowski / Luiza Wojnicz (eds.), Multi-level Governance w Unii Europejskiej [Multi-level Governance in European Union], Wrocław 2013, 19–60.

9 See Mazur, Współzarządzanie, Loc. Cit. (Note 1), 17–37.

10 The analysis presented here is the result of the research project "Trust beyond Borders. Spree-Neisse-Bober Euroregion in Perspective of Integrating Processes in Polish-German Borderland" implemented in 2013 by researchers from the Institute of Sociology at the University of Zielona Góra and the Brandenburg University of Technology. This work was supported by the European Regional Development Fund as part of the Cross-border Cooperation Operational Programme – Poland (Lubuskie) – Brandenburg 2007–2013 under Grant 516/FMP/12.

structure data referring to the inhabitants of SNBE in 2010 published by the Central Statistical Office (Główny Urząd Statystyczny) and Statistisches Bundesamt. The age range, gender and the place of residence were controlled. 600 inhabitants of the Polish part of SNBE and 200 inhabitants of the German part took part in the survey. The opinions of the cross-border cooperation leaders were obtained by means of the unstructured interviews with the persons having the most impressive output in terms of the issues on which the current paper focuses. In total there were 70 interviews conducted, 50 with the Polish and 20 with the German leaders of the cross-border cooperation.

Due to the volume of transcription of the statements made by the leaders of the cross-border cooperation we aborted their citation, but in the appropriate places in the analysis, we make references to the unstructured interviews. The audio recording and the interview transcripts are stored in the Faculty of Education, Psychology, and Sociology of the University of Zielona Góra. In the current text, the interviews which include the premises for the conclusions being drawn have been tagged (De – interviews with the German leaders, Pl – interviews with the Polish leaders).

The research uses also data from the analysis carried out in 2017 contenting content analysis covering the documents connected with the number and kind of euroregional projects being implemented (reports on the implementation of euroregional tasks for the period 2007–2013, analyzes commissioned to external companies) and the official web pages of the Euroregion.

Circumstances of Cross-border Cooperation in Polish-German Borderland

The characteristic features of the Polish-German borderland as the new reality constitute significant conditionality of the cooperation forms within SNBE and the relationships among the inhabitants. The changes taking place in the Polish-German borderland were shaped by the significant historical events of the international and even global importance. The most important were:

- The end of the Second World War and establishing the border on the Oder-Neisse line. The border delineated in 1945 was impermeable until 1972.[11] In the post-war period, the German population was almost totally displaced from the part of the Polish borderland and replaced by the new residents[12] re-

11 Bogdan Koszel, Die Außenpolitik der Volksrepublik Polen gegenüber der Bundesrepublik Deutschland 1949–1989, in: Jan-Pieter Barbian / Marek Zybura (eds.), Erlebte Nachbarschaften. Aspekte der deutsch-polnischen Beziehungen im 20. Jahrhundert, Wiesbaden 1999, 57–75.

12 Jacek Kurzępa, Otwarcie granicy a nielegalna działalność gospodarcza (Polska – Niemcy 1988–1998) [Opening of the Border and Illegal Business Activity (Poland – Germany 1988–1998)], in: Leszek Gołdyka (ed.), Transgraniczność w perspektywie socjologicznej. Kontynuacje [Cross-border in the Sociological Perspective. Continuations], Zielona Góra 1999, 255–270; Dorota Bazuń, Kształtowanie przestrzeni społecznej przez mieszkańców pogranicza zachodniego Polski. Wybrane zagadnienia [Shaping the Social Space by the Inhabitants of the Borderland of Western Poland. Selected Issues], in: Żywia Leszkowicz-Baczyńska (ed.), Transgraniczność w perspektywie socjologicznej. Nowe pogranicza? [Cross-border in the sociological perspective. New borderlands?], Zielona Góra 2006, 221–235.

settled from the different part of pre-war Poland.[13] The characteristic feature of the ethnic differentiation in the borderland was the lack of roots and the uncertainty of life in the recently repopulated area.[14]

- Opening the border in January 1972. The abolition of the visa and passport requirements caused the massive increase in contacts between the institutions and between the citizens. At the beginning of the 1970s, several million were crossing the border on the yearly average.[15] The convenient changes in the custom and foreign currency regulations contributed towards the development of the trade between the border situated companies.
- Poland taking a decision to suspend the visa-free tourism due to the political and economic changes in the second half of the eighties. Nevertheless, the process of opening the border in the political, social and cultural aspects, not without any impediments, was being continued. The diplomatic measures taken on both sides contributed towards the resumption of certain forms of cooperation what favored the already initiated mutual rapprochement of Poles and Germans living on the border.[16]
- The break-through of 1989. At that time the borders became the space where the new possibilities of cross-border mobility and cooperation emerged intensifying the appearance of spontaneous processes of territorial re-structurization in Europe.[17] The change in the Polish-German relations was enabled by the 1990 German-Polish Border Treaty[18] and the 1991 Treaty of Good Neighbourship and Friendly Cooperation.[19] The intensity of the changes was reinforced by the

---

13 Włodzimierz Borodziej / Stanisław Ciesielski / Jerzy Kochanowski, Wstęp [Introduction], in: Stanisław Ciesielski (ed.), Przesiedlenie ludności polskiej z kresów wschodnich do Polski 1944–1947 [Resettlement of the Polish population from the eastern borderlands to Poland in 1944–1947], Warszawa 1999, 5–51; Czesław Osękowski, Ziemie Odzyskane w latach 1945–2005. Społeczeństwo, władza, gospodarka [Recovered Territories in 1945–2005. Society, Power, Economy], Zielona Góra 2006.

14 Czesław Osękowski, Pionierzy w mundurach na Ziemi Lubuskiej [Pioneers in Uniforms on the Lubusz Land], Zielona Góra 1985; See Osękowski, Ziemie Odzyskane, Loc. Cit. (Note 16).

15 Stanisław Ciok, Pogranicze polsko-niemieckie: problemy współpracy transgranicznej [The Polish-German Borderland: Problems of Cross-border Cooperation], Wrocław 2004.

16 Józef Fiszer, Stosunki polsko-niemieckie w latach 1970–1989 – uwarunkowania i bilans [Polish-German Relations in the Years 1970–1989 – Conditions and Balance], in: Jerzy Holzer/ Józef Fiszer (eds.), Stosunki polsko-niemieckie w latach 1970–1995. Próba bilansu i perspektywy rozwoju [Polish-German relations in the years 1970–1995. An attempt to balance and development prospects], Warszawa 1998, 11–29; Czesław Osękowski / Hieronim Szczegóła, Pogranicze polsko-niemieckie w okresie transformacji (1989–1997) [The Polish-German Borderland during the Transformation (1989–1997)], Zielona Góra 1999.

17 Arnaud Lechevalier / Jan Wielgohs (ed.), Borders and Border Regions in Europe. Changes, Challenges and Chances [online]. Bielefeld 2013, http://www.transcript-verlag.de/ts2442/ts2442_1.pdf [Accessed: 03.07.2014].

18 Treaty between the Federal Republic of Germany and the Republic of Poland on the confirmation of the frontier between them, 14 November 1990. The source: isap.sejm.gov.pl/Down load?id=WDU19920140054&type=2 [Accessed: 30.07.2015].

19 The Polish-German Treaty of Good Neighbourship and Friendly Cooperation was signed between the Federal Republic of Germany and the Republic of Poland on 17 June 1991. It supplemented the German-Polish Border Treaty signed in 1990. In the treaty both countries agreed to respect the rights of national minorities living on the other side of the border, and to promote cultural contacts, particularly among young people. The source: http://www.traktaty.msz.gov.pl/fd.aspx?f=P0000006258.pdf [Accessed: 30.07.2015].

system transformations in Poland and Germany (the transition from socialist to the democratic system in Poland and the unification of Germany). The abolition of visa requirement resulted in the unprecedented intensity border traffic between Poland and Germany in the 1990s. Additionally the participation of Poland in the Phare CBC[20] programme accelerated the establishment of favorable conditions for the development of Polish-German cooperation.

- Poland accession to the European Union in May 2004 and the Schengen Treaty in 2007. The process of opening the border finished in 2007 with the Schengen Treaty. The increase of the border traffic and of the number of Polish-German connections served the exchange of material goods (markets on the Polish side, short supply goods on the German side) as well as the exchange of the non-materialistic assets (values, patterns).[21]

The economic development of the borderland towns initiated in the nineties of the previous century was observable due to the (1) development of the small trade (the German customers were interested in shopping in the border markets) and (2) the attractiveness of the borderland premises for the foreign investors which was connected with the relatively short distance from Berlin, one of the main European capitals, the availability of cheap labour force and the possibility of suitable fiscal and administrative conditions for business operation.[22] In spite of it, the relations between the inhabitants of the borderland were formed by the economic, political, social and cultural differences.[23] They included the difference of the size of the national budgets as well as the difference between the average household budgets, the different rules of local economy transformation and the specificity of understanding the national border and its reception[24] in the awareness of the inhabitants, the differences of pro-active attitudes in the labour market on both sides of the border, the low confidence in social relations within the Euroregion, the lack of long-term experience in the local self-governance, the economic disparities within the Euroregion, as well as between the region and

20 The programme of Cross-border Cooperation introduced by the European Parliament in 1994 in order to support the cooperation between the Eastern and Middle European countries and their EU neighbors (Sylwia Dołzbłasz / Andrzej Raczyk, Współpraca transgraniczna w Polsce po akcesji do UE, Kraków 2010.).

21 Leszek Gołdyka, Miasto pogranicza polsko-niemieckiego jako środowisko wychowawcze [A City of the Polish-German Borderland as an Educational Environment], in: Leszek Gołdyka / Jerzy Leszkowicz-Baczyński / Lech Szczegóła / Maria Zielińska (eds.), Transgraniczność w perspektywie socjologicznej [Cross-border in the sociological perspective], Zielona Góra 1999, 153–163.

22 Zbigniew Kurcz, Pogranicze polsko-niemieckie a "polnische Wirtschaft" [Polish-German Borderland and "Polnische Wirtschaft"], in: Leszek Gołdyka (ed.), Transgraniczność w perspektywie socjologicznej. Kontynuacje [Cross-border in the sociological perspective. Continuations], Zielona Góra 1999, 219–233.

23 Leszek Gołdyka, Pogranicze polsko-niemieckie jako przestrzeń socjalizacji [The Polish-German borderland as a space for socialization], Warszawa 2013.

24 For the Germans the border with a less-off neighbour was a source of problems, for Poles it was a chance to improve the economic standards of living in micro and mezzo scale from the very beginning (Jarosław Jańczak / Magdalena Musiał-Krąg (eds.), Pogranicze polsko-niemieckie po 2004 roku. Nowa jakość sąsiedztwa? Toruń 2009).

other EU countries.[25] For example, in 2003 the value of GDI per capita in the Polish part of the SNBE came to 23,1 % of the GDI per capita in the German part (SNBE Action and Development Plan). The recognition of the asymmetry in the level of economic development[26] was one of the reasons of looking for the innovative methods of economic resourcefulness by the Poles, including the density of pathological phenomena (thefts, smuggling, prostitution).[27]

The above-mentioned conditions had an impact on the functioning of the Euroregions emerging on the Polish-German borderland in the nineties. The creation of the Euroregions was possible due to the system changes in Poland especially the institutionalization of the self-governance idea. SBNE which is the issue being discussed here is one of the oldest in Poland.[28] It was created in 1993. There are three premises for the choice of the Euroregion as a case for the current analyses. The first of them refers to its origins. Its creation had a bottom-up character. As one the few it was initiated by the local political elites.[29] The second is connected with the experience of implementing the EU cohesion policy. In

---

25 Marianna Greta / Robert Stanisławski, The significance of euroregions in the process of achieving social and economic cohesion in the European Union, in: Robert Stanisławski / Marianna Greta / Aleksandra Maciaszczyk (eds.), Structural funds for the socio-economic development of the Lodz Region in the perspective of experiences of polish regions, Łódź 2008, 213–225.

26 See Gołdyka, Miasto pogranicza polsko-niemieckiego, Loc. Cit. (Note 24), 153–163; See Kurcz, Pogranicze polsko-niemieckie a "polnische Wirtschaft", Loc. Cit. (Note 25), 219–233; See Michelle Brym, The Integration of European Union Borderlands: A Case Study of Polish Opinions on Cross-Border, in: Cooperation along the Polish-German Border, The University of the Fraser Valley Research Review 3 3 [online] (2011), 15–33, http://journals.ufv.ca/rr/RR33/article-PDFs/2-brym.pdf [Accessed: 07.04.2015].

27 Zbigniew Kurcz, Procesy integracji i dezintegracji społecznej w miastach pogranicza [Processes of Social Integration and Disintegration in Borderland Cities], in: Zbigniew Kurcz (ed.), Problemy społeczno-gospodarcze miast pogranicza polsko-niemieckiego [Social and Economic Problems of Cities in the Polish-German Borderland], Wrocław 1992, 59–89; Władysław Misiak, Dirty togetherness: phenomena of social pathology in borderland areas at Polish-German and Polish-Czech frontiers, Warsaw 1999; Jacek Kurzępa, Młodzież pogranicza – "Juma" [Borderland Youth – "Juma"], Zielona Góra 1998; Jacek Kurzępa, Młodzież pogranicza – "Świnki", czyli o prostytucji nieletnich [Youth of the borderland – "Świnki", the Mrostitution of Minors], Kraków 2001.

28 SNBE is situated in the central part of the Polish-German borderland. It comprises The Association of the Communes of the Republic of Poland of the Euroregion "Sprewa-Nysa-Bóbr" and the Association Spree-Neiβe-Bober. The Polish part of the Euroregion – the southern part of the province is twice the size. It occupies an area of 8,709 km^2 with 654,352 inhabitants. It includes 55 communes (gmina) and 7 counties (powiat) as ordinary members and provincial governor (Wojewoda Lubuski) as a supporting member. The German part – the southern part of Brandenburg and the northern part of Saxony has 27 members (communes, social organizations, educational institutions, economic institutions, associations, and individuals). It occupies 1,812 km^2 and has 229,221 inhabitants. The source: http://euroregion-snb.pl/o_nas/wladze [Accessed: 01.08.2017].

29 The Euroregions in Poland were initiated from the bottom up by the political elites or top-down by the national authorities (Marek Sobczyński, Percepcja współpracy transgranicznej Polski z sąsiadami pośród mieszkańców pograniczy [Perception of Poland's Cross-border Cooperation with its Neighbors among Borderland Residents], in: Marian Malikowski / Dariusz Wojakowski (eds.), Granice i pogranicza nowej Unii Europejskiej. Z badań regionalnych, etnicznych i lokalnych [Borders and Borderlines of the New European Union. From Regional, Ethnic and Local Research], Kraków 2005.

the pre-accession period, SNBE was characterized by high efficiency in absorbing the European resources targeted at the candidate countries.[30] The third is linked with the activities of the Euroregion's representatives in disseminating the idea of cross-border cooperation. The leading role of the Euroregion in Poland is displayed in integrating and educating the environment and in this respect the SNBE representatives were members of The Polish Borderland Regions Forum, Association of European Border Regions, Cross-Border Cooperation Committee.

Dimensions of the functional interdependence in SNBE

Euroregions were formed as a response to the challenges of European integration. Those challenges included satisfying needs and resolving problems of neighboring local communities on Member States borderlands. Currently they are part of a multi level governance in the EU. The activities undertaken by the administration of Euroregions are primarily the management and disposal of the Small Projects Fund (SPF). The implementation of the MLG idea by European regions depends not only on the efficiency of the European funds disposal, but mostly on achieving the intended results of their implementation. SPF measures are primarily spent on the implementation of the so-called meeting projects. Their expected effect is a promotion of the relationship between the Euroregions' inhabitants – individuals, but also representatives of institutions and organizations. However, close-up of the latter should result in the spread of the cooperation in various aspects of life in the local borderland communities – the formation and development of functional interdependence which would fulfill the needs and solve problems specific to such areas i. e. transportation, labor market and economy. This was included in the aims of the SNBE activities contained in the Euroregion establishing documents.

The activity of the Euroregion, specified in the founding documents, is focused on the pursuit to prosperity of the borderland, and refers to such spheres of functioning of local communities as:

- spatial management,
- environmental protection,
- economy and aligning the living standards of the inhabitants,
- cross-border infrastructure,
- prevention and fight against effects of natural disasters,
- cross-border traffic and tourist traffic,
- culture and cultural heritage protection,
- education of children and youth,
- civil contacts,
- cross-border cooperation.[31]

The Euroregional involvement spheres shown above cover a significant part of the local community life of the German-Polish border. They refer to the key as-

30 Sylwia Dołzbłasz /Andrzej Raczyk, Współpraca transgraniczna w Polsce po akcesji do UE [Cross-border Cooperation in Poland after Accession to the EU], Kraków 2010.

31 The contract for the formation of the Euroregion Spree-Neisse-Bober, section 1 § 1, http://pliki.euroregion-snb.pl/umowa_snb.pdf [Accessed: 3 October, 2018].

pects. From here we believe that the assumptions underlying the basis of SNBE focus on the support of regional development and should set their directions. They are the basis for the implementation of the MLG idea in the Euroregion and contribute to the formation and development of functional interdependence of borderland institutions or organizations. Below are the results of the search for a functional interdependence between the SNBE and borderland communities in three dimensions: subjective, territorial, and structural.

The subjective aspect concerns the issues dealt regarded by cross-border partnerships. It manifests in the projects' themes. In the years 2007–2013 in SNBE there were 421 cross-border partnerships that implemented 1,181 projects financed by SFP.[32] Figure 8.1 presents the contribution of individual aspects of the borderland local communities in the themes adopted for the implementation of cross-border projects. The spheres of involvement of the Euroregion we determined primarily on the basis of the themes of projects carried out by cross-border partnerships during the EU reference period 2007–2013. Nearly half (47 %) of the projects concerned culture and cultural heritage. Besides, the partnerships mostly ran the projects on sport (19 %) and directed to youth (11 %) or in the field of education (8 %) (chart).

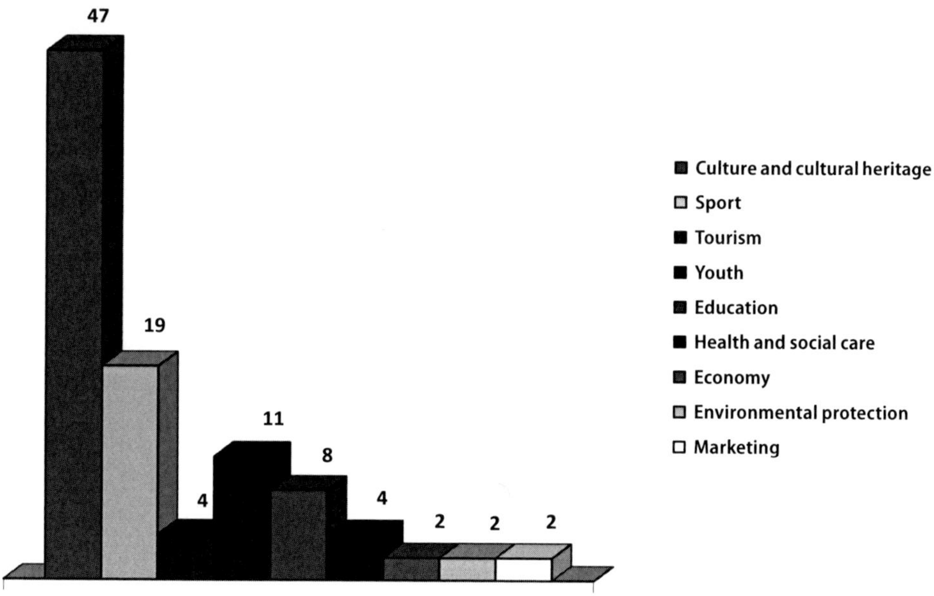

Figure 8.1: Thematic scope of SPF 2007–2013 in SNBE (%). Source: own elaboration based on Katja Sarmiento-Mirwald, Analysis of German-Polish partnerships [Analysis of Polish-German partnerships], http://euroregion-snb.pl/aktualnosci/1120/Analiza_polsko_niemieckich_partnerstw [Accessed: 03.08.2018].

32 Katja Sarmiento-Mirwald, Analiza polsko-niemieckich partnerstw [Analysis of Polish-German partnerships], http://euroregion-snb.pl/aktualnosci/1120/Analiza_polsko_niemieckich_partnerstw [Accessed: 03.08.2018].

Collected data indicate a concentration of activities of cross-border partnerships in certain thematic areas. These are the culture, sports and various activities directed mainly to young people, including educational projects. In other spheres of life of the local community, such as transport, labor market and spatial management, a lower level of activity of Euroregion participants can be noticed. What are the effects of actions taken? Between 2007–2013 the expected effects of the Euroregion activities included, inter alia, supporting the relationship between its inhabitants. Therefore, here are the results of search for signs of the impact of cooperation of Polish and German partners in two related areas. The first concerns the mutual attitudes, trust, and contacts between the Euroregion inhabitants, which are an important factor in the social relationships quality, the second concerns cooperation between institutions and organizations functioning in the Euroregion local communities.

A research we carried out in 2013–2014 indicates the domination of a positive attitude of the Euroregion residents to themselves, and a relatively high level of mutual trust. We also noted that both Poles and Germans find mutual contacts relatively highly important. However, the Polish responses on the question of personal attitude toward Germans differed from the response of the Germans on the same question. Respondents from Germany more often declared fondness of Poles (83.5 %) than the Poles of Germans (38.7 %). The dominant attitude of Poles towards Germans is indifference (52.7 %). It should be noted that the level of dislike towards neighbors from abroad was relatively low among all respondents (Poles 5.5 %, Germans 1.0 %). Declarations of respondents coming from the German part of ESNB on the attitude towards Poles were relatively homogeneous. They did not differentiate: belonging to different age categories, gender, place of residence. Responses of respondents from Poland stood out in this context. The liking for Germans was most often declared by people aged 40–49 (51.1 %).

The results regarding the trust of the SNBE inhabitants to each other are consistent with trends relating to the personal attitude towards Germans/Poles. The respondents living in the German part of Euroregion more often declared that they trust the neighbors from across the eastern border (81.5 %). The share of Germans declaring that they definitely trust Poles, was almost twice as high (31.5 %) as the share of Poles firmly trusting Germans (16.7 %). The percentage of people declaring distrust to Germans was more than four times higher than the percentage of people claiming that they do not trust Poles (total answers "probably not" and "definitely not"; Poles 25.8 %; Germans 5.8 %). The percentage of women declaring that one could trust Germans amounted to 78.7 % and was 10 % higher than the percentage of men who gave such an answer (69.7 %). Representatives of the oldest age category of Poles stood out in relation to other people. The oldest Polish respondents were the least likely to trust Germans (47.3 %). Most often such declarations were made by respondents aged 50–59 (72.3 %). Compared to the information about the trust of participants in the study against Germans and Poles, the answers to the question whether Germans generally trust Poles and whether Poles trust Germans appeared less frequently. Among the Poles participating in the research there were fewer people who expected that Germany trusted them than among German respondents expecting trust from Poles. In the Polish part of the ESNB, the majority were people who assumed that the Germans rather did not trust Poles (37.9 %), while in the German part the respondents most often believed that the Poles rather trusted them (54.0 %). The share of people who expected that the neighbors from abroad definitely trust them, was again more than twice higher among respondents from Germany (14.0 %) than among respondents with Polish (5.8 %). The percentage of Polish respondents who answered "definitely not" to the question whether Germans trust Poles was 12.0 %. The percentage of German respondents who gave the same answer to the same question was 1 %.

The last indicator discussed here concerns the direct contacts of the Euroregion inhabitants. The question of keeping any contacts with Germans/Poles, was more frequently answered "never" by the respondents from the Polish part of SNBE than the participants in the German part of the study (46.2 % and 34.5 %). The percentage of people that claimed to meet with neighbors from across the border about once a month or more often was almost twice as high among German than Polish respondents (36.0 % and 18.7 %). The majority of Poles and Germans participating in studies considered contacts with friends from behind the Lusatian Neisse as important. However, Germans more often than Poles declared that meeting with friends from a neighboring country are very important (41.7 % and 26.7 %). The number of Poles, who found contacts with friends from across the border rather unimportant, was four times higher than the number of Germans expressing the same opinion (16.8 % and 4.2 %).

The result described above regarding the inhabitants of the Polish part of SNBE differs significantly from the results of surveys carried out on a representative sample of adult Poles by the CBOS in 2014.[33] Although, the level of positive feelings towards Germans remained relatively similar (39 %), the more significant differences revealed in the responses declaring indifference and dislike. The national studies respondents declared indifference to Germans significantly less frequently (27 %) than the borderland respondents while the percentage of reluctant respondents was significantly higher (30 %). Bearing in mind the methodological differences of the studies, their results can be carefully explained by the borderland effect. This effect is seen in negative attitudes. In borderland they are given up in favor of indifference. It was accompanied by the process, characteristic of the post-Communist countries of Central and Eastern Europe, of gradual opening of Poles on foreigners after 1989.[34] Specifying a foreigner as a "stranger" is followed by a process of reducing the psychological distance to people of a different nationality. Consciousness of Poles tends to recognize different culturally foreigners rather as "others" than "strangers". This process is reinforced on the borderland by the relatively more frequent contacts with foreigners and ability to verify usually negative generalized knowledge about them (stereotypes). This results in the occurrence of not much more positive, but less negative, and specifically the domination of the indifferent attitudes towards neighbors from behind

---

33 Polish Attitude to other Nationalities, the report of the CBOS, http://www.cbos.pl/SPISKOM.POL/2014/K_020_14.PDF [Accessed: 22.02.2014].

34 Renata Siemieńska, Narody Wschodniej i Środkowej Europy o sobie i innych [The nations of Eastern and Central Europe about themselves and others], in: Aleksandra Jasińska-Kania (ed.), Trudne sąsiedztwa. Z socjologii konfliktów narodowościowych [Difficult neighborhoods. From the sociology of national conflicts], Warszawa 2001.

the Oder and Neisse River among the inhabitants of the Polish part of SNBE. This effect is considered positive and its occurrence, according to the statements of the cross-border cooperation leaders, who took part in our research, to some extend is found to be the impact of Euroregion.[35]

Another effects of promoting the relations between the inhabitants of the Euroregion is a developing cooperation in various areas including the functioning of the local communities on the borderland. The course of interaction and decision-making processes is here a function of the ability of euroregional institutions to include entities operating in the public sphere in the implementation of goals set for Euroregions. Their activity in the area of multi level governance manifests itself in the diversity of organizations operating in the area of tasks and programs implemented by euroregions and ways of using resources of cooperating entities. As a manifestation of the dissemination of the cross-border cooperation we adopted the number and scope of projects from the ETC resources made by the cross-border partnerships participants. Between 2007–2013 19 of SNBE implemented 37 projects, of which 17 have been embedded in tourism, 4 in education and transport. In other areas (infrastructure, spatial management, economy, science, environmental protection, cultural heritage and science) 1–2 projects were implemented. In our view, the analyses showed a narrow range of issues undertaken in the projects.

With the results obtained, it is possible to formulate at least two conclusions. The first one concerns the concentration and efficiency of cross-border partnerships activities in the sphere of the promotion of social capital, in accordance with the intended purpose of the SPF. The possibility of ensuring conditions that enable creation and strengthening of the relationship between the inhabitants results in creating and maintaining a positive image of neighbors, sympathy, mutual trust. The second observation concerns the implementation of other cross-border cooperation objectives within the Euroregion. In relation to the sphere of economy, spatial planning, communication and others, we notice significantly lower activity of partnerships, both in the area of supporting of institutional and organizational links and implementation of joint projects in the scope of social needs.

The territorial dimension of the cross-border partnerships impact is important to determine the meaning of the Euroregion for local development and the presence of functional interdependence between its actors. Euroregion, especially on the Polish side, covers a large area. It includes municipalities located far away from the border. Admission that cross-border partnerships promote functional interdependence in the SNBE requires the presence of links between Polish and German municipalities in its whole area. The analysis of the territorial distribution of partnerships has demonstrated the characteristics both favorable and unfavorable from the point of view of Euroregion governance and the impact of cross-border cooperation on meeting the comprehensive needs of inhabitants.

35 Joanna Frątczak-Müller / Anna Mielczarek-Żejmo, Zwischen Sympathie und Gleichgültigkeit. Die Einstellung der Einwohner der Euroregion Spree-Neiße-Bober zu ihren Nachbarn, in: Uta Bretschneider / Frank Sönke / Ira Spieker (eds.), Verordnete Nachbarschaften: Transformationsprozesse im deutsch-polnisch-tschechischen Grenzraum seit dem Zweiten Weltkrieg, Dresden 2016, 165–179.

The persistent links throughout the Euroregion (in each county), also away from the border can be found beneficial. Two partnerships from Czerwieńsk and Drebkau, and one from Zbąszynek and Peitz, municipalities significantly distant from the Polish-German border, were among the five most active in the Euroregion between 2007–2017.[36] These partnerships are characterized by a significant number of projects and the relatively long "experience" of cooperation. There were relatively few territorial units, which did not implement any project between 2007–2017. They were only on the Polish side. They were located close to the border (municipalities of Tuplice, Bobrowice and the town of Gozdnica) as well as at some distance from it (municipalities of Kolsko, Siedlisko, Brzeźnica, Nowa Sól and Żagań).

However, distribution of partnerships in the Euroregion is not balanced. The concentration of partnerships and the projects carried out looks adversely. There are two trends. The first is a higher density of partnerships and projects in the border districts and the second – in the big cities. The areas where the most partnerships operate include Krosno Odrzańskie County, as well as the cities of Cottbus and Zielona Góra (more than 75). But it is worth noting that Krosno Odrzańskie County owes a high rate of cooperation due to the border town Gubin, which is the sister unit for the German town Guben. Between 2007–2017 the town offices of Guben and Gubin jointly carried out 56 projects, achieving the best result in the SNBE. The number of partnerships in the counties decreases with the distance from the border. At the German side, the least partnerships are located in the municipalities Spreewald, Kolkwitz, Drebkau, Welzow and Neuhasen/Spree. On the Polish side the lowest result was reached by Wschowa County, furthest to the East, and two municipalities located in the North of the Euroregion: Cybinka and Torzym. The last two units distinguish in the SNBE. These are the municipalities that are part of counties in two Euroregions: SNBE, and Euroregion Pro Europe Viadrina.

The location of the leaders of the projects from the SPF, and ETC resources was also analyzed. The results regarding the location of such projects' leaders confirm the preliminary trends to focus cooperation in certain areas. Leaders of nearly ⅓ of small projects came from big cities. In the cities and municipalities by the border, there were 13 % of the leaders. Between 2007–2013 a total of 37 projects were carried out funded by ETC. The most leaders (17) had their headquarters in the border municipality of Gubin, 11 in big cities. Only 9 leaders came from other municipalities, however the partnerships with considerable achievement in the implementation of small projects did not implement projects within the ETC.

The tendency to concentrate activities of partnerships in border towns and big cities results from two different circumstances. The first is the availability of partners and ease of contact in the border municipalities, especially in the "twin cities" (eg. Guben and Gubin). The close location promotes regularity and frequency of meetings which positively influence the durability of the relationship. An important factor is also the possibility of direct contacts that lead to personal relationships that exceptionally, under the conditions of the cross-border cooperation are among the factors contributing not only to the sustainability of

36 See Sarmiento-Mirwald, Analiza polsko-niemieckich partnerstw. Loc. Cit. (Note 35).

partnerships, but their development and achievements.[37] The financial and organizational resources are an important factor contributing to the development of cross-border cooperation in big cities. Support for EU projects, their development, implementation and settlement is associated with a significant effort. The ability to provide adequate staff to manage projects is available primarily to large units. It is also an important factor in the regularity of the actions taken and durability of the bonds. It is the advantage of large cities and results in the concentration of a considerable part of the partnerships and projects in their area.

The last analyzed dimension relates to the structure of entities making decisions on the shape of cross-border cooperation in the Euroregion. It refers to the condition of a public sphere management through a network of institutions and organisations, which is to enable the non-governmental and private sector representatives in the decision-making process.[38] In this article we analyze the participation of entities representing various sectors among leaders and among the members of the decision-making bodies of the Euroregion.

Cross-border projects in Poland are usually coordinated by local government units and other public sphere bodies. Between 2007–2013 among the leaders of cross-border projects financed from the FMP on Polish side of SNBE[39] was 18 % of the non-governmental sector organizations representing. We consider this share relatively high, especially in the context of significantly limited financial and organizational resources at their disposal and their role in the Euroregion decision-making.

The rules for selecting representatives of the SNBE entities to decision-making bodies are different in Poland and Germany. Participants in the Polish part of the Euroregion, due to the current legal status in Poland,[40] are only local authorities (municipalities and counties). It must be noticed that organisations representing civil and economic sector within the decision-making bodies totally lack opportunities to participate in decision-making. Members of the Association of the German side can be entities belonging to all sectors. These are local governments, legal persons that represent the citizens and businesses as well as individuals. In 2017, the Association had 10 local governments, 6 non-governmental organizations, 7 enterprises and 3 individuals. All members belong to the Assembly. However, the votes in the Assembly are not in proportion to the participation of the representatives of the different sectors. Under the Statute, the territorial units' representatives are entitled to 10 votes, legal persons (except associations) 2 votes, the remaining members have 1 vote.

A demand for public decisions being made by representatives of all sectors is accompanied by a belief in the positive effects of broadening participation in decision-making bodies. Expected advantages of incorporating the non-governmental and private sectors representatives in creation of public policies include (1) better adaption of measures to the inhabitants' needs, (2) the increase in the

37 See Frątczak-Müller / Mielczarek-Żejmo, Cross-border partnerships, Loc. Cit. (Note 4), 77–97.

38 Simona Piattoni, The theory of multi-level governance: conceptual, empirical, and normative challenges, New York 2010.

39 While the creation of the article only data on projects implemented through the Office of the Polish part of the Euroregion were available.

40 The Local Government Act of 8 March 1990.

level of legitimacy of decision makers by opening up to the voice of the different groups and the indirect management of local communities, (3) strengthening of civil society, and (4) of the social capital[41]. The analyses presented above suggest that the level of activity of the non-governmental sector in applying for funds and implementation of projects is relatively high in the SNBE. The conclusion on their contribution to decision-making about objectives and development strategies of the Euroregion is quite a contrary. In the Polish part of Euroregion, entrepreneurs and representatives of social organizations are completely excluded from participation in decision-making committees. In the German part, their participation is decreasing with the increase of general importance of considered cases.

Final conclusions

Institutionalization of cross-border cooperation and establishment of Euroregions had been preceded by a common activity undertaken by local communities of European borderlands for solving important problems and meeting the needs of inhabitants.[42] It had concerned spheres which are essential for local communities, such as transport, labor market, spatial management. Authorization of the Euroregions was based on designs developed bottom-up and was supposed to disseminate the idea of cooperation between neighbouring local communities to enhance the cross-border regions.

The aim of this article is to investigate principles of governance in contemporary Euroregions. The reference model adopted here is the MLG which favors functional interdependence between the institutions and organisations involved. The analyses were meant to search its manifestations in terms of (1) subjective aspect (sphere of functioning of cross-border partnerships), (2) territorial (the area of action taken) and (3) structural (representatives of all sectors in decision-making). The discussed thesis concerned the existence of restrictions on the functional interdependence in the dimensions mentioned above. In the SNBE, which was the subject of the presented analyses, we find conditions beneficial to broadening a range of local communities' needs and issues on the German-Polish borderland in the institution's activities. However, barriers for the implementation of this postulate in the development strategies of the region also exist.

The conditions conducive to deepening functional interdependence include, first, the concentration of activities on the development of social capital among the inhabitants of the German-Polish border. A high level of social capital contributes significantly to the well-being of local communities.[43] In the case of Euroregions it is a prerequisite for the development of cross-border cooperation. Secondly, an important factor is a territorial scope of cooperation. Network of

41 Michał Żabiński, Governance vs. Network Governance in Local Government, in: Stanisław Mazur, Public Governance, Warszawa 2015, 171–193.

42 Hiroshi Tanaka, Carpathian Euroregion and Cross-Border Cooperation, The Journal of Comparative Economic Studies 2 (2006).

43 Piotr Gliński / Barbara Lewenstein / Andrzej Siciński (eds.), cooperation: Piotr Frączak, Samoorganizacja społeczeństwa Polski: trzeci sektor [Self-organization of the Polish society: the third sector], Warsaw 2002.

partnerships covers the entire area of the Euroregion. Persistent and active partnerships are found in all its parts. Thirdly, social organizations are an important participant in the cross-border cooperation. Between 2007–2013 they coordinated nearly 20 % of the projects. In this way, their representatives directly decided on the shape of the co-operation between the inhabitants of the Euroregion.

The barriers are primarily (1) a relatively rare cooperation in such areas, essential to local communities, as transport, labor market and spatial management. In further research aimed at explanation of diagnosed limitations we propose examining the two potential causes of their occurrence. The first is the lack of patterns and experience in cross-border cooperation of the relevant institutions and organizations and, as a result, lack of motivation to seek out new ways to meet local needs and solve problems. The second concerns the lack or ignoring spheres of local communities lives demanding the intervention, cooperation of the relevant actors on both sides of the border. Another barrier is (2) uneven distribution of partnerships and projects. The concentration of cross-border cooperation at the border and in major cities has objective grounds (availability of partners in border cities and financial and organization resources of large cities). However, it leads to recognize the functional interdependence in Euroregion as spot and/or discontinuous (e. g. permanent partnership located away from the border). The last factor that negatively impacts on closer cooperation of the local communities on the German-Polish borderland concerns (3) relatively low participation of non-governmental and private sector in making key decisions for the development of the Euroregion. The existence of formal barriers for membership of non-governmental organizations and entrepreneurs to decision-making bodies may result in a mismatch between the implemented solutions to both the needs and potentials of the third sector representatives and lowering the level of identification with the objectives of the Euroregion among activists and residents, which they represent.

The importance of the regions to meet the needs of inhabitants and solve social problems is increasing now. At the same time, a relevant way of creating social policies requires the involvement of all sectors (particularly the non-governmental), the authorities at different levels, and a non-herarchical form of the relationship between decision-making participants. Despite the mentioned barriers, Euroregions work to create a community based on a bond that meets the needs of their participants and borderland residents. The problem-solving and meeting the social needs of their inhabitants requires the mobilisation of actors from various sectors and different levels around common issues, which are increasingly more likely to be dealt with in regions.

Abstract

The purpose of the article is to analyze how the rules of euroregional institutions' co-governance are implemented. The subject of the presented study is the effective aspect of the European regions' functioning in terms of management. The area of reference is the Polish-German Euroregion Spree-Neisse-Bober.

Governance is understood as an interaction of people and institutions based on norms aimed on supporting political or economic units and achieving their goals. It is considered in EU as multilevel governance based on public authority partnership with social subjects, representing citizens' interest (e. g. NGOs, professional and economic associations, business and the media). Referring to the principles of governance accepted in literature, authors formulate a thesis of the limitations of cross-border policy objectives and the principle of multilevel governance, which are manifested in three dimensions: *subjective* (issue of actions taken), *territorial* (distribution of partnerships and a range of functional interdependence), *structural* (representatives of each sector in the activities of the Euroregion).

The analysis is based on the research conducted in 2013. It used content analysis, survey (800 respondents) and unstructured interviews (70 experts from Poland and Germany) methods. The authors also use data from the analysis carried out in 2017 containing content analysis covering the documents of euroregional projects published on official web pages.

Conflict and cooperation at European Borders

Birte Wassenberg

In Europe, the Schengen crisis, spurred off by the unexpected migration flow in 2015, led to a re-questioning of the functions of "borders" in European Integration.[1] Especially the ideal of a "Europe without borders" is crumbling, which has been propagated by the European Union (EU) since the ambitious project of the Single European Market in 1987. It is the heart and spirit of the Schengen agreement abolishing internal border checks of EU citizens which is now at stake.[2] The re-introduction of "border controls" in several EU Member States not only slows down the process of European Integration, but it also represents an obstacle to cross-border cooperation in Europe: the "separation" function of the border is being reinforced and "the pertinence of the border" seems being largely confirmed.[3] One of the main consequences of this crisis is also growing Euroscepticism and a new "fear of integration" which might even lead to the disintegration of the EU.[4]

Indeed, Euroscepticism does not stop at the border regions of Europe. It is precisely in cross-border spaces that the problems, which have surfaced in many areas because of gaps or a lack of European Integration, become visible.[5] Administrative, legal, psychological and linguistic barriers emerge when borders are crossed, when the political and administrative structures of neighbouring countries come up against each other. The lack of knowledge about the historical and cultural context of one's neighbour regularly leads to misunderstandings and

---

1 Sabine Saurugger, Crise de l'Union européenne ou crise de la démocratie, in: Politique étrangère 1 (2017), 23–33.

2 Elspeth Guild / Evelien Brouwer / Kees Groeneduk / Sergio Carrera, What is happening to the Schengen borders?, in: CEPS Paper in Liberty and Security in Europe Vol. 85 (December 2015), 1–26; Internal border controls in the Schengen area: is Schengen crisis-proof?, in: Study for the LIBE committee, European Parliament, June 2016. http://www.europarl.europa.eu/RegData/etudes/ STUD/2016/571356/IPOL_ STU(2016)571356_EN.pdf [Accessed: 02.03.2017].

3 Birte Wassenberg, La frontière, objet d'intégration ou cicatrice de l'Histoire. L'étude du cas de l'espace du Rhin supérieur, in: Revue RECERQ Vol. 1 spécial (2017), http://recerc.eu/wp-content/uploads/2017/10/R9birte.pdf.

4 See Patrick Moreau / Birte Wassenberg (eds.), European Integration and New Anti-Europeanism, Vol. 1 and 2, Stuttgart 2016.

5 Birte Wassenberg, Can Cross-Border Cooperation Provoke Opposition to Europe? The Example of the Upper Rhine Region, in: Birte Wassenberg / Frédéric Clavert / Philippe Hamman (eds.), Anti-européisme, euroscepticisme et alter-européisme dans la construction européenne de 1945 à nos jours 1: les concepts (2010), 285–307.

even to intercultural conflicts between citizens living on borders.[6] Even with its ideal of a united Europe, the existence of the EU is not necessarily a guarantee against the insecurity and fear of "the other" beyond the border, which is more specifically felt in Euroregions since it is there that close contacts can be established with the other and otherness.[7] Furthermore, when looking at the historical development of cross-border cooperation and its link with European Integration, it clearly appears that the conscience of the "border" as an obstacle had always existed in border regions and was even the "object" of cooperation itself: to overcome the border as "a scar of history" was the main incentive for many border regions to start cooperation.[8] Only from the 1990s, with the introduction of the Interreg programme by the European Commission, cross-border cooperation was increasingly put forward as a tool in order to implement the ideal of a "borderless Europe".[9] However, paradoxically, the more cross-border cooperation developed, the more the persistence of the border was felt in border regions. There seems thus to be a general ambivalence between the role of cross-border cooperation as a "model" for European Integration and the persistence of obstacles to overcome the border in border regions.[10]

In order to examine more in detail this dichotomy, the Jean Monnet project "Conflict and cooperation in EU Border Regions (EU-Front)" aimed at an exchange of experience and debate on the role of the border in the process of European Integration.[11] The idea was to examine the border in its dialectical function between separation and *rapprochement* and to discuss the consequences of this for the EU. Concretely, the project consisted in the organization of four so called "Castle-talks on cross-border cooperation" at the château Pourtalès, in Strasbourg, be-tween 2012–2016: *Cross-border Cooperation and International Relations* (6 December 2012), *Borders and Governance* (3 December 2013), *Fear of Integration: The Pertinence of the Border* (8–9 December 2014) and *The Border: Source of Conflict or a Place of Reconciliation?* (7–8 December 2015). Each Castle-talk dealt with a current border problem (immigration crisis, the reintroduction of border controls etc.) and examined selected cases studies of cross-border regions for a comparative analysis.[12] The choice of these

6 Anne Dussap-Köhler, Les sensibilités interculturelles dans les régions transfrontalières, in: Birte Wassenberg, Joachim Beck, Vivre et penser la coopération transfrontalière 4: les régions frontalières sensibles (2011), 129–145.

7 Jens Gabbe, Sensibilität in europäischen Grenzregionen, in: Birte Wassenberg / Joachim Beck (eds.), Vivre et penser la coopération transfrontalière 4: les régions frontalières sensibles, 93–105.

8 Alfred Mozer, Entwicklungspolitik zu Hause, Entwicklungsregionen in der EWG, in: Schriften der Bundeszentrale für politische Bildung (1973), 14.

9 Bernard Reitel / Birte Wassenberg / Jean Peyrony, European Territorial Cooperation, in: Eduardo Medeiros (ed.), European Territorial Cooperation. Theoretical Approaches to the process and impacts of Cross-Border and Transnational Cooperation in Europe, Heidelberg 2018, 7.

10 Cf. Emmanuel Brunet Jailly, Borders and the EU: The consequences of the Schengen crisis, Communication at the 2nd ABS World Conference, Budapest-Vienne, 10–14.07.2018.

11 The Jean Monnet project Conflits et coopérations aux frontières de l'UE, Réf: 574769-EPP-1-2016-1-FR-EPPJMO-PROJECT, was supported by the EU Erasmus + program for the period between 2016–2018.

12 These case-studies were: the Upper Rhine Region (France, Germany, Switzerland), the Mont Blanc Space (France, Switzerland, Italy), the Calais-Dover Region and Eurometropolis Lille

regions was justified by a representativeness both in geographical (internal and external borders, Schengen) and policy field terms (migration problems, cross-border crime, Franco-German reconciliation, East-West cooperation, Euro-metropoles, etc.). The debates and the comparative analysis were also interdisciplinary and associated researchers, PHD students, European and International students, but also cross-border actors (at political and administrative level) and representatives of European Organizations (Council of Europe, European Parliament, Committee of Regions).

The approach was innovative: the concept of the "Castle-talks on Cross-border Cooperation" was in fact first introduced in 2012–2013.[13] Its objective was to deepen research and to encourage interest of young researchers in the field of Border Studies at the *Institut d'études politiques* (IEP) of the University of Strasbourg, especially for the Master 2 in *Relations Internationales et processus d'intégration régionale* (International Relations and Processes of Regional Integration) and for the American students of the CEPA study abroad program at the château Pourtalès. The title "Castle-talks on Cross-border Cooperation" was invented at the second seminar, in December 2013, on "Borders and Governance". Key note speaker Karl-Heinz Lambertz, then Minster-President of the German Community of Belgium, talked about "the contribution of cross-border cooperation to foreign policy".[14] He mentioned that, "in the past history of Europe, Foreign policy has often been discussed in castles" and that, maybe "a castle ghost at the château Pourtalès" was listening to these talks on cross-border cooperation".[15] The terminology was forged: from then onwards, the seminars were called "Castle-talks on cross-border cooperation". The concept of the castle-talks was as follows: the seminars presented an occasion both for researchers to present papers on a specific aspect of cross-border cooperation and for European and American students from the Master 2 on International Relations of the IEP in Strasbourg, the University West Virginia and Georgia State University to exchange on these subjects. The idea was also to draw from this experience and open up the seminars to other scientific disciplines and researchers coming from other border regions in the world. The encounter between renown Border Studies researchers, European and American Master students and young researchers/PhD candidates presented an ideal framework for a fruitful interdisciplinary discussion on cross-border cooperation.

The results of the project "Conflict and cooperation at European Borders" were published in 2018, in a volume, which took up the title of the third Castle-talk in 2014: "*Fear of Integration? The pertinence of the border*", because it well reflected the current changes in the perception of borders and their meaning for European

---

(France, Belgium, United Kingdom), the Region Ireland/Northern Ireland, the Cieszyn Region (Czech Republic, Poland), the Euroregion Viadrina (Germany, Poland), the Catalan Region (Spain, France, Andorra) and the Slovenia-Austria-Italy Border Region.

13 In the framework of my Jean Monnet Chair on the contribution of cross-border cooperation to the European Neighbourhood Policy supported by the EU Erasmus + program for the period between 2013–2016.

14 Karl-Heinz Lambertz, Communication at the second Castle-talk on cross-border cooperation "Borders and Governance", Strasbourg 3 December 2013.

15 Ibid.

Integration and cross-border cooperation.[16] First of all, the benefit of the publication was to establish a link between three so far not well connected interdisciplinary research fields: Border Studies, Cross-border Cooperation and European Integration. Indeed, Border Studies are a discipline in International Relations, which focusses on the analysis of the border and its (geopolitical) functions in the world. They have been initially launched in the United States in 1976, when a network of researchers, mainly geographers, set up the Association for Borderland Studies (ABS), which then developed and spread internationally. ABS regularly publishes the *Journal of Borderland studies*, which deals with very diverse subjects related to the border.[17] In Europe, the border has also been subject of a large number of research works and the historiography on the matter is abundant.[18] Geographers often put the accent on the (geo-)political dimension of the border which becomes apparent with its territorial affirmation, i. e. the articulation of politics and of space, as Michel Foucher explains it.[19] More recently, Border Studies in Europe have been analysed in this sense by Marie-Christine Fourny and Anne-Laure Amilhat-Szary.[20] But this dimension has also been stressed by political scientists such as Malcolm Anderson and Eberhart Bort, who have studied the Western and the Eastern European borders.[21] The historical dimension of the border has been recently examined in two books, one edited by Sabine Dullin and Sophie Cœuré on the *Frontières du communisme* (Frontiers of communism) and the other by Michael Gehler and Andreas Pudlat on *Grenzen in Europa* (Borders in Europe).[22]

Cross-border Cooperation, on the other hand, is a relatively new research field which has been developed as a "European" branch of Border Studies. The study of these relations below state level that have been established after the Second World War alongside European borders has been initiated in the 1970s. The first multidisciplinary studies were in fact launched by Raimondo Strassoldo and his colleagues at the International Sociological Institute of Gorizia created a network of researchers who led a scientific study on cross-border relations and cooperation at local and regional level in Europe.[23] Since then, other scientific disciplines have shown an interest for the field of cross-border cooperation: geographers mainly

16 Birte Wassenberg (ed.), Castle-talks on Cross-Border Cooperation. Fear of Integration? The Pertinence of the Border, Stuttgart 2018.

17 See http://absborderlands.org/journal-of-borderlands-studies [Accessed: 02.01.2019].

18 Bernard Reitel, Villes et frontières. Un jeu de construction de territoires, Bâle, Berlin-Strasbourg-University of Paris 2010, largely reports on the scope and scale of geographic works on the notion of the border.

19 Michel Foucher, Fronts et frontières, Paris 1986.

20 Anne-Laure Amihat-Szary / Marie-Christine Foruny (eds.), Après la frontière, avec la frontière : nouvelles dynamiques transfrontalières en Europe, Paris 2006.

21 Malcolm Anderson, Frontier regions in Western Europe, London 1983; Malcolm Anderson / Bort Eberhart, Boundaries and identities: the Eastern frontier of the European Union, Edinburgh, Social Science Institute 1996.

22 Sandrine Dullin / Sabine Coeré, Frontières du communisme. Mythologies et réalités de la division de l'Europe de la révolution d'Octobre au mur de Berlin, Paris 2007; Michael Gehler / Andreas Pudlat (eds.), Grenzen in Europa, Hildesheim-Zürich-New York 2009.

23 Raimondo Strassoldo, Bounderies and regions, International Sociological Institute de Gorizia, Trieste 1973.

analyse the functions and effects of borders; law specialists examine the legal tools and problems of cooperation; political and administrative scientists regard the cooperation in relation with the subject of governance, federal and regional studies; economists study the economic disparities and flows between border regions and historians look at the origins and the development of neighbourhood relations in cross-border areas.[24] The first attempts to study Cross-border Cooperation with regard to European Integration were made by political scientists in the mid-1990s who regarded the cooperation in relation with the subject of a "Europe of Regions", where local and regional actors were the central focus of European Integration, because they seemed to represent the "most ideal" level of governance for achieving a united Europe closest to the citizen.[25] In this context, Cross-border Cooperation was mainly identified as a means to implement the Single European Market and to establish a "Europe without borders" with free movement of goods, services, capital and people.[26]

"Conflict and cooperation at European Borders" indeed confirms the potential for cooperation and rapprochement in border regions. Until the recent crises of the EU culminating in the Brexit decision of 2016, the positive link between cross-border cooperation and European Integration did seem to make sense. Especially since the completion of the single market in 1992 the effects of integration have been directly felt in Europe's border regions. And it is notably for this reason that they have increasingly been identified, both in theory and in practice, as "models" of the process of European unification[27]. Indeed, 40 % of the EU's territory is covered by border regions containing approximately 30 % of the EU population. The effects of the progress of European Integration can therefore be studied here: horizontal mobility of goods, capital and people are very obvious in border regions.[28] As a result, from having previously been rated as outlying, peripheral and disadvantaged areas, border regions have been elevated to the rank of central spaces in the process of European unification where the effects of integration have become measurable "on a small scale" and were representative of the whole Community.[29]

---

24 For the bibliographical references of the different disciplines, see Birte Wassenberg, Historiographie de la coopération transfrontalière, in: Birte Wassenberg (ed.), L'approche pluridisciplinaire de la coopération transfrontalière. Les jalons pour un travail de recherche interdisciplinaire, Cahier FARE Vol. 5 (2015), 9–15.

25 Ingrid Grom, Die grenzüberschreitende Zusammenarbeit als Beitrag zur Förderung der europäischen Integration, Berlin, 1995; Silvia Raich, Grenzüberschreitende und interregionale Zusammenarbeit in einem Europa der Regionen, Baden-Baden 1995.

26 Charles Ricq, Les Cantons frontaliers et l'intégration européenne, Acte Unique européen, 1992, report from the symposium of 28.10.1988 in Geneva, Council of Europe, Strasbourg 1990.

27 Karl-Heinz Lambertz (ed.), Die Grenzregionen als Labor und Motor kontinentaler Entwicklungen in Europa. Berichte und Dokumente des Europarates sowie Reden zur grenzüberschreitenden Zusammenarbeit in Europa, Zürich-Baden-Baden 2010.

28 Joachim Beck, Introduction, in: Joachim Beck / Birte Wassenberg (eds.), Vivre et penser la coopération territoriale en Europe 6: vers une cohésion territoriale?, Stuttgart 2014, 37 ff.

29 Christian Mestre, Les incidences de l'achèvement du Marché unique sur les régions transfrontalières, Conseil de l'Europe, Strasbourg 1992.

For border regions, the border represents both a place of governance and cross-border cooperation a possible tool of a "new foreign policy"[30] or a "small neighbourhood policy".[31] Today, with the ongoing process of globalization, local and regional actors in EU border regions are interested in positioning their cross-border space not only as contributing to the process of European Integration, but more generally to international cooperation. Depending on their local and regional interests, this might mean to complement or to counteract existing bilateral relations between their respective central governments. Cross-border governance or "secondary foreign policy" in border regions is therefore the expression of a new tendency in the development of international cooperation or "diplomacy" performed by non-state government actors.[32] Local and regional actors in European border regions have therefore progressively constructed an institutional cooperation governance system which can be qualified as *sui generis*. They are however not necessarily always linked to EU.[33] Constantly changing institutional challenges and specific preconditions have in each border region led to the development of specific solutions of the respective cross-border governance structures.[34] The project on "conflict and cooperation at European borders" has indeed identified several examples of cross-border cooperation governance systems which are more or less successful depending on the geopolitical situation and the issues at stake. In the Channel/La Manche Region between France and the UK, for example, cross-border cooperation has succeeded where sub-national authorities have been able to capitalize on opportunities to address functional policy challenges, but has failed when policy issues "become embroiled in 'high politics' at the national level".[35] In contrast to this, the "participatory governance" model of the Viadrina Region at the German-Polish border seems to be more promising. Participation results indeed in higher legitimation of the EU and more effective, smart and multi-stakeholder cross-border governance seems to be impeding nationalist uprisings.[36] Similarly, at the Czech-Slovak border, institutionalization of cross-border governance under the umbrella of the legal tool of the European Grouping of Territorial Cooperation (EGTC) has improved mutual cooperation.[37]

---

30 Karl-Heinz Lambertz, Cross-Border Governance in Europe: A New Foreign Policy?, in: Birte Wassenberg (ed.), Castle-talks on Cross-Border Cooperation, 103–109.

31 See special issue by Martin Klatt / Birte Wassenberg, Secondary Foreign policy – local international relations: can, local cross border cooperation function as a tool to peace-building and reconciliation?, in: Regional and Federal Studies 27 3 (2017), 205–358.

32 Birte Wassenberg, The Place of Cross-border Cooperation in International Relations, in: Luiz Dominguez / Iva Pires (eds.), Cross-border Cooperation Structures, Learning form the Past to the Future, Bruxelles 2014, 67–81.

33 Joachim Beck, Territorial Institutionalism and the European Administrative Space. A Conceptual Framing for Capturing the Institutional Dynamics of Cross-Border Cooperation.

34 See examples in: Joachim Beck / Birte Wassenberg (eds.), Grenzüberschreitende Zusammenarbeit leben und erforschen 2: Governance in deutschen Grenzregionen, Stuttgart 2011.

35 Christopher Huggins, Building Cross-Border Governance in the Channel/La Manche Region, in: Wassenberg, Castletalks, Loc. Cit. (Note 16), 137–153.

36 Marcin Krymuski / Peter Ulrich, Actor's Participation in Cross-Border Governance Structures at the German-Polish Border, in: Wassenberg, Castletalks, Loc. Cit. (Note 16), 153–183.

37 Hynek Böhm, Networks as Functional New Micro-diplomacy Tools Supporting Cross-border Co-operation, in: Wassenberg, Castletalks, Loc. Cit. (Note 16), 183–201.

Beyond the function of mutual cooperation, cross-border governance has also served and still serves an important function of reconciliation in Europe, which has already been identified by the pioneers of cross-border cooperation, for example Alfred Mozer who described the borders in Europe as "scars of history which should be overcome".[38] The specificity of the function of the border as a place of reconciliation can be traced back to very beginning of cross-border cooperation in Europe.[39] It mainly started at the Franco-German border in the Upper Rhine or the Saar-Lor-Lux Region as a bottom-up approach. It is thus different compared to the more top-down national reconciliation frameworks which were established, for example, by the Treaty of Elysée between France and Germany in 1963.[40] Interviews with key actors from the Upper Rhine Region asking them about their perceptions of European integration, cross-border cooperation and intercultural relations with their neighbours indeed reveal the positive results of this bottom-up reconciliation process which has led to stable friendly relations in an area that has been particularly marked in the past by the "scars" of the Franco-German wars.[41] The positive effect of reconciliation can even be illustrated by comparing shopping behaviour, for example at the Franco-German border between Alsace and the Palatinate or the Polish-German border in Slubice.[42] However, whereas cross-border shopping is certainly an indicator of dynamic cross-border relations, it does not necessarily result in sustainable regional integration, nor in the total elimination of stereotypes and distrust towards the other. In any case, cross-border reconciliation at the Eastern borders is different: it was first hampered by the beginning of the Cold War, so that the peace-building process at the Polish-German border, for instance, had to wait until after the fall of the Berlin wall in the early 1990s.[43] According to some researchers in this field, the process of reconciliation actually worked both from a psychological point of view and taking into account the historical heritage in Europe of WWI and II and of the Cold War.[44] Others,

---

38 See Mozer, Entwicklungspolitik, Loc. Cit. (Note 8), 14.

39 Birte Wassenberg, Secondary foreign policy as a peace-building tool? The contribution of cross-border cooperation to reconciliation and stability in Europe, in: Martin Klatt / Birte Wassenberg, Secondary Foreign policy – local international relations: can, local cross border cooperation function as a tool to peace-building and reconciliation?, in: Regional and Federal Studies 27 3 (2017), 219–237.

40 Birte Wassenberg, Grenzorte: von der Konfrontation zur Kooperation. Das Beispiel des Oberrheins, in: Corinne Defrance / Ulrich Pfeil (eds.), Verständigung und Versöhnung nach dem "Zvilisationsbruch"?, Brussels 2016a, 349.

41 Birte Wassenberg, The Rhine: A Border of Peace? Memories from Key Players in the Upper Rhine Region, in: Wassenberg, Castletalks, Loc. Cit. (Note 16), 281–295.

42 Bernhard Küppen, Beyond "Erbfeind" and after Reconciliation. Shopping? A Comparative Study on French-German and Polish-German Cross-Border Tourism as a Common, Integrative Routine, in: Wassenberg, Castletalks, Loc. Cit. (Note 16), 295–305.

43 Elzbieta Opilowska, Reconciliation through Europeanization: Secondary foreign policy in the Germa-Polish borderlands, 283–303; Hynek Böhm / Emil Drápela, Cross-border cooperation as a reconciliation tool: Example from the east Czecj-Polish borders, 35–319, in: Martin Klatt / Birte Wassenberg, Secondary Foreign policy – local international relations: can, local cross border cooperation function as a tool to peace-building and reconciliation?, in: Regional and Federal Studies 27 3 (2017).

44 Gerhard Besier, Mental Borders Create Limited Minds: How to Overcome Prejudices, Stereotypes and Concepts of an "Enemy" in the Second Decade of the 21st Century, in: Wassenberg, Castletalks, Loc. Cit. (Note 16), 265–281.

however, show more scepticism about its success. In the border regions between Germany and Poland, for example, the EU, with its political and financial instruments, might thus have facilitated the creation of a "peaceful neighbourhood"[45] and political borders have become more permeable, but cultural and symbolic boundaries often remain an obstacle in trans-border relations which ultimately take on a very "insular"[46] character. The reconciliation process is thus far from being completed. This also counts for external EU borders regions such as the Finnish-Russian one, which, in spite of cross-border interaction, continues to represent a strongly hermetic border between Eastern and Western Europe.[47]

However, despite cooperation and reconciliation, conflict also remains a key characteristic in European border regions. First of all, the effects of the border crises induced by excessive migration flows and terrorist threats since 2015 have become extremely palpable in Europe's border regions. What used to be "models of integration" might now represent how it looks like when "the border comes back in Europe", as images of newly imposed border controls in well integrated cross-border spaces such as the Oresund region or the Strasbourg-Kehl/Ortenau Eurodistrict illustrate.[48]

The project "conflict and cooperation at European borders" has therefore also drawn its attention to the conflict side of neighbourhood relations to the function of borders as gatekeepers of sovereignty and security, a function which has gained in significance since the migration crisis and with the international terrorist threat.[49] At the internal and external borders of the EU, security issues have become again of crucial importance and local and regional actors are increasingly interested in the control function of the border in order to prevent cross-border crime, increase internal security and to contribute to the European Neighborhood Policy.[50] However, this function of the border is still mainly reserved for the national States who watch over this competence as an expression of their exclusive competence in Foreign and Defense Policy and as a safeguard of their national sovereignty.[51] Therefore, the Member States of the EU are reluctant to

45 Beata Halicka, Polish-German Border: A Laboratory of Transnational Cooperation, in: Wassenberg, Castletalks, Loc. Cit. (Note 16), 305–321.

46 Ibid.

47 Katarzyna Stoklosa, The Finnish-Russian Border between Myth and Reality, in: Wassenberg, Castletalks, Loc. Cit. (Note 16), 321–331.

48 Birte Wassenberg, The "myth" of a Europe without borders and its consequences for European Integration and cross-border cooperation in the EU, Communication at the ABS Annual Conference "Bridges or Walls? The Case for Open Borders in the XXI Century", San Francisco 12–15.04.2017.

49 Noe Cornago, Diplomacy and Paradiplomacy in the Redefinition of International Security: Dimensions of Conflict and Co-operation, in: Fransisco Aldecoa / Michael Keating (eds.), Paradiplomacy in Action. The Foreign Relations of Subnational Governments, London-Portland 1999, 40–57.

50 Birte Wassenberg, Le voisinage de proximité: les eurorégions "géopolitiques" aux frontières externes de l'UE (1993–2009), in: Denis Rolland / Jean-Christophe Romer (eds.), "Espaces de voisinage", Les espaces de voisinage. De Monroe à la politique européenne de voisinage. Identité et altérité, Matériaux pour l'histoire de notre temps, 97 & 98, janvier–juin 2010, 45–49.

51 Joachim Blatter / Matthias Kreutzer / Michaela Rentl / Jan Thiele, The Foreign Relations of European Regions: Competences and Strategies, in: West European Politics 31 3 (2008), 464–490.

share power with European Institutions (Schengen Information System, Europol, Frontex) on the management of the national border for security reasons and they do not favor participation by local and regional authorities either.[52] Military experts highlight this function of national borders as an "invaluable asset for a nation to exercise sovereign powers within its territory".[53] The Westphalian border has indeed always been highly relevant from a security and geopolitical perspective, even if borders between post-modern states have lost some of their geopolitical relevance due to globalisation, world-wide mobility and transnational interactions. For borders are not only permeable with respect to the flow of goods, services and information, but also let admit crime and violence and they still serve an important security function. It is true however, that, from a legal point of view, globalization has modified the very definition of borders. They have now acquired a new function as they serve the EU's strategy to influence world trade liberalization pushing its external (legal) borders way beyond the geographical limits of the European continent. They thus become "lines that redistribute the world map according to legal closeness, rather than by political separation".[54] The mobility of these borders and their new locations are a sign of the EU's normative enlargement and hence mark a new way to ensure the area's security. It can indeed be argued that the Westphalian order of borders has in no way been overcome in Europe, as the EU is not at all "immune to sovereignty and territorial conflicts".[55] These conflicts may be of a sub-national, national, or supranational nature as can be illustrated with the examples of Northern Ireland, the Brexit referendum or the Gibraltar issue. Borders as gatekeepers of sovereignty therefore still matter. This point can equally be confirmed when looking at the external borders of the EU. Switzerland, for instance, is holding on to its national borders as gatekeepers of sovereignty and rejects the EU with its principle of free movement of people.[56] By dissociating themselves from their neighbours and the European unification process, the Swiss are also "drawing up borders in their minds", with no connection to the economic and cultural realities of interdependency.[57]

Not only do neighbouring States cling to the function of the border as a gatekeeper against conflict, but at the borders in Europe, one can still observe many border conflicts, barriers and resistance to cooperation. Compared to other regional spaces, border regions are characterized by a very specific structural situation: natural and/or socio-economic phenomena like mountains, rivers, seas, unemployment, migration, criminality, pollution, etc. have typically a border-

52 With the notable exception maybe of the regional State level of government in those Member States of the EU which have a federal political structure, especially concerning the German Länder.

53 See for example the welcome speech by the Deputy Commander of the Eurocorps in Strasbourg at one of the Casteltalks: Walter Spindler, Borders, Security and Geopolitical Aspects, in: Wassenberg, Castletalks, Loc. Cit. (Note 16), 201–219

54 Antoine Ullestad, Protecting the Security of the EU through its External Borders, in: Wassenberg, Castletalks, Loc. Cit. (Note 16), 219–239.

55 Jaume Castan Pinos, Conflicts over Sovereignty in Europe in the so-called Post-Sovereignty Era, in: Wassenberg, Castletalks, Loc. Cit. (Note 16), 239–353.

56 Manuel Firesecke, The Pertinence of the External EU Border: A Swiss Point of View, in: Wassenberg, Castletalks, Loc. Cit. (Note 16), 253–265.

57 Ibid.

crossing dimension directly affecting the neighboring states.[58] The resulting structural or everyday policy problems require close cross-border co-operation between those actors, which are competent and responsible for problem resolution within the institutional context of the respective national state. But there are often still latent conflicts, persistent barriers or even resistance to cross-border cooperation. Indeed, in contrast to a national context, where regional cooperation is taking place within a uniform legal, institutional and financial context, cross-border governance is characterized by the challenge to manage the working together of politico-administrative systems which have a distinctive legal basis and share a different degree of vertical differentiation both in terms of structure, resources equipment and autonomy of action.[59] In addition, cross-border cooperation is still confronted and finds itself sometimes in conflict with the principle of territorial sovereignty of the respective national states.[60] Even in those regions where the degree of cooperation is well developed, cross-border cooperation is therefore still marked by administrative, political and cultural obstacles and decisions often have to be taken outside the cross-border governance sphere.[61]

Indeed, many obstacles to cross-border cooperation still have to be overcome. In order to implement the EU's cohesion policy in border regions a set of measures is first needed to eliminate barriers to cross-border cooperation.[62] The EU should thus focus on the learning of the neighbor's language, on the development of interpersonal links through micro project funds, on the building of sustainable cross-border observation systems, on cross border media, on intercultural training and capitalization and on projects in the field of education to develop a sense of belonging and common visions. Practical solutions can also be offered by specialized training, counselling and support, adapted to the specific characteristics of each frontier.[63] Capacity-building in cross-border contexts, for example, allows to overcome obstacles to cooperation that remain due to lack of knowledge vis-a-vis the "other" and the lack of appropriate methods for cross-border project management and intercultural work.[64] Linguistic differences are also often identified as one of the main obstacles to cross-border cooperation.

58 Karl-Heinz Lambertz / Joëlle Ramakers, Vielfalt und Hürden kennzeichnen die grenzüberschreitende Zusammenarbeit in Europa, in: Joachim Beck / Birte Wassenberg (eds.), Grenzüberschreitende Zusammenarbeit leben und erforschen 5: Integration und (trans-)regionale Identitäten, Stuttgart 2013, 61–73.

59 Ewald Eisenberg, Learning form Cultural Experiences and Interactions: Cross-Border Administrative Cultures, in: Franz Thedieck (ed.), Foundations of Administrative Culture in Europe, Baden-Baden 2007.

60 Joachim Beck / Eddie Pradier, Governance in der transnationalen Regionalpolitik: Bestandsaufnahme und Perspektiven der Kooperationsbeziehungen in grenzüberschreitenden Verflechtungsräumen, in: Beck / Wassenberg, Zusammenarbeit, Loc. Cit. (Note 34), 107.

61 Joachim Beck, Cross-border cooperation in Europe – The example of the Upper-Rhine, in: Klaus König / Scott Fosler (eds.), Regionalization below State-level in Germany and the United States, Deutsches Forschungsinstitut für öffentliche Verwaltung 1999, 137.

62 Jean Peurony, Integration in Cross-Border Regions: Obstacles and Solutions, in: Wassenberg, Castletalks, Loc. Cit. (Note 16), 331–347.

63 This is for example the case of the Transborder Euro-Institute Network (TEIN) which brings together 14 training organizations and universities from 8 regions in the EU.

64 Anne Thevenet, Capacity-Building as a Tool to Overcome Obstacles in Border Regions, in: Wassenberg, Castletalks, Loc. Cit. (Note 16), 347–369.

However, whereas linguistic diversity might constitute a barrier to communication, it might also be a cultural asset: minority languages such as Catalan can in fact present an opportunity as a cultural bridge in a former unified regional space now separated by two Nation States.[65]

In some cross-border spaces, there are not only barriers to cooperation, but political conflicts still heavily weigh on neighborhood relations. The Northern Ireland conflict is such a case, where European Integration as well as support to cross-border cooperation may help to overcome the border as a "scar of history". The reconciliation process was indeed largely facilitated by the EU membership of Ireland and the UK and the support given by the Structural Funds.[66] The Interreg and Peace programs have therefore played a positive role since the 1990s for the resolution of the conflict, a role now threatened by the Brexit decision.[67] Brexit indeed causes a new threat of disintegration in this border region – which might spread to other areas in the EU (Scotland, Catalonia, etc.). Another case of prevailing conflict is the border region between Bulgaria and Rumania. It suffers from important deficits hindering cross-border cooperation, such as financial, economic and transport difficulties, but there are also more sensitive issues: corruption, organized crime, trafficking of weapons, drugs and human beings thus constitute serious threats to good neighborhood relations and to the security at the border.[68] Since 1989, the EU's operational programs have progressively put in place the conditions for developing cross-border strategic concepts and provide ground for investment interventions aimed at minimizing the border obstacles and at resolving issues of common concern. However, the recent migration and terrorist crises in the EU have more than ever questioned the direction of these policies, especially if the emphasis is to be placed again on border controls. Should the barrier function of EU borders be privileged in future with regard to that of free circulation? Does this function result in more reassurance and security or in more mistrust and conflict?

The project "conflict and cooperation at European borders" does not give a definite answer to these questions. But the different contributions show the diversity of functions, positive or negative, that the border might take in the process of European Integration and in International Relations.[69] It therefore moves away from a too one-sided, positivist approach to cross-border cooperation as a necessary contribution to European Integration. Instead, it re-establishes the research field of Cross-Border Cooperation as a specific branch of Border Studies which may help to explain the process of European Integration – but also a possible process of disintegration. It also repositions the theoretical approach to cross-border

65 Jordi Cicres / Sílvia Llach, The Role of Languages in Cross-Border Cooperation: Obstacle or Opportunity?, in: Wassenberg, Castletalks, Loc. Cit. (Note 16), 369–389.

66 Andy Pollack, Irish-British Relations, 1998–2012: From Provincial Conflict to European Tensions, in: Wassenberg, Castletalks, Loc. Cit. (Note 16), 389–397.

67 Ruth Taillon, Cross-Border Cooperation and Peace-Building in Ireland, in: Wassenberg, Castletalks, Loc. Cit. (Note 16), 397–407.

68 Alessandro Torello, Barriers to the Bulgarian Cross-Border Cooperation with Rumania, in: Wassenberg, Castletalks, Loc. Cit. (Note 16), 407–427.

69 Wassenberg, The Place of Cross-border Cooperation in International Relations, in: Dominguez / Pires (eds.), Cross-border Cooperation Structures, Loc. Cit. (Note 32), 67–81.

cooperation from three different perspectives. First, cross-border cooperation can be identified as a specific case within the field of Area Studies.[70] Second, as European frontiers have clearly developed from a border regime ruled by the Nation States to a cross-border regime defined by the EU, a link can be established between the EU as an international actor and cross-border cooperation.[71] Third, despite having no specific border dispute policies, the EU has acted to resolve and limit border disputes since the very beginning of the European Integration process. This does not prevent the sovereign and guarding functions of borders from being maintained and territorial, positional and functional disputes may still exist in the EU – a reason to encourage further cross-border cooperation. This by itself fosters a strong connection between Border Studies and European Integration.[72]

All contributions to the project "conflict and cooperation at European borders" confirm three major tendencies: first, the pertinence of the border exists and is currently being reinforced by the European crises of migration and terrorism. Second, the myth of a "Europe without borders" propagated by the EU is about to be dismantled, revealing borders as a crucial part to be re-reflected when developing any future project on European Integration. Third, cross-border cooperation does not always and necessarily contribute to the European Integration process: border regions can be "models for integration" but they can also be mirrors of a growing Euroscepticism or a place where "fear of Integration" persists.

Abstract

In Europe, the Schengen crisis, spurred off by the unexpected migration flow in 2015, led to a re-questioning of the functions of "borders" in European Integration. The re-introduction of "border controls" in several EU Member States not only slows down the process of European Integration, but it also represents an obstacle to cross-border cooperation in Europe. There seems thus to be a general ambivalence between the role of cross-border cooperation as a "model" for European Integration and the persistence of obstacles to overcome the border in border regions. In order to examine more in detail this dichotomy, the Jean Monnet project "Conflict and cooperation in EU Border Regions (EU-Front)", which was led by the University of Strasbourg between 2016 and 2018, aimed at an exchange of experience and debate on the role of the border in the process of European Integration. The idea was to examine the border in its dialectical function between separation and rapprochement and to discuss the consequences of this for the EU. Overall, throughout four research seminars, the project confirmed three major tendencies in Europe: first, the pertinence of the border exists and is currently being reinforced by the European crises of migration and terrorism. Second, the myth of a "Europe without borders" propagated by the EU is about to be dismantled, revealing borders as a crucial part to be re-reflected when developing any future project on European

70 Jean-Christophe Romer, International Relations and Area Studies, in: Wassenberg, Castletalks, Loc. Cit. (Note 16), 59–69.

71 Bernard Reitel, "Cross-Border Cooperation and International Relations: Towards the Emergence of a Cross-Border Regime?", in: Wassenberg, Castletalks, Loc. Cit. (Note 16), 69–85.

72 Emmanuel Brunet Jailly, Borders and Border Disputes in Europe, in: Wassenberg, Castletalks, Loc. Cit. (Note 16), 85–103.

Integration. Third, cross-border cooperation does not always and necessarily contribute to the European Integration process: border regions can be "models for integration" but they can also be mirrors of a growing Euroscepticism or a place where "fear of Integration" persists. The contributions to this project also showed the diversity of functions, positive or negative, that the border might take in the process of European Integration and in International Relations. As a result, it is recommended to move away from a too one-sided, positivist approach to cross-border cooperation as a necessary contribution to European Integration. Instead, one should re-establish the research field of Cross-Border Cooperation as a specific branch of Border Studies which may help to explain the process of European Integration – but also a possible process of disintegration.

Abstracts

Jenni Merovuo, Persistent operation – Memories of border work during transition periods, p. 1–16

The article studies the border work in the Eastern Finnish borderland during two transition periods of the first half of the 20th century. Border work is understood as a controversial social process of strengthening official national borders. First, after Finland became independent in 1917, and second, after the border shift of 1940 (reasserted in 1944), the border work aimed to establish new borders and to inhibit border crossings. The main source material consists of the interviews with the former border guards and the borderland civilians. To establish strong borders, the border guards educated, helped, controlled and disciplined the borderland community. The most successful cooperation between the border guards and the civilians built around neighborhood and utility. However, conflicts were inevitable as the local community resisted submitting to the new order. Though the trouble was reluctantly discussed in the interviews, the border work is remembered to have caused controversy of personal and professional nature. In the local community, the border guards were considered as the 'internal other' but in time they became trusted members of the community whose presence increased the sense of security. Thus, the dividing national borders did not fall into place naturally, but they have formed gradually in a complex and continuous social process.

Chloe Wells, The 'lost city' of Vyborg and the construction of remembered borders between Finland and Russia, p. 17–30

This article examines collective ideas, memories and postmemories, and socio-spatial frameworks concerning the Finnish-Russian border. The article focuses on the formerly Finnish borderland city of Viipuri (today Vyborg, Russia). Before World War Two (WWII) Vyborg was Finland's second city and the capital of Finnish Karelia. Its loss to the Soviet Union at the conclusion of the Fenno-Soviet Winter War in March 1940 and again (after a brief re-occupation by Finnish forces) in June 1944 is often represented in Finnish discourses as an historical injustice. This idea of injustice is framed by conceptions of a 'holy' Finnish Eastern border and maintained by processes of spatial socialisation, especially the representations of Vyborg and the events of WWII in Finnish popular media. Successive Finnish governments have never officially raised the question of 'getting Vyborg back.' Vyborg being returned is not now thought by the majority to be realistic or feasible but the idea that things 'should have been different' lingers.

Vyborg's Finnish era is conceptualised in terms of nostalgic longing. An idealised, mythic, 'golden Finnish Vyborg' is presented in stark contrast to its sudden, traumatic loss and its current Russian identity. Memories of Vyborg in Finland are informed and shaped by the 'loss' of the city and by an understanding of Vyborg as, historically, a Swedish / Finnish place, an 'outpost of the West against the East.' Alongside an analysis of Finnish media portrayals of Vyborg this article presents the preliminary results of new research with Finnish youth, airing their neglected opinions and thoughts on these issues. This article examines whether today's Finnish youth have adopted the idea circulating in Finnish popular and familial discourses that Vyborg, Russian now for over 70 years and only part of the independent state of Finland for around 20 years, 'should' be part of Finland, and that the loss of Vyborg was an historical injustice.

Olga Ilyukha, Soviet and post-Soviet borders in texts for children and as perceived by children – Symbolic figures, images, meanings, p. 31–50

This paper deals with the children-targeted version of the myth about Soviet borders generated through texts of various genres, the techniques of impressing it upon children. The lingo and implications of the governmental and pedagogical discourses on the subject are exposed. An attempt is made, relying on texts published both in editions for children and in those meant for school teachers, youth organization leaders, day-care teachers, to identify the characteristics of the Soviet canon for representing the border and its later modifications. The paper describes how the notion of the border was explained to children in the Soviet time. It also demonstrates how games were used as a tool to shape a mythologized worldview in Soviet schoolchildren.

The lines of post-Soviet border-related reflections are outlined, and the opposition and intertwining of the Soviet discourse with the post-Soviet one, targeted at erasing borders and building 'cultural bridges', are shown. The author used her own collection of children's drawings on the subject to disclose the notions of the border maintained by contemporary children, the surviving stereotypes and the new trends.

Dorte Jagetić Andersen, Making Space for the Future? – Reconstructing Spatial Identities after Armed Conflict, p. 51–66

The article problematizes the way in which war heritage is used to solidify the image of the Croatian town Vukovar as a national symbol and how this affects the town-scape and its population. Focus is on post-war initiatives to develop new heritage infrastructures, disseminating narratives of national identity at everyday level. The author mobilizes the concepts of spatial identity, particularly the national, and war heritage, showing how the town has frozen in time because of its task to represent the ultimate sacrifice for the nation. Despite of attempts at reinventing the town's image differently it is left devastated. Through the exemplary case of Vukovar, the article contributes to research investigating relations between nation-building and heritage by showing how the use of war to solidify national identity prevents restoration and, not the least, over-coming ethnic conflicts.

Steffen Höhne, Trieste and Chernivtsi – Prologues on urban monument policy, p. 67–90

Based on case studies examining Trieste and Chernivtsi, this article explores different cities' policies regarding monuments and memorials, looking back to the 19th century and through to the present-day. In the process, it is revealed how, in the first instance, local references and living environments were increasingly replaced by selected national monuments in Trieste and (somewhat belatedly) in Chernivtsi over the course of the 19th century, leading to the domination of nationalist and ideologically-based monument policies, especially in the aftermath of 1918. It is not until that critical year of change, 1989 and subsequently, that a heightened recourse in monumental policy starts to emerge, looking back to the Habsburg era, as well as to those cities' multi-national and multi-lingual traditions.

Volodymyr Kravchenko, Ukrainian-Russian Border after Euromaidan – Regional Perspective, p. 91–108

The Euromaidan revolution of 2014 followed by the Russian annexation of the Crimea and a military conflict on Donbas is a watershed in the history of Ukraine and Ukrainian-Russian relations. Both of these countries are going on the road of "nationalization" of the former Soviet nation and its symbolic space. Russia has advanced far beyond Ukraine in this direction. The erosion of Soviet space and clash of the Russian neo-imperialist with Ukrainian ethnic-cultural doctrines contributed to symbolic heterogenization of Ukrainian border territory and emergence of regional discourses. They played an important role in the process of re-bordering and transformation of Ukrainian-Russian borderland. At the same time, Ukrainian regional discourses were marginalized by the Ukrainian and Russian national projects. The interplay between regional, national, and border discourses on Ukrainian-Russian borderland can contribute to the updating of methodological arsenal of respective disciplines.

Gerhard Besier, "So close and yet so far"? – Experiences from the Polish-Russian and Ukrainian-Russian border regions, p. 109–116

Which factors trigger a feeling of togetherness and which one of separateness? Phrases like "So close and yet so far" and "So far and yet so close" can have a similar impact – dependent on our perceptions of communality. This cognition of similarities is mostly based on lifestyles, professions and a sense of mutual understanding. Factors need not be realistic but are perceived as genuine. If the reason why your counterpart seems likeable is unclear, you will be keen to look for reasonable justification of your opinion, thus fostering your sympathy. In such cases, you will be able to ignore or bridge obvious objections and gaps between your mental state and theirs. Remember, for instance, the baffling friendship between the former German Chancellor, Gerhard Schröder, and the Russian President, Vladimir Putin. Furthermore: Felt closeness, as well as strangeness, can be both attractive and repellent. Your mood can easily change from the one to the other. In this respect, propaganda and selective disinformation, which denies or disputes fundamental facts, likewise play a central role like people's constant willingness to believe in the most absurd of constructs. So what? I am going to analyse some of the arguments in the field of social sciences in favour of a good and friendly neighbourhood or, alternately, an adverse demarcation and will base my analysis on the examples of Polish-Russian and Ukrainian-Russian cross border co-operation.

Joanna Frątczak-Müller and Anna Mielczarek-Żejmo, Euroregion, governance, community – Analysis of functional interdependence on the example of the Euroregion Spree-Neisse-Bober, p. 117–134

The purpose of the article is to analyze how the rules of euroregional institutions' co-governance are implemented. The subject of the presented study is the effective aspect of the European regions' functioning in terms of management. The area of reference is the Polish-German Euroregion Spree-Neisse-Bober.

Governance is understood as an interaction of people and institutions based on norms aimed on supporting political or economic units and achieving their goals. It is considered in EU as multilevel governance based on public authority partnership with social subjects, representing citizens' interest (e.g. NGOs, professional and economic associations, business and the media). Referring to the principles of governance accepted in literature, authors formulate a thesis of the limitations of cross-border policy objectives and the principle of multilevel governance, which are manifested in three dimensions: *subjective* (issue of actions taken), *territorial* (distribution of partnerships and a range of functional interdependence), *structural* (representatives of each sector in the activities of the Euroregion).

The analysis is based on the research conducted in 2013. It used content analysis, survey (800 respondents) and unstructured interviews (70 experts from Poland and Germany) methods. The authors also use data from the analysis carried out in 2017 containing content analysis covering the documents of euroregional projects published on official web pages.

Birte Wassenberg, Conflict and cooperation at European Borders, p. 135–148

In Europe, the Schengen crisis, spurred off by the unexpected migration flow in 2015, led to a re-questioning of the functions of "borders" in European Integration. The re-introduction of "border controls" in several EU Member States not only slows down the process of European Integration, but it also represents an obstacle to cross-border cooperation in Europe. There seems thus to be a general ambivalence between the role of cross-border cooperation as a "model" for European Integration and the persistence of obstacles to overcome the border in border regions. In order to examine more in detail this dichotomy, the Jean Monnet project "Conflict and cooperation in EU Border Regions (EU-Front)", which was led by the University of Strasbourg between 2016 and 2018, aimed at an exchange of experience and debate on the role of the border in the process of European Integration. The idea was to examine the border in its dialectical function between separation and rapprochement and to discuss the consequences of this for the EU. Overall, throughout four research seminars, the project confirmed three major tendencies in Europe: first, the pertinence of the border exists and is currently being reinforced by the European crises of migration and terrorism. Second, the myth of a "Europe without borders" propagated by the EU is about to be dismantled, revealing borders as a crucial part to be re-reflected when developing any future project on European Integration. Third, cross-border cooperation does not always and necessarily contribute to the European Integration process: border regions can be "models for integration" but they can also be mirrors of a growing Euroscepticism or a place where "fear of Integration" persists. The contributions to this project also showed the diversity of functions, positive or negative, that the border might take in the process of European Integration and in International Relations. As a result, it is recommended to move away from a too one-sided, positivist approach to cross-border cooperation as a necessary contribution to European Integration. Instead, one should re-establish the research field of Cross-Border Cooperation as a specific branch of Border Studies which may help to explain the process of European Integration – but also a possible process of disintegration.

Index of Names

Index of Places

Mittel- und Ostmitteleuropastudien

hrsg. von Gerhard Besier und Katarzyna Stokłosa (TU Dresden)

Kimmo Katajala (Ed.)
Meanings of an Urban Space
Understanding the historical layers of Vyborg
vol. 12, 2016, 308 pp., 34,90 €, pb., ISBN 978-3-643-90784-4

Kimmo Katajala; Maria Lähteenmäki (Eds.)
Imagined, Negotiated, Remembered
Constructing European Borders and Borderlands
vol. 11, 2012, 232 pp., 29,90 €, pb., ISBN 978-3-643-90257-3

Gerhard Besier (Hg.)
20 Jahre neue Bundesrepublik
Kontinuitäten und Diskontinuitäten
Bd. 10, 2011, 272 S., 29,90 €, br., ISBN 978-3-643-11423-5

Gerhard Besier; Katarzyna Stokłosa (Hg.)
Geschichtsbilder in den postdiktatorischen Ländern Europas
Auf der Suche nach historisch-politischen Identitäten
Bd. 9, 2009, 192 S., 19,90 €, br., ISBN 978-3-643-10230-0

Mike Schmeitzner; Katarzyna Stokłosa (Hg..)
Partner oder Kontrahenten?
Deutsch-polnische Nachbarschaft im Jahrhundert der Diktaturen
Bd. 8, 2008, 240 S., 19,90 €, br., ISBN 978-3-8258-1254-6

Krzysztof Ruchniewicz
„Noch ist Polen nicht verloren"
Das historische Denken der Polen
Bd. 7, 2007, 104 S., 19,90 €, br., ISBN 978-3-8258-0893-8

Gerhard Besier; Agnieszka Debska; Zbigniew Gluza; Katarzyna Stokłosa; Anna Zinserling (Hg.)
Deutsche und Polen während und nach dem Zweiten Weltkrieg
Gemeinsame Geschichte gemeinsam erinnern
Bd. 6, 2007, 304 S., 19,90 €, br., ISBN 978-3-8258-0504-3

Dominik Trutkowski
Der Sturz der Diktatur
Opposition in Polen und der DDR 1988/89
Bd. 5, 2007, 168 S., 14,90 €, br., ISBN 978-3-8258-0416-9

Gerhard Besier; Katarzyna Stokłosa (Hg.)
15 Jahre Deutsche Einheit
Was ist geworden?
Bd. 4, 2007, 184 S., 14,90 €, br., ISBN 978-3-8258-0207-3

Andrew Chandler; Katarzyna Stokłosa; Jutta Vinzent (Eds.)
Exile and Patronage
Cross-cultural negotiations beyond the Third Reich
vol. 3, 2006, 216 pp., 29,90 €, pb., ISBN 3-8258-0014-8

Gerhard Besier; Francesca Piombo; Katarzyna Stokłosa (Hg.)
Fascism, Communism and the Consolidation of Democracy
Comparison of European Dictatorships
. 2006, 120 pp., 19,90 €, br., ISBN 3-8258-9657-9

LIT Verlag Berlin – Münster – Wien – Zürich – London
ieferung Deutschland / Österreich / Schweiz: siehe Impressumsseite